SPIRITUALLY DYSFUNCTIONAL

ALSO BY FRED SINGER

*Change Your Mind, Save Your Life: How Your Mind Affects Your
Health and What You Can Do About It,*
Colonial House Press, 1991.

OTHER TITLES IN THE CAPITAL CURRENTS SERIES:

The Ambassador: Inside the Life of a Working Diplomat
by John Shaw

*Baby at Risk: The Uncertain Legacies of Medical Miracles for Babies,
Families, and Society* by Ruth Levy Guyer

*David, Goliath and the Beach Cleaning Machine: How a Small
Polluted Beach Town Fought an Oil Giant—And Won!*
by Barbara Wolcott

*March to a Promised Land: The Civil Rights Files of a White
Reporter 1952-1968* by Al Kuettner

*The $100,000 Teacher: A Teacher's Solution to America's Declining
Public School System* by Brian Crosby

*The Other Side of Welfare: A Former Single Welfare Mother Speaks
Out* by Pamela L. Cave

*Serving Our Children: Charter Schools and the Reform of American
Public Education* by Kevin Chavous

Suffer the Child: How the Health Care System Is Failing Our Future
by Lidia Wasowicz Pringle

*Torn Between Two Cultures: An Afghan-American Woman Speaks
Out* by Maryam Qudrat Aseel

SPIRITUALLY DYSFUNCTIONAL

being the true and amazing story of
how a confirmed jewish atheist and his
seriously catholic wife explore the meaning
of life, god, the universe, and their own
relationship with the help of one demented
uncle, the great minds of the past, and
some odd characters from the bronx

fred singer

CAPITAL
BOOKS, INC.
Sterling, Virginia

Capital Books, Inc.
P.O. Box 605
Herndon, Virginia 20172-0605

ISBN 10: 1-933102-34-9 (alk. paper)
ISBN 13: 978-1-933102-34-4

Grateful acknowledgment is made for permission to reprint the following:
A 115-word excerpt from *The Thorn Birds*, by Colleen McCullough. Copyright © 1977 by Colleen McCullough. Reprinted by permission of HarperCollins Publishers.
Assorted excerpts (824 words) from *Tuesdays With Morrie*, by Mitch Albom. Copyright © 1997 by Mitch Albom. Reprinted by permission of Doubleday, a division of Random House, Inc.

Library of Congress Cataloging-in-Publication Data
Singer, Fred.
Spiritually dysfunctional : being the true and amazing story of how a confirmed Jewish atheist and his seriously Catholic wife explore the meaning of life, God, the universe, and their own relationship with the help of one demented uncle, the great minds of the past, and some odd characters from the Bronx / Fred Singer. – 1st ed.
p. cm. – (Capital's life series)
Includes bibliographical references.
ISBN-13: 978-1-933102-34-4 (alk. paper)
ISBN-10: 1-933102-34-9 (alk. paper)
1. Spiritual life. I. Title. II. Series.

BL624.S5346 2006
204–dc22

2006030811

Printed in the United States of America on acid-free paper that meets the American National Standards Institute Z39-48 Standard.

First Edition

10 9 8 7 6 5 4 3 2 1

For my parents
Bertrand B. Singer and Ruth Singer
And in memory of the Linets:
Millie, Sonny, Richard, and Johnathan

The Poisoned Pool

Above my uncle's bed at Garden Square Assisted Living was a painting called, "The Poisoned Pool." It was painted by his father—my grandfather—in 1913. My uncle loved his father; in some ways he idolized him. He may have been remembering the past more fondly than it actually was, but in his mind his father was "a wonderful man," and he talked about him often during the time he was with us in Colorado.

In the painting, two men are at a desert water hole. Around the hole are the bones of animals, indicating that the water is poisoned. One man is struggling to drink the water; the other man is restraining him in an attempt to save his life.

We will never know what happened to these two men, conjured up in my grandfather's mind almost a century ago; but I do know this—most of us thirst for salvation in its many and varied forms; but so often when we drink from what we think is the pool of life, we hurt ourselves instead. When our thirst is out of control, we do not hear the restraining voices–from within and without–trying to save us from ourselves.

contents

Prologue: Do Not Yoke Yourselves in a Mismatch with
      Unbelievers   xiii
Introduction: A Stormy Night in Venice   xvii

PART 1

AN ASSORTMENT OF CHARACTERS ON THE SPIRITUALITY SPECTRUM

1	First Date: Love and Evolution 1974	3
2	His Miserable Life Was an Inspiration	11
3	If This Is the Best of All Possible Worlds, Then How the Heck Can I Get Off?	19
4	Second Date: Mere Christianity	29
5	Odd Characters in the Bronx	39
6	To Hell and Back	47
7	Johnnie, Death, and God	53
8	Popcorn and Free Will	65
9	Some New Characters on the Spirituality Spectrum Arrive on the Scene	71
10	Roaming Around in the Past with Ashlie	81
11	Do Things Happen for a Reason?	91
12	Uncle Sonny Contemplates the Universe or How Can We Go On If We Don't Believe in God?	99
13	Uncle Sonny and the Little Old Ladies	109
14	Uncle Sonny Deals with the Big Question: Who Am I?	115

PART 2

THE QUEST FOR IMMORTALITY

15	A Brief History of Modern Spirituality	125
16	What Do People Want?	133

contents

17   Image Boosting   139
18   I Will Not Be Anything Other Than What I Am   145
19   Immortality Projects   151
20   Heroism   161
21   The Holy Missions of War and Revolution   171
22   Feasting on Ambrosia: Good Immortality Projects   179
23   Waiting for the Secular Messiah   185
24   Thomas Aquinas Weighs-In on Immortality Projects   195
25   The Joy of Martyrdom Versus Veal Piccata Sautéed
     Lightly in a Lemon Sauce   201
26   Mandy in the Middle   209
27   Ernest Becker and Temple Grandin: A Slam Dunk
     Confirmation of Spiritual Hunger   217

PART 3
FROM THE BRONX TO THE ALAMO

28   September 11th   225
29   The Quest for Significance in the Bronx   229
30   Strangers in a Strange Land   237
31   Chaos as the Road to Salvation   245
32   A Candle at Thanksgiving   253
33   Thorn Birds at the Alamo   259

PART 4
LIFE, LOVE, AND DEATH

34   Mother Melanie Contemplates Her Life in 2081   271
35   Life Begins at Sixty (But Death Begins on Day One)   279
36   Significance, Disease, and Death   285
37   A Bridge Is Broken   291
38   A Short Visit to a Parallel Universe   301
39   Morrie Returns from the Dead for One Last Chapter   309
40   The Childhood of Eternity   317

Notes   323

acknowledgments

Many of the ideas expressed in this book have been built upon the thoughts of others who have come before. Two thinkers in particular, who passed away a generation ago, deserve special recognition. Anyone interested in the ideas in this book should run out to the bookstore to purchase a copy of Ernest Becker's, *The Denial of Death*. The truth of who we are seems to shout out to the reader on every page.

In 1951, a self-educated longshoreman, Eric Hoffer, described the psychological profile of the fanatic in concise and brilliant detail. Although he didn't use the phrase, spiritually dysfunctional, his book, *The True Believer*, clearly fits that category.

This book could not have existed without the Linets—Sonny, Millie, Richard, and Jonathan—who are all gone now; but whose lives can, perhaps, gain the meaning in death that seemed beyond them in life.

Among the living there are a few hardy souls who made a difference.

First, as always, is my wife Becky, who put up with my nightly retreats to the den for most of our married life; and then, in an unexpected twist, became first a character in this book and then provided her own theological input. Thus, to say this book could not have existed without her is more than a cliché; it is the reality of what we produced together.

The publisher of Capital Books, Kathleen Hughes, gambled with this book because it's different from the practical line of books they usually publish and because it is, in places, unorthodox. Thanks for taking a chance, Kathleen.

Having worked alone these many years, it was indeed strange to have an outside force read it, process it, analyze it, refocus it, and, most painfully of all for the author, to take the editor's blue pencil to it. All of this was done by the senior editor at Capital Books, Amy

acknowledgments

Fries, whose perceptive eye vastly improved the content and organization. I had heard from various sources that an author should not expect much editorial help; publishers want a finished product. I was, therefore, delighted to get genuine expert advice, and the book is far better as a result.

The last person I would like to thank could be termed, "a famous and accomplished writer." In 1968, thirty-eight years ago, as a young and aspiring writer, I sent what I thought was a humorous piece to Russell Baker, who wrote a syndicated satirical column for the *New York Times*. To my surprise, Baker responded with a little bit of praise and a lot of suggestions, among them the advice that I was not yet ready to write professionally. Seventeen years later, Baker responded to my newspaper columns, this time having lots of good things to say. During this almost four decades, Baker won two Pulitzer Prizes, while this writer won a ton of rejection slips. Now that I'm a senior citizen and Baker is retired, I'd like to publicly thank him for the generosity, encouragement, and advice he offered so long ago.

do not yoke yourselves in a mismatch with unbelievers

Late October 1976, early evening in the kitchen of my small apartment in Germany. We were breaking up for perhaps the hundredth time.

This one, however, would end it once and for all. Sometimes the conversations about god (little g for me, big G for Becky) and man's place in the cosmos were interesting, sometimes agonizing, sometimes exhausting. But the time for theological debate was over. The school year was only two months old, and we were at it again. Now what?

I stood in the kitchen looking at Becky. "If you go now it's over." We both had tears in our eyes. The sun was dropping fast outside the big window over the table. "If you walk out the door I swear I'll never call you, never. I'll never go to your apartment. I'll never pick you up at your classroom. I'll never talk to you again. Never. It's over if you leave. I can't go through this anymore."

I turned and sat at the kitchen table, emotionally drained. At the age of thirty-three it was hard to imagine starting all over again. Going to the O club, taking phone numbers, calling for dates, doing the getting-to-know-you-conversations. Maybe I'll never get married, never have kids, maybe I'll live alone in bachelor apartments forever. How could we ever have thought this would work? I sighed and turned. She was gone. Actually gone. Out-the-door-gone. End-of-relationship-gone. The front door was wide open. I looked out the window. There she was walking to her car.

She had really done it, really walked out.

The whole thing had been ridiculous from the start. I had always been contemptuous of religious people; they were ignorant, superstitious peasants; they were serfs; they were people unable to reason, unable to live life on their own terms without that supernatural crutch. I was Jewish and didn't believe in that either. How could I possibly spend two years with someone who was not only religious, but some kind of super Christian?

Just the month before Becky had consulted God about our relationship. Opening the Bible at random, she ran her finger down the page and got the answer she was looking for.

> *Do not yoke yourselves in a mismatch with unbelievers.*
> *After all, what do righteousness and lawlessness have*
> *in common, or what fellowship can light have with darkness?*
> *What accord is there between Christ and Belial, what*
> *common lot between believer and unbeliever?*
> —2 CORINTHIANS 6:14-15

There it was. The Supreme Judge of the Universe had given a Celestial Thumbs Down to the relationship. That should have been enough to end it. But in spite of God's warning, we stayed together.

Until that day in the kitchen. Now I knew it was over.

Thank god. Finally. What a relief. I'm so tired of these conversations. I could think of two or three girls who I would call tomorrow who had no religious baggage. Finished, finished, *finished.* It's over.

The next day I went through the motions in school and then headed for Foodland, which happened to be right across the street from the Fliegerhorst chapel. I knew she'd be there and she was. Her green Capri was out front. She was inside praying, asking for guidance; maybe she wanted a different answer than "Do not yoke yourself in a mismatch . . ."

I walked past the minister who had been meeting with us for months, trying to work things out. "What if she wants to go to church Sunday morning, and you want to stay in bed and fool around?" he had asked. "Are you okay with having *Catholic* children?"

He started to say something, but I brushed past him. It always seemed that making the decision to marry would be incredibly hard. The world was full of women. Which one? How can anyone make that lifetime commitment?

Prologue

"Becky!"

She turned, shocked to see me. "How did you know I was here?"

"I knew."

We were both crying now. I didn't make any jokes about what god had to say. I had no idea what *I* was going to say. I was in a daze. I just couldn't let her go. "Are you going to be my wife?" I asked. "Are we going to live together forever?" The words came out of my mouth but were somehow disconnected from my brain. I was hearing myself say these things.

The rest of the world was a blur. There was only the two of us standing in the back of the church. The gloomy late afternoon light made its way dimly through the stained-glass windows.

We embraced, we kissed, we cried. I caught a glimpse of the minister turning away; and for a flickering moment, I wondered about those Sunday mornings and those unborn children—*Catholic* children. There would be a lifetime of churches, priests, confessions, crosses and . . . *Jesus,* for crying out loud.

But all of that was secondary to the moment. Emotion trumped reason and there was no turning back.

After two years of this turmoil, getting married would be a piece of cake.

It wasn't.

INTRODUCTION

a stormy night in venice

Over six hundred years ago, on a stormy night in Venice, Francesco Petrarch, known to history as the father of Renaissance humanism, sat in a tower watching ships cast off for foreign ports. The old man dipped his pen in the ink and jotted down a thought: ". . . at this moment, with all the stars hidden by clouds, as my walls and roofs were shaken by the wind, as the sea roared hellishly below, the ships cast loose from the quay and set forth on their journey."[1] He wondered why men take risks and deal so carelessly with their lives. Petrarch paused, looked out at the slanting rain, and was struck by a thought.

> I had got thus far, and was thinking of what to say next, and as my habit is, I was pricking the paper idly with my pen. And I thought how, between one dip of the pen and the next, time goes on, and I hurry, drive myself, and speed toward death. We are always dying. I while I write, you while you read and others while they listen or stop their ears, they are all dying.

Ironically, Petrarch had missed the point. The answer to his query lay in his musings. Men take risks and are careless with their lives because they are pressed by time to make their marks on life. The sailors casting off into the menacing sea and the old man in the tower compelled to produce manuscripts were driven by the same existential needs.

To varying degrees we all set sail for foreign ports, we all take risks, we are all driven, we are all afraid, we are all pressed for time, and we all want the same thing.

The purpose of this book is to explain this compulsion—a psychological and spiritual force—which I believe is the root of human behavior and which goes a long way in answering Life's Big Questions. This force is the carrot on the stick that holds out the promise of salvation in its many and varied forms in front, while simultaneously is the grinning skull of death that chases us from behind.

But how should this story be told? I've written hundreds of thousands of words on the subject, trying to find the right voice. Voluminous academic tracts didn't work. Publishers want books that connect with real people, not with college professors. I had been searching for the right approach for decades, and then in the spring of 2003 . . .

Nobody Cares

"I really don't think anyone cares that you've written hundreds of thousands of words," said my wife upon reading the manuscript. "They're not interested in your problems. It's not worth saying."

I sighed. "I don't think you understand what I'm trying to do in this book. *My* problems, as you put it, are a perfect example of *secular* spirituality. To have pursued a singular goal for the better part of forty years has that religious, existential, reason-to-be dimension. What I'm trying to do in my own personal life is in the same category as the sailors in Venice and the old man in the tower—racing against death to give my life meaning. It's what we all do."

Becky paused for a long, drawn-out moment. "But it's not what I do."

"Of course you do," I said, feeling the conversation edging up a notch. "Are you telling me you don't want your life to be meaningful?"

"*Fred,* of course I want a meaningful life, and I get it from God."

"I understand what you're saying, but the fact is, god isn't enough, even for you."

Becky remained even-tempered as usual, as she calmly hurled a dart right back at me. "How do you know what's enough for me?"

"Because," I said, choosing my words carefully, "when you get a compliment for having done a good job on a project, you feel good about yourself; and if someone criticizes you, you feel bad. It's not just about god. Here on earth you want people's approval too."

"Well, of course I do," she replied steadily. "I'm a human being, I have feelings. Of course I want people to think well of me. But unlike Petrarch, I don't feel pressed by time to make my mark."

I shook my head. Statements like that drive me crazy.

"Are you telling me," I said accusingly, "that you don't care if you die?"

"No, that's not what I'm saying. What I'm saying is that death doesn't frighten me because I know that God exists. My life has meaning in Him."

"And that," I said triumphantly, "is the whole point of this book. We all hunger for meaning, we all want our lives to have counted for something in the greater scheme of creation. You have it built in because of god; me, I have to write books."

It was late September 2003. Early afternoon. We sat at the dining room table of our Colorado home. Through the window summer was still in full bloom. We were at it again. After twenty-nine years, we were still hacking away at each other's core beliefs.

"Why are we having this conversation?" I asked. "All I wanted was a little feedback."

"And I gave it to you," she said.

"But I disagree with you," I said right back at her. "I'm going to leave it in."

So How Should This Story Be Told?

So, how should this story be told? I had been searching for the right approach for decades, and then in the spring of 2003, two old and ailing men impinged on my consciousness, suggesting another angle. These two old guys entered the picture at exactly the same time. One was famous, the other obscure. One cheerful, one bitter. One philosophical about death, the other fearful of it. One happy, the other miserable. And it led me to realize that the key to discussing our spiritual nature and our hunger for salvation, lay right before my eyes with Uncle Sonny and Morrie.

And then, of course, there was Becky

PART 1

An Assortment of Characters on the Spirituality Spectrum

A * <————————————————> B**

Going from Point A to Point B

I turned to speak to God
About the world's despair;
But to make bad matters worse
I found God wasn't there.
—Robert Frost, "Not All There"

For I am certain that neither death nor life, neither angels nor principalities, neither the present nor the future, nor powers, neither height nor depth nor any other creature, will be able to separate us from the love of God that comes to us in Christ Jesus, our Lord.

—Romans 8:38-39

*A - Atheist
**B - Believer

1

first date:
love and evolution 1974

. . . since man was made out of the dust of the earth . . . there is nothing else, your honor, that has caused the difference of opinion, of bitterness, of hatred, of war, of cruelty, that religion has caused.
—Clarence Darrow at the Scopes Trial, 1925

In 1974, I was thirty-one and she was twenty-three. Becky needed someone "older" because she had been an adult since around the age of four; while I, being a normal male, had been an actual grown-up for about a year. By then I had been overseas for six years and had seen the capitals of the world—Tokyo, Bangkok, Hong Kong, Taipei, Paris, Rome, Geneva, Casablanca, Jerusalem, Madrid, Cairo, Tunis, and Marrakech. She was fresh out of Paola, Kansas. We were teaching in Germany in schools for the children of military personnel stationed overseas and were both newly arrived in Hanau, Germany.

Checking Out the New Crop of Female Teachers

We met at a Friday afternoon happy hour at the Rhein Main Officers' Club, early in September. It was a perfect time and place to check out the new crop of female teachers, many of whom were looking for the perfect place to check out the young officers and pilots. Becky's presence at a happy hour—in an actual bar—was about as rare as snow in May. But her friends were going, and, well, there she was. I had been edging in the direction of a very shapely teacher with long blonde hair when I landed, for a moment, at the booth where Becky was sitting with a cluster of girls.

"You're a new arrival here, aren't you?"

She said she was. So we got to talking. A half hour later we were embroiled in a conversation about the civil rights movement. She was saying something, and I thought to myself that here is someone I could marry. I actually articulated those thoughts. What she had was substance. Maybe it was that natural maturity or obvious intelligence. It had such an appeal. No frivolousness, no adolescent flirting, just good conversation. While so many girls seemed hollow, or mentally vacuous, or self–focused, or drenched in affectations, or insecure–she was the opposite: deep, full, introspective yet outer-focused, and genuine. I asked if she would like to have dinner with me. She said she'd love to. And as the evening progressed, it became apparent that we were incompatible, that we inhabited different universes, and that this relationship was going to die at the very moment of its inception.

During dinner, at a table below us, I noticed Diane, a teacher at Becky's school. Diane was cute and perky. I had met her at the officers' club in Stuttgart two years before (yes, the O Club was indeed a great source of dates) and suggested we head downtown where we found a German beer hall with a loud brass German band playing the usual beer hall songs. In the course of the conversation, Diane told me that up until the year before she had never had a date. I figured I hadn't heard correctly. She was cute, warm, and friendly and quick to hold my hand. She must have had plenty of dates. "That's right," she said, shouting over the din, muttering something about "her sisters."

"What?" I asked, leaning forward and putting down my beer. The brass band drowned out everything.

"I was a member of the Ursuline Sisters," she shouted.

"What does that mean?"

"Up until last year I was a nun!"

I was stunned. Nuns were colorless old women who rapped the knuckles of kids in Catholic school. It blew me away.

Back in the relative quiet of the Rhein Main O Club, I pointed Diane out to Becky and told her about Diane's sordid past. She didn't seem surprised.

"Some nuns return to a secular life."

"How do you know?" I asked

"In Paola, I used to visit the sisters at the convent."

"Oh," I said, trying not to sound too interested. "Why's that?"

She hesitated, weighing her response. "I was lonely in Paola, and they were my friends."

She was friends with nuns.

The steaks arrived, the band played on. We talked about nuns.

"I've never understood how someone could give up a normal life to live like that," I said.

"But for them it is normal."

"Giving up sex is not normal."

She looked straight at me, amused and challenging. "It's not so hard."

"Did you ever think about becoming a nun?" I asked.

"Not really, but I'm converting to Catholicism."

"From what?"

"My mother's family was Southern Baptist. My dad's was Methodist."

I asked her why she was converting, but she demurred, implying it was too personal to talk about with strangers. "Maybe some other time."

This is ridiculous, I thought. *She's converting to Catholicism.* Religion must be important to her. It was meaningless to me. Catholics inhabited an alien world. In elementary school the "Catholic" kids were in the minority. Most people in the world were Jewish. In high school, I looked with amusement at the Italian girls crossing themselves when the elevator train passed a church. Catholics used words like "baptism" and "Jesus," and they wore big crosses and had black hair. They had Italian and Irish names. The super of our building was Catholic.

And so was Becky.

We made a date for Sunday.

Green Pants

I picked her up at the Hanau train station Sunday morning. All was quiet out on the platform by Track 4. Very few people were out and about on this warm September morning. I sat on the wooden bench, looking occasionally in the direction of the train, knowing full well that it would come exactly on time as trains always did in Germany.

I looked down the track and knew she could be the one. At thirty-one I was ready. My parents were back in New York thinking I'd never do it. In my early twenties I couldn't imagine getting married. I was having too much fun. I had a lifetime to be married. But now, with two serious girlfriends fitting into the mosaic of the past, it was time. The biological clock wasn't ticking, but the psychological one was making a lot of noise.

She was a possibility all right; but I hadn't gotten a good look at the entire package. The night before she had worn some kind of a smock. The lights had been dim, and, well, I wanted to get a better look. So I shook myself from the reverie of this peaceful Sunday morning and walked down the stairs of the platform where all passengers arrive. The train came into the station, and a surprising number of people departed and marched swiftly and quietly—in good German order—down the stairs. I spotted her and came up behind to get a good look. She was wearing green pants. *Beautiful* green pants. And that whole "Catholic" business ceased to be all that important.

"Don't you *dare* put that in there," she said in 2003.

"Why not? That's exactly the way it happened."

"I don't care. You are not going to write about my rear end in any book. It's not necessary. It has nothing to do with getting at the truth of life."

"But it's part of the story, part of the whole picture."

"Fred, that's just ridiculous. You sneaking up behind me at the train station has nothing to do with *your* version of the eternal truths."

"But it does, because if you didn't have the right shape, then we wouldn't have gotten married and had all those conversations, and my mind and my life would have gone in different directions and . . ."

By this time she was tickling and pinching me, and I was screaming for mercy.

Evolution on Trial

That night, on our first date, we went to see the local community production of *Inherit the Wind,* the fictionalized story of the Scopes Monkey Trial.[1] It was the perfect vehicle to set us off.

Teaching evolution was against the law in Tennessee. In 1925, a young biology teacher in Dayton, Tennessee, with the support of the American Civil Liberties Union (ACLU), challenged the law and was put on trial for teaching evolution. The case attracted nationwide attention because two of America's most famous men were the opposing attorneys. William Jennings Bryan, the former secretary of state and three-time unsuccessful candidate for President of the United States, offered his services to the prosecution. Clarence Darrow, the most prominent defense attorney in the nation, fresh from his highly publicized triumph in the Leopold and Loeb murder trial, came to Dayton to defend Scopes.

It was to be a clash of giants, a made-for-TV special before TV. Both men wanted to use the case as a national forum for their views on evolution. Darrow, at sixty-eight, was the prototype of the modern attorney who takes high-profile cases to feed his megalomania. He was an admitted agnostic who considered Christian fundamentalists to be small town ignoramuses. Bryan, at sixty-five, was deeply religious and appalled by the insidiousness of the theory of evolution that, by implication, questioned the existence of God and the special place and purpose of man in the universe.

Darrow typified the liberal city lawyer—well-spoken on a variety of subjects, sharp-tongued, flamboyant, and urbane. Bryan was kind-hearted and rural, a crusader with a zealot's hyperbolic style. Darrow was big-boned, with a craggy, lined face, a hoarse voice, and limp gray hair. Bryan was flaccid, fat, and bald with a graying fringe around the back of his head.

Both men owed their fame to fighting righteous causes against difficult odds. Bryan had been a champion of the long-suffering farmers, while Darrow defended labor leaders, communists, anarchists, and murderers. Bryan challenged entrenched power and money. Darrow played the gadfly, attacking prejudice and ignorance.

Bryan came to prominence in 1896 when he gained the Democratic nomination for president at the tender age of thirty-six, on the strength of his booming voice and a crusading zeal for the plight of farmers.

Bryan was an orator of rare ability. Before the advent of microphones, his booming voice could fill up a convention hall. His youth, his vigor, and his conviction were inspiring and electric. Although he never achieved the presidency, he became addicted to crusades and heroic stands. At various times he opposed World War I, championed women's suffrage, and supported prohibition. But the issue that earned him immortality was his war on evolution.

Sitting across the courtroom in Dayton, Tennessee, was Clarence Darrow, the tough, raspy-voiced, caustic, big city, liberal defense lawyer ready to give his all for Darwin and evolution. "Everybody's for something," Darrow once said. "I'm just against." He claimed to oppose ignorance, prejudice, inequality, and privilege. He was a liberal's liberal, and like Bryan, clearly enjoyed his role as a champion of great causes. During his defense of the accused assassins of the governor of Idaho in 1907, he had grandly proclaimed, "I speak for the poor, for the weak, for the weary, for that long line of men, who, in darkness and despair, have borne the labors of the human race."

But his real goal was self-promotion. As the prototype of the flamboyant, self-serving attorney, he sought high profile cases. In 1895, his defense of labor leader and later socialist, Eugene V. Debs, brought him national prominence. Like Bryan, he was hooked on causes that brought him fame. He defended labor leaders, communists, anarchists, and murderers, many of whom were guilty. Nevertheless, the year before the Scopes trial, this champion of the poor defended Nathan Leopold and Richard Loeb, two rich and brilliant boys, ages seventeen and eighteen, who had kidnapped and murdered a fourteen-year-old boy for "the sake of thrill."

The following year, at the height of his powers and fame, Clarence Darrow arrived in Dayton, Tennessee, to defend John Scopes, take on William Jennings Bryan, and gain the spotlight in what possibly was the highest profile trial in American history.

Bryan deplored evolution. "The brute standards (the evolutionists) advocate would rob man of his high standards and drag him down to the brute basis. Evolution is a stagnant pool, the center of disease and death, and revealed religion is a flowing spring, giving forth all the time that which refreshes and invigorates."

Darrow, on the other hand, had no use for religion or the Bible. "Since man was made out of the dust of the earth," said Darrow, ". . . there is nothing else . . . that has caused the differences of opinion, of bitterness, of hatred, of war, of cruelty, that religion has caused." Another time he referred to Christianity as "your fool religion."

It was called the Scopes "Monkey" Trial because evolution and man's supposed descent from apes was on trial. But in a larger sense, it was a debate about man's place in the cosmos. If evolution was true, then man might be a biological accident, and by implication, god may not exist. Clarence Darrow was basically there to say just that. Bryan, who had an abiding faith in God and accepted the Bible literally, was there to defend the idea that God is in Heaven, man is His creation, and every one of us has a part in God's plan.

Microcosm

I didn't know it at the time, but the Scopes Monkey Trial was a microcosm of ideas for which I was just beginning to search. Darrow's publicity-seeking and joy at "going against" and Bryan's lifetime of crusading were manifestations of *the human need for heroism, defiance, purpose, and significance.* While each man played the role of just wanting to do what's right, of helping people in need, of fighting for justice, or of going against convention, their primary need was to make their own lives worthy, to gain the approval and admiration of their fellow men, and to do all this before death overtook them. They both derived an essential joy in fighting the good fight.

While Bryan was the "religious nut," and Darrow the "atheist leftist lawyer," Darrow was—if not conventionally religious—then as hungry for spiritual purpose as Bryan. For as we shall see, *spirituality takes many forms,* and it is this hunger for spiritual purpose that drives us. In Bryan, we see the appeal of a crusading heroism; in Darrow we see the joy of defiance. Both are powerful manifestations of the human hunger for meaning. In that sense, their needs were no different than the rest of us; they were just more public.

A few days after the trial, while still in Dayton, after a midday Sunday dinner, William Jennings Bryan went upstairs for a nap and quietly died in his sleep. Darrow callously suggested that Bryan died "from a busted belly," although it was probably from a broken heart. His life was over. At the trial, Darrow had made a fool of him in front of the entire country; his beloved Bible was shown to be indefensible. But perhaps, most importantly, there was nothing left for him to do; there would be no more crusades, no more glory. Life was over; it was time to die.

The trial was among the most public and dramatic examples of the resistance to evolution that is going on today, and which could be defined as *existential dread.* For if Darwin was correct that we are a biological accident, then god and heaven are negated, along with any cosmic purpose for the human race in general and we as individuals. What that means is that the history of mankind—all the armies that

9

have marched, all the lives and loves and ambitions of every single individual who has come and gone, all the ideas, all the thought, all the prayer, all the faith in god, all the poignancy of life—is utterly meaningless in a universe that is incomprehensibly vast. If we are, as Voltaire said, just "atoms on a ball of mud," if all of human history is a speck on a speck lost in a galaxy among billions of galaxies, then everything we do is meaningless, and how can we cope with that?

Let's Go Back to My Apartment for Some Wine and Music

But on that Sunday night early in September 1974, I wasn't thinking about those things, and after the play I asked Becky if she would like to go back to my apartment for some wine, music, and conversation.

"I'd rather not," she said.

Of course, I knew she wouldn't. She was solid and soft and intelligent and pleasant and virtuous, and she wasn't going back to someone's apartment on the first date. But what annoyed me was that I was a perfectly decent guy, and I did have a nice apartment, and it was a nice place to go after a date just to talk. All of which I told her. "My intentions are completely honorable," I said. "Really, it's just a nice place to go."

"I'd really rather not."

I drove her home.

We stood in front of her house in Erlensee. The streetlights provided the usual symmetrical illumination with pockets of dark and umbrellas of light. The early September air was warm. The little suburban German town was particularly quiet on this Sunday night. Her hands were on her hips. Her waist was tiny. A slightly amused smile was on her face. She wore the same green pants from that morning.

"Are you angry with me?" she asked.

"No, I'm not angry," I said, sounding like a broken record. "I just thought it would be a nice place to go."

Her hands were still on her hips. "Well, I don't feel comfortable doing that."

"Well, I'll see you then." And I knew I would. We were teaching in the same building. We frequented the same officers' club.

There was no kiss goodnight.

It was our first date and our first break-up.

2

his miserable life
was an inspiration

There is only one question which really matters: why do bad things
happen to good people? All other theological conversation is intel-
lectually diverting. . . . Virtually every meaningful conversation I
have ever had with people on the subject of God and religion has
either started with this question, or gotten around to it before long.[1]
—Rabbi Harold Kushner, *When Bad Things Happen to Good People*

At the end of April 2003, we flew to New York to bring my uncle back
to Colorado to spend the rest of his life. We were also in the midst of
reading the blockbuster bestseller *Tuesdays With Morrie* together at night,
and those two events seemed to be a good starting point to tackle
those eternal questions.

In *Tuesdays With Morrie,* a dying Morrie Schwartz talks every week
with a former student, imparting to him lessons for living. The old-
man/young-man relationship was clear. Sportswriter Mitch Albom
connected with his old professor in the final months of his life. Mitch
was hustling, he was making money, he was on the move; but by the
end of the book, he had learned life's lessons from Morrie as the older
man's life drained away. The book sold gazillions of copies. The testi-
monials on the back cover oozed superlatives.

> This book is an incredible treasure. One's sense of our mortality
> is a great teacher and source of enlightenment. To have a teacher
> share this experience provides us with a profound wisdom and
> insight. I laughed, cried and ordered five copies for our children.
> —Bernie S. Siegel, MD, author of *Love, Medicine and Miracles*

Tuesdays with Morrie is a sweet and gentle tribute to age and aging. Thanks, Mitch Albom, for introducing me to Morrie Schwartz. His dignity and frankness stirred me. His good humor and zest left me smiling.

–Alex Kotlowitz, author of There Are No Children Here

Every page of this beautiful moving little book shines with the warmth of unembarrassed love.

–Rabbi Harold Kushner, author of When Bad Things Happen To Good People

Then there was Uncle Sonny. *Good humor? Enlightenment? Wisdom? Zest? Unembarrassed love?* I don't think so. He was not going gentle into that good night.

Just the year before we had the following phone conversation:

Me: Hello?
Uncle Sonny: You f-----, c---, s------, son-of-a-bich, mother f------ piece of s---. You f------ bastard. You f---, you f---. I'll kill you, you f------ c--- s-----."
Me: Uncle Sonny, is there something bothering you? Please, don't hold back. Tell me what's *really* on your mind.

It was one of his paranoid, alcoholic rages. He would sit in his apartment night after night ruminating on how everyone was cheating him. Some other family members got the same treatment. So did his neighbor Steve, the one-eyed man with an eye patch over his right eye, whom Uncle Sonny had punched in the face in the hall of their apartment building.

The old-man/young-man angle, which made *Tuesday's with Morrie* so compelling, would certainly be a stretch in this case because although my uncle was eighty-three, at fifty-nine I wasn't exactly young, and I certainly wasn't going to get any wisdom from Uncle Sonny. He had little in common with Morrie Schwartz whose touching death and relationship with Mitch Albom became the gigantic bestseller. Morrie was warm, intelligent, educated, open, friendly, lovable, interesting, and courageous in the face of death. My uncle, by contrast, was a chain-smoking alcoholic at the end of a tragic life. He was profane, bitter, angry, emotionally erratic, and afraid of death. While Morrie was focused on other people, Sonny was focused on himself. The only thing they had in common was that they were old.

Morrie's life was uplifting; my uncle's was tragic. What could reviewers say about *this* book? "Sonny's profanity, alcoholism, and depression left me smiling."

Or how about: "Thanks for introducing me to Sonny Linet. His miserable life was an inspiration."

But it wasn't always miserable. There was a time, long ago, when his life held promise.

Storming the Beaches of Normandy

Back in 1944, we had a somewhat different relationship. I was a six-month-old infant and he was a twenty-five-year-old GI stationed in England. He stormed the beaches of Normandy about a month after the D-Day invasion and saw little action—at least on the battlefield. His war stories involved sex and fights, and I more or less helped him out. "I carried a picture of you in my wallet," he told me fifty-five years later. "I'd show all the English girls, and they'd say, 'Oh, isn't he cute,' and then I'd get them in bed."

Within a half hour of arriving in Liverpool, he told me, "I was messing around . . . The English girls were very loose." He saw little fighting in France, but ended up in a few haylofts. He was not bragging or showing off or looking for approval or respect when he told

UNCLE SONNY DRINKING AND SMOKING IN A MANCHESTER PUB, 1944.

these stories; he just wanted to tell them. When you come to the end of your life, you want to pass it on to the next generation. You know it's over, and whatever you did and whoever you are will be lost to eternity.

Like so many young men in time of war, he drank, brawled, swore, and chased women. One night in Manchester, he went downtown on the "Negro's night." That's the way it was back then. Whites and blacks went to town on different nights, and Uncle Sonny found himself surrounded by angry black men. But he also had many friends among them, and one insisted that they leave him alone. If he had been knifed to death that night, we all would have been spared the tragedy that developed later.

Richard and Johnnie

The tragedy was that both of his children died of muscular dystrophy. Slowly. After the war he married my Aunt Millie who was short, cute, and chatty, with dark hair and dark eyes. Her brother had died from the disease, and the doctors feared that the female carried it while the male contracted it.

They were afraid to have children and waited seven years. My aunt wanted to adopt. My uncle wanted children of his own. The doctors told them to go ahead–the outcome was unknown.

When I was twelve, sitting in the back of the car looking up at my parents looming large in the front seat, my mother said, "So it's true,

JOHNNIE (L) AND RICHARD, BRONX, NEW YORK, AROUND 1960.

14

PREGNANT AGAIN, 1958.

Millie's pregnant." Wow, I thought, a new person coming into the world. A cousin. I memorized the moment, and now in retrospect it was a cruel kind of irony—to be so excited about new life and for that life to already be doomed from the moment of conception.

But we didn't know that then.

Soon after Richard was born, my proud uncle stood over him, moving his finger back and forth in front of the infant's face. Uncle Sonny grinned through his cigarette. His head was already shiny and devoid of hair, except for the brown fringe.

"See how he follows with his eyes. He's so alert."

The doctors told them that Richard was fine and to go ahead and have another. But the doctors were wrong. Richard had the disease and was also autistic. He would not grow up. There would be no school plays, no ball games, no helping with homework, no watching him mature. He was already dying. And Millie was pregnant again.

Still they hoped. Maybe the doctors were wrong. Maybe the next one would be a girl. Maybe not *all* boys got the disease. But *maybes* are often in the category of desperate hope. When we start with the maybes, we are often kidding ourselves.

Johnnie was born two years after Richard, and it was soon apparent he shared a similar fate. The disease was less debilitating in Johnnie. Richard was never normal. He physically and mentally curled in upon

15

himself and died at thirteen, but Johnnie did better. Unlike Richard, his mind was sound. He went to school, but was shunted off into special classes for the disabled where he learned little. But at least he was there, which offered a semblance of normality.

Unfortunately, the deterioration was steady and relentless. At the age of fourteen, Johnnie could no longer walk and resigned himself to a wheelchair. At twenty, while at a summer camp for the handicapped, he had a breathing attack, and they stuffed a tube down his throat. He looked like a fish on a hook, helpless and afraid. His eyes were wild with terror. The doctors explained that the only way he could breathe was with a tracheotomy, and that he would have to be attached to a machine for the rest of his life. Did they want him to do it? Johnnie nodded as best he could. "Yes, yes, yes," he seemed to be saying. "I want to live, please, I want to live."

That was the first tube. By the time he died ten years later, he had a tube for everything–food, toilet, and breathing. He could talk, although somewhat breathlessly, and could move his tongue. Otherwise he was immobilized. He had no muscles, he was emaciated, and almost always frightened. They rigged a contraption near his face he could touch with his tongue to trigger an alarm at the nurse's station. He was continually testing to see if his tongue would reach, or if it indeed triggered a response.

Meanwhile, Uncle Sonny went to pieces. He drank, quit work, and never went back. He went on welfare. For years they lived in "the projects," low-rent housing in the Bronx.

What was it like all those years? I don't know much. Taking care of Johnnie was a full-time job. They would get up several times a night just to shift his position. They had to take him to the bathroom. Every year he weakened until that day at camp in 1978 when they moved him permanently to Goldwater Memorial Hospital on Roosevelt Island in the East River.

By the time Johnnie was moved to Goldwater, I had already been teaching overseas for ten years, so I more or less absolved myself of the burden. During the summers we occasionally visited them with my parents; but the visits were always unpleasant, and we were all glad when they ended. Aunt Millie's chattiness had evolved into ongoing jabber. She talked and talked and talked, often not finishing a thought as she went on to the next one.

Becky Critiques This Book

"It's not a very interesting story," my wife said after reading up to this point.

"Well, I'm not writing a novel," I said defensively. "I'm just telling it straight out, just as it happened."

"But where are you going with it?" she asked. "What's the point? What does Uncle Sonny have to do with the meaning of life?"

"Well, I'm going to use Uncle Sonny's life as a jumping-off place to answer the Eternal Questions. It's an attempt to personalize these ideas."

"When you say, 'Eternal Questions,' you're talking about God," she said accusingly.

"That's part of it, but it's much more than that. It's a book about purpose, and death, and the fear of death. It's about the universe and our place in it. But it's really a book about spirituality, about how we are all religious beings."

She wasn't surprised. During our twenty-seven years of marriage we had talked quite a bit about religion, rarely agreeing on anything. No, she wasn't surprised that I would take a stab at explaining human behavior and human psychological hungers. *That* she could deal with. But me as an expert on spirituality was something else again.

"So, a Jewish atheist is going to write about the importance of religion."

"No, no, no, that's not the point. It's not religion that I'm writing about. Religion is just one manifestation of spirituality. Besides, only someone like me can have a reasonably objective perspective. Your average everyday Christian has so much psychic and existential energy infused in his beliefs, that he couldn't possibly see the forest for the trees. It's not about religion. It's not even about theology. It's about our deepest fears and our deepest needs."

"So you're saying I'm too blinded by faith to be rational."

"Becky, that's not what I meant. My point is . . ."

"But you just said that Christians can't see the forest for the trees. I would say the same about you. God is right there in front of you, and you can't see it."

As usual, our discussion edged up into friendly and not-so-friendly banter. "But my point—if you'll let me finish—is that Christians can only give one interpretation to spirituality, and I'm trying to point out that we *all* need spirituality, even if it's expressed in secular form. When most people think of spirituality, they think of the supernatural, like god or the tooth fairy. . ."

"You know, I really don't appreciate you putting God and the tooth fairy in the same sentence."

I shook my head. "*Becky*, I'm not trying to make fun of god. All I'm saying is that . . ."

"*Fred*, that's exactly what you're doing. When you equate God and the tooth fairy, you are trivializing Him."

I took a breath. "That's not what I meant to do. Would you please just back off and let me finish what I was saying?"

"No, I won't back off."

"Look, I'm very sorry; I apologize. I beg your forgiveness. I admit it—god is much more important than the tooth fairy. As a matter of fact, there wouldn't even be teeth if it wasn't for god."

Becky was smiling now, satisfied that she had made me grovel once again. "Okay, finish your point."

"The point I wanted to make is that spirituality can be anything that gives people a sense of meaning or purpose. It's not just guru stuff or even god stuff. We all know that we're going to die, and that we have limited time to live fully and well. If we're satisfied with our lives we can die with some sense of contentment, knowing we have added something to the cosmos. This to me is at the heart of spirituality."

So, Where Are You Going with It?

"So where are you going with it?" Becky asked. "Is it going to be uplifting? Are there insights about how to live? Poignant death scenes? Spiritual messages? Uncle Sonny is not exactly Morrie."

"Uncle Sonny's life," I said slowly, "represents the one unanswerable question. Until that question is answered successfully, as far as I'm concerned, all discussion of god is in the realm of fantasy."

"Human suffering," she offered, knowing where I was going with this.

I nodded. "If god is a benevolent and loving Creator, then why did he create cancer and earthquakes? Why does he allow little girls to be gang-raped and murdered? Why did he ruin Uncle Sonny's life by giving him two boys with fatal diseases? I want to know *why*."

3

if this is the best of all possible worlds, then how the heck can I get off?

Ah, best of worlds, where are you?

—Voltaire, *Candide*

I read the Book of Job last night—I don't think God comes well out of it.

—Virginia Wolf

On November 1, 1755, at 9:40 a.m., an earthquake, tidal wave, and fire destroyed the city of Lisbon. Fifteen thousand were killed in six minutes. Another fifteen thousand died later of injuries. And the people of Lisbon lifted their faces to Heaven and asked, "Why?"

God could not have chosen a more inopportune time. November 1st was All Saints Day, and the good Catholic people of Lisbon were in church praying to the God who watched impassively as they were crushed, burned, and drowned.

Some were tempted to say, as people often do, that the disaster was God's way of punishing sin. But the people of Lisbon were certainly less sinful than, say, the cosmopolitans of Paris. And besides, they were after all, in church . . . praying . . . to God . . . on a Holy day. Nine-forty a.m. was *prime time*. Everyone was inside where they were more vulnerable. Why did this happen?

When Bad Things Happen to Good People

Reconciling a benevolent and loving god with the ubiquity of human suffering is a question that never goes away because the answers are somehow never satisfying and because the world that god created continues to be surfeited with natural disasters and disease. On December 26, 2004, a tsunami washed away 280,000 people in South East Asia. The following year, hurricane Katrina killed almost 2,000 Americans, destroyed New Orleans, and displaced many more. Soon after that, an earthquake crushed over 50,000 in Pakistan. In every case, the inevitable question surfaced: What role does God play in human suffering? "Did God let this happen," asked Sergeant Tyrone Short, a Colorado National Guardsman helping in New Orleans, "or is this God's handiwork?"[1]

The most widely read book on the subject was the 1981 bestseller *When Bad Things Happen To Good People* by Rabbi Harold Kushner. Kushner's son Aaron was born with progeria or rapid-aging disease. The doctor explained that "Aaron would never grow much beyond three feet in height, would have no hair on his head or body, would look like a little old man while he was still a child, and would die in his early teens."[2]

The rabbi was a good person. Why did this happen to him? Why do bad things happen to good people? How can God allow such seemingly arbitrary evil? "If God existed," Rabbi Kushner mused, "if He was minimally fair, let alone loving and forgiving, how could he do this to me?" It is one hard question to answer.

The most interesting discussion on the subject took place in the wake of the Lisbon earthquake of 1755. Europe was in the midst of "the Enlightenment," a secular, intellectual, and creative explosion that frowned on superstition and religion and made Reason the new god. The atmosphere in Europe was electric with creative thought and towering intellects, and it's not surprising then, that the leading lights of the time rolled up their sleeves to engage each other in an Olympian debate on the meaning of human suffering.

The prevailing outlook of the time, "Philosophical Optimism," explained it this way: God is infallible. He is omnipotent and perfect. He can't make mistakes. If He wrote in the great book of life and death that thirty thousand people must die in an earthquake, then not only is it not a bad thing, but also it's all for the best. On the surface it may seem terrible, but ultimately only good can come from it because God, the Ultimate Good, would not allow it to happen or cause it to happen unless it had a positive outcome. If God could have made the world without evil and suffering, He would have. But since He did not, and He is perfect, then this world, although not the best as perceived by us, is at least the *best possible* that God could have made.

Everything happens for a reason, even if we mere mortals cannot see it. What seems to be disorder is really part of His Grand Design. What seems evil will eventually lead to good. No matter how vile, tragic, arbitrary, or chaotic an incident may seem, its ultimate result will be desirable and positive. Therefore, instead of whining about the unfairness of life, we should accept the fact that God knows what He is doing, and in the end, everything works out for the best. Or as poet Alexander Pope put it in the 1730s in his poem "Essay on Man, Epistle 1": "Whatever is, is right."

The world we live in, with its wars disease, rapes, murders, savagery and uncertainties is the best possible world that God could make?

I don't think Uncle Sonny—watching his sons deteriorate and die—would have bought that line of reasoning, and frankly neither did I.

Voltaire Tells It Like It Is

Voltaire didn't buy it either. At the time of the Lisbon earthquake, he was sixty-one years old and probably France's most celebrated citizen. He was a playwright, poet, and philosopher with a predilection for satire. Voltaire was the leading light of the European Enlightenment, and to him, Philosophical Optimism was a delusion. It was a way to explain the inexplicable. To the Grand Old Man of Letters, evil was evil, not some hidden good. And he said as much in his satirical story, *Zadig*.

Zadig—a well-meaning, well-educated, bright, and philosophical young man—is forced to endure a series of misadventures because of the stupidity, selfishness, and ignorance of others.

Late in the story, Zadig meets a hermit. They are lodged in a generous man's home. The next day the hermit says, "I wish to leave this man a token of my regard and affection," and proceeds to burn down the man's house. Later, they are put up by a widow and her charming fourteen-year-old nephew. While walking with the boy over a bridge, the hermit says, "Come, I must prove my gratitude to your aunt," which he does by drowning the boy.

Zadig is appalled, but the hermit, who is really an angel, explains how these seemingly evil acts really work out for the best. Burning down the man's house will reveal buried treasure. In another year, the boy would have killed his aunt. "There is no evil from which some good does not spring," the angel instructs. Men can never understand the ramifications of every evil, but in the end, everything works out for the best.

As the angel talks, Zadig, speaking for Voltaire, interrupts with a series of "buts . . ."

"But . . . would it not have been better to have corrected this youth, and to have made him virtuous, than to drown him?" No, says the angel. "If he had been virtuous, and had continued to live, it would have been his destiny to be murdered himself, together with the wife he was to marry, and the son whom she was to bear." His drowning was the best solution in the best of all possible worlds. Men think that the boy drowned by accident, said the angel, ". . . but there is no such thing as accident; all that takes place is either a trial, or a punishment, or a reward or a foretelling."

Zadig's "buts" were a cry against submitting to destiny. We are victims of the vagaries of fortune, but we do not have to submit to it by blindly believing that suffering has some positive function. There is no hidden good in evil. We desperately want to believe in God and His goodness and His Plan, but since it makes no sense in the face of thousands of years of ongoing misery and suffering, we insert the square peg into the round hole, insisting that it fits. Evil, we are told, is really good.

Voltaire responded to the Lisbon earthquake with an epic poem in which he heaped scorn on the idea that everything works out for the best. The Optimists, he argued in verse, are telling the women and children who are crushed, mangled, torn, and slowly dying that their suffering will ultimately have positive consequences. Basically, Voltaire is telling them to shut up. "I'm crushed and dying and you're telling me it's all for the best?" Or, as he put it: "From consolation you increase my pain."

The "best of all possible worlds" argument is far from satisfying.

Explaining Robert

What would Robert have thought about this best of all possible worlds? In the fall of 2003, I visited a high school classroom for the severely handicapped. Some were very slow, some retarded, while others were confined in wheelchairs. An eight-year-old boy with the mental age of three months sat on the floor waving his arms and screaming. But most of all there was Robert. And if I could, I would ask god about him. Since god is silent, I would ask Rick Warren.

Robert was probably the ugliest human being I had ever seen. He was completely immobilized and strapped to a wheelchair. He breathed through a tube in his throat and communicated through an electronic device. His tongue hung out of a gaping, drooling mouth. But his eyes were the worst part––they were more than double the normal size and protruded about an inch from his face, giving the impression of eye-stalks. Robert looked like an alien being. But he was not a vegetable; he had a mind. He was able to maneuver his wheelchair; he had voli-tion; he was cognizant of life around him and responded to it.

My heart ached for Robert. We all know that life is unfair, but for Robert, and Rabbi Kushner's son, the word *unfair* hardly suffices. *Cosmic injustice* comes a bit closer, but that phrase takes us back to god. We want this universe to make sense, and this kind of suffering is an ongoing reminder that god's world is often cruel, and we don't know why.

The week I visited Robert's room, I was finally reading Rick Warren's gigantic bestseller, *The Purpose Driven Life*. "The book," said an article in the *Denver Post*, "is more than a best seller. It's become a movement." It had already been read by 1.5 million people at 4,500 churches in twenty countries.[3] It obviously hit a nerve, met some need. The subtitle gives us a clue. The book is going to answer this question: "What on earth am I here for?"

Here's what Rick Warren says about you and me and Robert[4]:

You are not an accident. Your birth was no mistake or mishap, and your life is no fluke of nature. Your parents may not have planned you, but God did. He was not at all surprised by your birth. In fact, He expected it.

God created Robert. He wasn't a fluke. This is what God wanted. Long before you were conceived by your parents, you were con-ceived in the mind of God. He thought of you first. It is not fate, nor chance, nor luck, nor coincidence that you are breathing at this very moment. You are alive because God wanted to create you!

Robert is paralyzed and breathing through a tube because God created him that way.

> God prescribed every single detail of your body. He deliberately chose your race, the color of your skin, your hair, and every other feature. He custom made your body just the way He wanted it.

God sat down one fine day in heaven and "custom made" Robert's body. He deliberately crippled this poor child and gave him eyestalks. Could it have been a mistake? No chance. "God," says Rick Warren, "... never makes mistakes. He has a reason for everything He creates. Every plant and every animal was planned by God, and every person was designed with a purpose in mind."

It all sounds so confirming and comforting when we think of ourselves, and how god has a specific interest for us, a plan for us, and a purpose for our lives. We like ourselves very much and can easily imagine god creating us. But the whole idea falls to pieces when we turn our eyes to heaven and ask, yet again, "What possible purpose could god have for Robert, and for that matter, for Johnnie?

Rabbi Kushner Has an Answer

So what did Rabbi Kushner have to say about human suffering? After going through the litany of possible explanations, he concludes that "God can't do everything," which means that God is not the God we thought He was. To the sick person whose prayers for healing go unanswered, Rabbi Kushner says, "God does not want you to be sick or crippled. He didn't make you have this problem, and He doesn't want you to go on having it, but *He can't make it go away.* That is something *too hard even for God"* (emphasis mine).[5]

What this means is that God is not omnipotent. Rabbi Kushner "recognize[s] His limitations. He is limited in what He can do by laws of nature and by the evolution of human nature and human moral freedom. I no longer hold God responsible for illnesses, accidents, and natural disasters, because I realize that I gain little and I lose so much when I blame God for these things. I can worship a God who hates suffering but cannot eliminate it, more easily than I can worship a God who chooses to make children suffer and die, for whatever exalted reason."[6]

The rabbi made a valiant effort to reconcile evil with God, something perhaps that he needed to do in response to his own suffering. But if God is not the omnipotent Being we thought He was, then He ceases to be God at all and needs to be redefined. The rabbi had wonderful things to say, but his answer is not satisfying.

God, the Benign Surgeon

Without a satisfactory explanation of how god can allow human suffering, all claims about the existence of god, from my point of view, are strained to the breaking point. Yet there is no shortage of explanations.

The great Christian writer, C.S. Lewis, compared God to a benign surgeon. "The kinder and more conscientious he is, the more inexorable he will go on cutting. If he yielded to your entreaties, if he stopped before the operation was complete, all the pain up to that point would have been useless."

But why pain at all? Why such ongoing horrors since the dawn of time? "Well," said Lewis, tackling the question head on, "take your choice. The tortures occur. If they are unnecessary, then there is no God or a bad one. If there is a good God, then these tortures are necessary. For not even a moderately good Being could possibly inflict or permit them if they weren't."[7]

Lewis's conclusion is that all this suffering is indeed necessary, but we mortals are not privy to the reason. God is good. He knows what he is doing, and we just have to accept the misery of this life without ever knowing why.

Lewis was a wonderfully articulate and interesting writer, but even his answer leaves one dissatisfied.

Psychologist Viktor Frankl, who survived years in a Nazi concentration camp, also tried to reconcile God with evil. One miserable night in the camps, as he and his fellow inmates lay exhausted and demoralized in the midst of ongoing horror, he asked whether an ape whose brain was repeatedly punctured to aid a medical discovery could ever understand the meaning of his suffering. Most people would say no, because the ape did not have the intelligence to understand. From its point of view, its suffering was meaningless. "Then," said Frankl, "I pushed forward with the following question:

And what about man? Are you sure that the human world is a terminal point in the evolution of the cosmos? Is it not conceivable

25

that there is still another dimension possible, a world beyond man's world; a world in which the question of an ultimate meaning of human suffering would find an answer?"[8]

It always seems to come back to that: *another dimension* beyond our understanding. We hope that our suffering has meaning, even though we can't "see" it. But vague references to an Ultimate Meaning or hope for "another dimension" or Zadig-like explanations of a hidden good in obvious evil are all somewhere between wishful thinking and desperation. We don't want nebulous hopes. We want answers. We want certainty. Any credible explanation one could give to prisoners in a Nazi camp would be welcome and wonderful, but looking at it objectively, Frankl's answer, like the others, fails to satisfy.

God Gives His Opinion on Suffering

So what does god say on the subject? Let's go to The Source. God speaks in the Bible in the Book of Job.

Although Job is "a thoroughly good man who never sins," God brings devastation upon him. He destroys the man's house and livestock and kills his children. He afflicts him with painful boils all over his body. Job doesn't understand why God would cause someone as righteous as he to suffer so horribly. After all, he says,

> *For I rescued the poor who cried out for help,*
> *the orphans, and the unassisted;*
> *The blessings of those in extremity came upon me,*
> *and the heart of the widow I made joyful.*
> *I wore honesty like a garment;*
> *justice was my robe and my turban.*

Job is beside himself. His suffering makes no sense. "Why me?" he cries to God. There must be sense in suffering. And yet, says Job, when "I cry to you . . . you do not answer." Instead, "you turn upon me without mercy."

Job goes on for page after page. Did I cheat on my wife? No. Did I steal food? No. Have I hurt the innocent? No. Was I greedy for gold? Did I take joy in destroying my enemy? No, no, no, and no! I want answers, says Job. "This is my final plea; let the Almighty answer me!"

And what does God answer? He says to Job, "Gird up your loins now, like a man. I will question you, and you tell me the answers!"

If I were Job, I'd be a little concerned at this point. Here I've been shaking my fist at God, and He doesn't sound too sympathetic. He's telling me to brace myself for what's to come. *Oy Vey!* He's saying to me, "I'm not gonna answer your questions, you little twit, but I have a few for you, AND I EXPECT ANSWERS!"

And then God lays it on him.

> *Where were you when I founded the earth?*
> *Tell me, if you have understanding.*
> *Who determined its size; do you know?*

If it's possible for god to be sarcastic, he's doing it here.

God goes on and on for several chapters, almost as if he's endured all of Job's complaining and now he's had enough and is going to give this little man an earful. Just who do you think made the clouds and the sea? says God. "Have you ever in your lifetime commanded the morning and shown the dawn its place?" What about that, Job, huh? "Can you send forth the lightnings on their way?" "Does the eagle fly up at your command to build its nest aloft?"

God ends by saying, "Will we have arguing with the Almighty by the critic? Let him who would correct God give answer!"

Eventually God restores Job to prosperity, but God, like a celestial politician, never actually answers the question. Telling Job that "I'm God, and you're a twit, so stop complaining about things you can't understand," isn't all that helpful. If I were Job, I would say this to God: "You created me with a brain. You gave me the ability to think and reason and question. You created me to crave order, to want the world to make sense, to expect justice, yet when I ask a reasonable question—and I do mean reasonable—you tell me to 'gird up my loins' and then you fire sarcastic questions at me like darts!"

Even God's words are not satisfying.

The Final Authority on Suffering—My Wife

Becky agreed that "suffering is the great unanswered question in life, but it seems to bring depth to a personality, a kind of maturity.

27

Expressions like 'he was born with a silver spoon in his mouth' are saying that a person is lacking in some way because he has never had to struggle. It is the *effect* of the suffering he is lacking, because without it a person cannot be fully complete."

"You're saying we can't fully appreciate life without some uncertainty, some struggle."

"Exactly," she said. "Suffering matures and deepens us. But it also opens a space for God; it dulls our taste for the noises and disorientations of the world."

"You seem to be saying that god makes us suffer so we will *need* him."

"Not quite. Suffering doesn't *create* our need, it only *reveals* it. When Saint Augustine said 'we are restless until we rest in you,' he meant that our souls desire Him in good times also, we just constantly substitute a variety of momentary pleasures for what we really long for."

Unfortunately, Becky's explanation, still doesn't sell me on the usefulness of suffering. Johnnie's suffering may have opened him up to God, but at what price? We look at Johnny and think, thank god it's not me, but Johnnie is thinking, "Why me, god?"

How did his debilitating disease make him better? Yes, Frankl, C.S. Lewis, and others have argued that we have the free will to respond admirably to suffering, but what if it destroys us instead? What if, like Uncle Sonny, we lack the emotional reserves to deal with it? Nothing positive came from the misery and death of my uncle's children; it just destroyed them all.

And yet . . . if there was a god, and he wanted us to appreciate the eternity into which we are heading, then giving us a life of pain, confusion, fear, and disease, and then bringing us into heaven would certainly make us appreciate our eternal existence. So perhaps this earthly life is a time to teach us how bad things can be before we learn how good they can be eternally. For we could not appreciate existence, heaven, and immortality without having feared that we would never get them, without having feared our own demise, and without having first survived the misery and uncertainty of this best of all possible worlds.

4

second date:
mere christianity

This man we are talking about [Jesus] either was (and is) just what
He said or else a lunatic, or something worse. Now it seems to me
obvious that He was neither a lunatic nor a fiend: and consequently,
however strange or terrifying or unlikely it may seem, I have to
accept the view that He was and is God. God has landed on this
enemy-occupied world in human form.[1]

—C.S. Lewis, *Mere Christianity*

On a Friday afternoon, late in September 1974, exhausted, I dragged
myself out of school, ready for the weekend. I was teaching in a junior
high for the first time and was shocked by the fidgeting, irrational
immaturity. With hormones raging and a sudden gut-wrenching fear
that they might not be accepted by their peers, these twelve- and thir-
teen-year-olds were often emotionally out of control.

I was ready for happy hour.

Walking in front of me with two other teachers and wearing a red
paisley straight dress, was Becky.

That's who I want to be with this weekend, I thought.

I had no shortage of dates. The young female teachers were on
the prowl. The next night I had a date with Michelle, a very attractive,
tall, slim, pleasant English teacher. I knew that *she* would go back to
my apartment.

Maybe Becky's going to happy hour at the air base again.

She was deep in conversation, heading for her car.

Maybe I should sidle up to her. "Ready for the weekend?" I would
say. "Hey, how are you? I haven't seen you for a while?" "I hear there's

29

going to be another play at the Five Pfennig Playhouse. Maybe you'd like to go."

But, alas, I dumped my bag in the back of my mint green Fiat, slumped in the seat, sighed deeply, and headed home.

Spaghetti Dinner

Two weeks later, Becky gave me an opening. "Sarah and I are having a spaghetti dinner at our house this Sunday for all the people we owe some thank yous. It's at two if you'd like to come."

Of course, she didn't *owe* me anything. What she really meant was, "I'd still like to go out with you, and this invitation is a way to ease back into that."

The usual elementary school teacher crowd milled about in her large living room. Most were single. Within a few years, many of them would be married; some would not. A couple of lieutenants, a warrant officer helicopter pilot, another junior high teacher, Diane the former nun, the school's principal, and Sarah's married boyfriend (an army sergeant named Ralph) rounded out the Sunday afternoon crowd.

I chatted somewhat impatiently with an assortment of people, scarfed down the spaghetti, garlic bread, and a piece of pie, and finally made my way over to Becky.

"Hi, how are you?"

"Good, how are you?"

"Good, how's school going?"

"Really good."

"Great, that's great."

This conversation was going nowhere.

"How are your classes?" Becky asked.

"Totally insane. The kids are all bouncing off the walls."

"It's a tough age," she said, adding, "What are you teaching?"

"Besides seventh grade social studies, I have two ninth grade world history classes. We were doing ancient Egyptian religion this week."

"I bet that's fascinating."

"It really is. When I was in Egypt [*I hope you're impressed by my worldliness*], I saw hundreds of yards of mummified bulls under the desert. It's amazing how much effort people put into religion."

"It's always been a powerful force," she said. "It's certainly an important part of my life."

"Really?" I said. "I didn't realize you worshipped mummified bulls."

She forced a smile.

"Are you still thinking of becoming a Christian?"

"Catholic Christian," she corrected. "I'm converting to *Catholicism.*"

Catholic, Christian, what's the difference? It was all a general blur.

"What's the appeal?" I asked, remembering that she had brushed off the question last time.

"It's long and complicated," she said, brushing it off again, "but there's a book that's helping me think through some of these issues. It's called *Mere Christianity.* Have you read it?"

Well, of course I've read it. I love Christian books. I can't get enough of them. I used to sneak them into Hebrew school when I was studying for my Bar Mitzvah.

"No," I said thoughtfully, "it doesn't sound familiar."

"It's really a wonderful book. I have an extra copy if you'd like to read it."

I'd rather watch the grass grow than read a religious book.

"Yeah, that would be great. Maybe after I read it we can get together and talk about it."

"I'd love that," she said.

Ah, she'd *love* that. Not *like* it but *love* it. What she really means is that she'd love to go out with me. And I'd love to go out with her. And every day that we aren't dating is a day wasted.

I was already in love. Or maybe I wasn't. Or maybe I just liked her *A Lot.* Then again, maybe it *was* love. Or was it just that my biological clock was ticking. But it wasn't ticking with Michelle. Do men even have biological clocks? And if they do, what time is it when you're thirty-one?

Death of Ambition, Birth of an Idea

Two weeks later, on our second date, with a copy of *Mere Christianity* held reverently between my fingers, we began in earnest to explore the meaning of it all.

After dinner at a local *gasthouse,* which included schnitzels, pommes frittes (French fries), and Coup Denmarks (vanilla ice cream with hot chocolate sauce), I popped the question. "Would you like to go back to my apartment to talk about the book?"

"Sure."

This is what's known as progress.

My apartment was furnished with Spartan German furniture. We sat on the hard leather couch, and with a Johnny Mathis album on the hi-fi (the ultimate make-out music) and some good German white *spatlese* wine on the table, we commenced firing. Unlike other couples who wrestled on the couch on their second date, we wrestled with eternity.

The last paragraph of *Mere Christianity* had grabbed my attention because—at that time—it made little sense. Ironically, over the ensuing decades, the idea of "ambition" became something of a cornerstone of what I came to believe. "But there must be a real giving up of the self," Lewis wrote:

> You must throw it away "blindly" so to speak . . . Give up your self, and you will find your real self. Lose your life and you will save it. Submit to death, death of your ambitions and favourite wishes every day and death of your whole body in the end; submit with every fiber of your being, and you will find eternal life. . . . Look for yourself, and you will find in the long run only hatred, loneliness, despair, rage, ruin, and decay. But look for Christ and you will find Him, and with Him everything else thrown in.[2]

"It seems to me," I said to Becky, "that since the beginning of time, human ambition and the desire to achieve is what makes the world go round. He says we'll find our real selves if we give it up, but our real selves are competitive and achievement oriented. We wouldn't be human if we gave it up."

Becky took a sip of wine. Johnny Mathis was singing, *a certain smile, a certain face, can lead two unsuspecting hearts on a merry chase . . .*

She paused for a moment and then began speaking. Her voice was clear. "I think you are missing the point. When you give up *your* ambitions, it's not that you become inactive, it's just that you stop demanding things you want. You don't say to the world, 'This is what I want, and I'm willing to do anything, to step on anybody to get it."

I wasn't sure how strongly I should argue. After all, the purpose of this little *tete-a-tete* was to foster a relationship, not to win an argument. On the other hand, I wasn't buying into her point. "Ambition,"

I said, "doesn't have to mean stepping on people; it doesn't have to be demanding or selfish. It's normal to want to do a good job, or rise up the corporate ladder, or get an A on a test. Ambition isn't a dirty word."

But in the hush of night, exactly like a bitter sweet refrain, comes that certain smile, to haunt your heart again.

"But any ambition not willing to be laid down, eventually has to come at the expense of someone else."

I took a sip of wine. "What does that mean, 'laid down'?"

"It means that if the ambition controls you to the point where you can't give it up, then it will ultimately harm others."

"But whether it controls you or not," I countered, "ambition means competition, and when people compete, some inevitably will lose. It's a competitive world. For every kid who makes the football team, others don't. Ambition and competition are *natural* to human life. I don't see how you can object to it."

"I understand," she said steadily, launching into a little speech. "Ambition *seems* natural, but it often causes others to suffer. For example, suppose a businessman who has a family wants to make a million dollars. Because he can't lay it down, his family will miss him and will be the worse for it. Because he can't say there is something bigger, greater than him—something more important—then his hunger will supersede everything. He may achieve it, but only at the expense of the loneliness and the unmet needs of his family.

"C.S. Lewis is not saying that you shouldn't have ambition, but when you enter into a relationship with God, you are conscious not only of what you want but of what God may be asking of you. Therefore, if you feel like He's asking you to do what was not part of your original plan, then you're willing to change it. If you only follow your own selfish desires and ignore God, then people around you may be hurt."

There was, I thought, a fatal flaw in that argument. "How can anyone know what God wants for his ambitions? It's all really guesswork, or even worse, wishful thinking. Like if somebody wants a promotion in a company, he can fool himself into saying 'Well, that's what god wants'."

"You're right, sometimes people see into God's wishes what they want to see, but those who are willing to lay it down, to give it up, are usually able to know the difference. If you're not willing to give it up, then you can't be open to hear what God desires."

Talking to Becky was somewhat exasperating. She always had a response. "It just doesn't seem realistic," I said, "or for that matter fair for god to expect anyone to give up their ambition. If someone has a passion for something, if they hunger to do something, and it doesn't hurt anyone, then they shouldn't have to lay it down."

"But Fred," she said earnestly, "if there is a God and an eternity, then our ambitions are set against a backdrop of eternity. The other issue is that people don't really know what will make them happy. We think we do, but we often don't. God, who knows us better than we know ourselves, has created each of us for good. But if we are not listening to Him, but instead are consumed by our own ambitions, then we will not hear him and will not find that good. Recognition in this life really doesn't matter."

I wasn't hearing everything she was saying because when people talk about what "God knows," I automatically write it off as irrelevant. However, I did jump on her last statement.

"But it does matter," I shot back at her. "You can *say* it doesn't matter, but people are driven by passions, by emotions. We want to be successful, we want to be admired, and we want to be recognized."

"Is that what you want?" she asked pleasantly.

That took me by surprise. I had been attacking her beliefs all night, and suddenly I was on the defensive.

I was tempted to hurl it back at her. *What's wrong with wanting to be successful? Or admired? Or recognized?* But instead of attacking, I used it as an opening in this getting-to-know-you-conversation to tell her who I really was.

"I have some overriding ambitions," I told her. "I want to be a writer. I've already written three novels."

"Really, what are they about?"

Now it was my turn to demur. "About a lot of things. Maybe you'd like to read them sometime."

"I'd love to."

Ah, there it is again. I love it when she says love.

Jesus, the Poached Egg

We talked about a lot of things that night. Just as we were about to leave my apartment, I asked her what it was about *Mere Christianity* that she liked so much, and she read the following:

A man who was merely a man and said the sort of things Jesus said would not be a great moral teacher. He would either be a lunatic—on a level with the man who says he is a poached egg—or else he would be the Devil of Hell. You must make your choice. Either this man was, and is, the Son of God: or else a madman or something worse.[3]

I nodded. "Anyone who thinks he's god would certainly be considered a fruitcake."

"Except He was the real thing."

"But how can you possibly know that?"

"Because He rose from the dead."

"Nobody rises from the dead."

"That's right. Nobody has, except Jesus of Nazareth."

"How do you know he rose from the dead?" I asked, not having the remotest idea what the Bible said. "Maybe the body didn't just disappear. Maybe his followers, who revered him so much, spirited away the body, and people think they saw him because they wanted him back so much."

"No, they couldn't have stolen the body. First, the tomb had been guarded by Roman soldiers. Any attempt would have resulted in a struggle at the very least, but none occurred. Second, the burial cloths that Jesus had been wrapped in were folded up and left in the tomb. People stealing the body certainly wouldn't have taken so much time to unwrap the body. Finally, the disciples saw Him numerous times in a resurrected form. They questioned him, and Thomas even initially doubted. But all maintained to the end the truth of what they saw and witnessed. Eleven of the apostles were martyred. It's hard to imagine that eleven men went willingly to such a death for something they absolutely knew to be a lie."

I could hardly wait until she finished her little discourse. "But Becky, just because they believed it doesn't make it true. It's just ridiculous to believe in anything supernatural."

Suddenly the room was silent.

The Johnny Mathis album had long-since ended.

She really believes all that! I thought that only Italian kids in the Bronx and peasants in Guatemala actually believed such superstition.

Becky picked up her purse. "It's getting late."

Does this mean we're not going to be making out?

35

We drove home in silence. My head was buzzing. As we turned into Erlensee I broke the silence. "I'm sorry. I shouldn't have said that."

"It's okay."

I pulled up to the front of her house. "You don't need to get out," she said.

"Okay, I won't," I said, getting out.

Her face was tight, sad perhaps. "You don't need to walk me in."

"Okay," I said, walking her in.

Becky stopped. She turned and looked at me. "I realize that you don't believe in God, and I also understand that you're Jewish, but this is at the core of who I am, and you have to understand that, too."

I'm really, really, really, really, really, really, really, very, very 100-percent-astronomically-out-into-the-cosmos sorry.

She turned and walked to her door. I was also 100-percent-astronomically-out-into-the-cosmos ready for some kind of physical contact—love, lust, affection, excitement, and mystery all swirled together.

"Well, I'll see you in school on Monday," I said cheerfully.

She ignored me and went in the house.

It was our second date and our second break-up.

False Gods

On the drive home, in the dark tranquility of a cool October evening, my mind wandered back to our discussion about ambition; it hung in my head like a cloud.

That conversation, now so long ago and so far away, with Johnny Mathis crooning in the background, stuck with me. It took a few decades to coalesce. To some extent, Becky and C.S. Lewis were right. So many of our destructive ambitions—our wars, our false heroics, our defiance against the greater forces in our lives, our willingness to destroy others for our own personal sense of accomplishment and importance—are more than just ambitions out of control, they are false gods, and the people who worship them are indeed spiritually dysfunctional.

I never imagined at the time that these ideas would apply to me. Those three never-to-be-published novels I had written in my twenties didn't hurt anyone. Why should I "lay it down?" The answer, of course, is exactly what C.S. Lewis had said: Ambition can sometimes

36

result in "hatred, loneliness, despair, rage, ruin, and decay," or at the very least, a fight with one's wife. Lewis was right. If we all "laid it down," gave ourselves up to god, concluded that this world is a fleeting and inconsequential moment in eternity, then the world would indeed be a better place—less brutal, selfish, irrational, and grasping. But god, it seems to me, is the one who made us hunger for respect, to want importance and recognition in the here and now. Our egos, our self-esteem, and our secular souls must be massaged in the present and just can't wait for a celestial pat on the back after we leave this earthly realm. Eternity may be looming, but the present—which is painful, poignant, compelling, and vital—makes existential demands on us that just can't wait.

An Obvious Solution

But most of that was hazy on this Saturday night in Germany. I was tired. I had a stack of papers to grade, and my landlady had been bugging me, in typical German fashion, to wash the windows. "Herr, Singer," she had said in German, "what will the neighbors think?"

As I pulled up to the house on a quiet street in Niederissigheim, noting the dirty windows with a touch of annoyance, I realized I was obviously going to have to be careful about what I said around Becky. Calling her core beliefs ridiculous was not going to win me any points. There was, however, an obvious solution. *We will never talk about that stuff again.* Now that we've had that little conversation about C.S. Lewis, there is no further need to discuss, say the Virgin Mary.

Perfect, I thought. *End of problem.* I suddenly felt very good about the whole thing. Becky's classroom was just a floor above mine at school. On Monday, at three o'clock, after the kids made their way to the busses, I'd kind of mosey on up to her fourth grade room, cheerful and friendly-like, I-just-happened-to-be passing-by-your-classroom-and-thought-I'd-stop-by-to-say-hi-and-see-how-things-are-going-with-your-class.

I was feeling quite positive, actually. I nodded to myself feeling a great sense of satisfaction at having so cleverly solved this problem. *We'll just never talk about religion again.*

5

odd characters
in the bronx

Four out of every five people surveyed had symptoms of psychiatric disorder; roughly one out of four had neuroses severe enough to disrupt their daily lives. And compared to the city-wide averages, midtown had twice as much suicide, accidental death, tuberculosis and juvenile delinquency, and three times as much alcoholism.[1]

—Results of a study of New Yorkers

"Do you remember what we talked about on our second date? I asked innocently, twenty-nine years later.

We were driving on Fordham Road in the Bronx on our fifth day back in New York City. Our mission was to bring Uncle Sonny home to Colorado. He had been deteriorating for years, and the combination of isolation, alcohol, paranoia, dementia, and the death of his wife eighteen months before was putting him over the edge.

Becky was driving. Since our arrival, we had visited him everyday in the VA nursing home where he'd been living for the past two months. And every day he was different. Tuesday he was happy to see us. Wednesday morning he was positive about moving to Colorado to be closer to us. Wednesday afternoon he said, "I'm scared about going." Late Wednesday afternoon he told us he would never go to Colorado, "and you can't make me go." Thursday we took him to Red Lobster. He enjoyed the meal and was ready to move to Colorado again.

"You mean the night we talked about *Mere Christianity*?" she answered.

"Right."

"Probably something about the idea that Jesus was either God or a lunatic," she said, honking at a driver blocking traffic. "What does he think he's doing?"

Traffic was always bumper-to-bumper. Double-parked cars made the right lane impossible, while turning cars made the left lane impossible. Everyone blasted their horns. It was reminiscent of Cairo or Naples. The Bronx was insane.

"What in the world made you think of that?" Becky asked in response to my question about our second date.

I had raised the question "innocently" because I already knew I was going to write this book, and I wanted it to play out naturally, without Becky knowing about it. The idea had taken hold just the week before, and was evolving by the moment.

"I dunno," I answered, turning up the air conditioning. And then in an attempt to change the subject, as we made our way past the Bronx Zoo, I said, "I never knew that about my grandfather's death."

"You mean," said Becky, "when his father said, 'well, I'll be a son-of-a-bitch.'"

"Right."

"He was obviously getting a glimpse of the afterlife. That kind of startled surprise had to be from something he was seeing."

"I knew you were going to say that."

"Well, I'll Be a Son-of-a-Bitch"

Two hours earlier, the three of us had been sitting in a booth at the nursing home canteen. Most of the place was closed off, this being Saturday, and with the exception of one man in a wheelchair putting coins in the ice cream machine, the canteen was deserted.

Uncle Sonny was talking about his father . . . again. We had been through this same conversation many times in the past months. "He was a wonderful man, my father. So talented. When I got out of the army I helped him in his sign-painting business. He could take a small picture and reproduce it on a huge billboard. That takes a lot of talent. He fell off a scaffold and never recovered. I remember the night he died. My parents had been fighting. They were always fighting. Horrible arguments. Anyway, my mother came in and said, 'Your father wants to see you.' I went in. He was having trouble breathing. I saw what was happening. I tried to give him mouth-to-mouth, but it was no use. Suddenly he reared up and said, 'Well, I'll be a son-of-a-bitch.' He was a wonderful man but he didn't have any great last words like your father did."

Was my grandfather—Uncle Sonny's father—amazed at the fact that he was dying, or did he get a glimpse of eternity?

"Look," I said as the traffic cleared on Pelham Parkway. "All these near death experiences about seeing lights and out-of-body trips are just the brain reacting to lack of blood or some such thing. It's wishful thinking. People want so much to believe in the afterlife that they'll interpret seeing lights or some brain malfunction as heaven. But they aren't seeing heaven because there is no heaven."

"So you say."

"Well, the burden of proof is on the claimant. You're the one who insists on it."

"Saying 'I'll be a son-of-a-bitch' is obviously an expression of amazement, like 'I'll be damned, there really is a God.'"

"Well, whatever he saw, it was a Fig Newton of his imagination."

She cast me a sideways glance over her sunglasses as if to say, "You're hopeless and stubborn." I looked back with raised eyebrows and open palms as if to say, "I'm right, and I'll never budge." I guess after twenty-seven years of marriage we communicate well with looks.

"But you know what really surprised me," I said. "He remembered my father's last words." Indeed. We were finding Uncle Sonny's dementia to be mostly short-term memory loss. And my father's last words in 1986 were not only dramatic, but a key concept of this book. What he said was reminiscent of Petrarch's musings on that stormy night in Venice over six hundred years ago.

"Dad, I Love You"

My dad was dying of lung and liver cancer at the age of seventy-one. Flying to Florida from Germany, I silently prayed. I was spiritually vulnerable. It's true, there *are* no atheists in foxholes. Of course, he died anyway.

He had been in a coma for several days when we stormed in directly from the airport. "Dad," I said. "Dad, we're here. I love you, Dad." He was bald, thin, gray, and in a diaper. His once robust frame had withered away. Every so often his face convulsed. It was at once fascinating, horrifying, and demoralizing, and reminded me of my own mortality. This man who had been so beefy and intelligent–the author of math texts–was physically and mentally reduced to nothing.

"Dad, how are you doing? We're here, Dad." I really didn't know what to say.

Almost immediately he came out of the coma and said something in a garbled voice.

I didn't understand. "What is it, Dad? What did you say?" He had mumbled something about "time."

I looked around helplessly and told him the time.

"No," said the nurse who was used to garbled speech. "He's not asking for the time."

"What did he say?"

The nurse bent down close to his face as he tried one more time.

"He said, 'Time is precious.'"

And he nodded.

Those were his last words.

He came out of a three day coma at the sound of my voice to tell me that.

In the nine months since he had been diagnosed with cancer, I suspect that in his methodical way, he had reviewed his entire life piece by piece and year by year. I visited him in Florida three times

Dad in 1973, at age fifty-eight, beefy and intelligent.

that year, and in conversations he made reference to various times in his life. "Every day was an adventure," he told me about his boyhood in the twenties. "One day you'd play ring-a-leav-eeo, another day you'd see *The Mark of Zorro*. It was the best time in my life," he said, but was quick to add, "except of course for my life with your mother."

He reviewed his life because he knew it would soon be over, and he must have marveled at how fast it went, and how we should cherish every day, and how we should not waste our time on petty hostilities, which he sometimes did. Was he trying to tell me not to make the same mistakes he did? I'll never know because he died three days later and never said another word.

Those three days were among the worst of my life. We knew it was coming, but the reality of being in that hospital every day and seeing his convulsions was emotionally wrenching. I finally understood what was meant by a "heavy heart." My chest was tight. My muscles ached. I would see people laughing in the cafeteria and wonder how anyone could laugh in a world so bleak. At the end of the hall in the waiting room, we called our three daughters who were staying with their grandparents in Germany. At ages eight, six, and three, the death of a grandparent was "just something that happens to old people." Talking to them on the phone was uplifting. They represented the future with their life, youth, and vigor. Knowing they were in the world and moving relentlessly forward made the death throes of my father down the hall somehow more bearable. On one end was life, on the other, death. And at forty-three I was squarely in the middle.

Of course we all know that time is precious. It goes so fast because we don't remember the details, just the outline. Who can remember what they did on April 12, 1973, for example. I spent that whole day doing something and could figure out in a general way what it was, but I can't remember the details. Thus, if I can't remember it, it's as if it didn't happen.

Petrarch bemoaned the fact that as he idly pricked pen to paper, time was passing, and he was racing relentlessly toward death. But what was my father trying to tell me? That he was sad to be out of time? That he could have made better use of his time? Or was he warning me to appreciate every moment? I don't know. I'll never know. But this much I believe to be true: *the preciousness of time and the awareness of our impending death is among those powerful forces driving us, haunting us, moving us, and making us a little crazy.*

A Huge Apartment Complex

Back at my uncle's apartment we continued packing his stuff. He lived on the nineteenth floor of a huge apartment complex in the Bronx overlooking the I-95. In a city that never sleeps, the roar on the highways produced an ongoing background rumble.

All his clothing went into boxes. He had some expensive plates with paintings on them; they went in the boxes. The paintings on the wall would also go. We doubted that he would ever be coming back. Moving him to Colorado was a risk. He might hate it. He might never adjust. He might not even get on the plane in the first place! After all, he had lived his entire life in New York. The clamor, the noise, the rudeness, the loud talking were normal to him. Could he make the move at the age of eighty-three? It seemed to us it had to be done. His children were dead. His wife was dead. Most of his friends were gone. We were the only ones available to help. His aide, a Jamaican woman named Norma, had been a godsend for the last five years but was finding it impossible to deal with his alcoholism and sporadic paranoia.

Norma had been indispensable. With no formal training, but with common sense and street savvy, she'd kept my uncle and aunt functioning. She shopped, cooked, drove them around, gave them medication. She shaved him, bathed them, and when the Alzheimer's crept into my aunt, she cleaned up the messes.

Their neighbor Steve was sixty-three, bald with that classic fringe, and looked like Robert Duvall with an eye patch. Steve wanted to be helpful. He had nothing else to do. He didn't work. Norma told us that many a time she had found Steve listening through the garbage room, which was adjacent to my uncle's apartment. Often when we visited, we would find Steve in the hall "by coincidence." He wanted to tell us what was going on in the deteriorating situation. But I suspect he wanted to talk to us because we were fresh faces from out of town. Perhaps he wanted us to see him as a human being, a good person, a normal person. And to some extent we did, but we also found him making many trips to the garbage room. Becky began whispering to me as if we were international spies and the room was bugged. Whenever she thought he might be listening she would open the door and check the garbage room. Once she found him hovering outside the door. "I was just throwing out some garbage," he said proffering the newspapers in his hand. "I was just waiting for Fred to come home," she said, giving him tit for tat.

A Haitian woman who lived on the eighteenth floor came up to the apartment to point out the pieces of furniture she would like to have when we closed down the apartment. "Why don't you just leave me the key," she suggested. "And I'll take care of things."

But the most destructive people were Rose and Eddie, who sound like a couple of Muppets or the latest sitcom. ("It's the *Rose and Eddie Show*, starring those two lovable old alcoholics. In tonight's episode Eddie brings Uncle Sonny his ration of cigarettes and wine, in return for hundreds of dollars. Don't miss next week's hilarious episode where Rose and Eddie hire a lawyer to prevent his family from taking him from his beloved Bronx, to take him to the miserable mountains and fresh air of Colorado.)

We were never sure what went on between Uncle Sonny and Rose and Eddie. They visited him a number of times at the VA nursing home; the aides told us he was always agitated after their visits.

"Fred," Becky whispered to me just in case Steve was listening in the garbage room, "These people are all a little crazy. You never know what they're thinking or what they want."

We had to get him out of there.

Several months before, when in a drunken stupor, he had been admitted to the VA hospital. After he dried out, they refused to let him return home. We flew to New York and had him admitted to the adjacent nursing home. Two months later, we were back. He wanted to return to his apartment, but if he did that he would drink himself into more rages and paranoid fears.

He could stay in the VA nursing home, but it was nothing more than a bed in a hospital room. He was much too ambulatory for that. In Colorado he would have a life. He would interact with normal people in an assisted living facility. He would have family nearby, and my daughters would be part of his family.

He had to go to Colorado.

6

to hell and back

For the love of heaven, who will take him? Please, Mr. Lewis, help me, help my child.

—Aunt Millie, 1962

Bringing Uncle Sonny to Colorado was something of a long shot. Seeing him for the first time at the VA nursing home in the Bronx, standing in his pajamas, hunched over his walker, so small and alone, I became flushed with sympathy. He was happy to see us and wanted to get out. At eighty-three, he looked very old. He had been to hell and back.

Jerry Lewis

As a kid, Uncle Sonny was hit by a car. In the army he contracted spinal meningitis. He was a life-long diabetic, a life-long smoker, and an alcoholic. By 1963, with both his children doomed, he went to pieces and spent two five-month periods in the veterans hospital. After that, he never worked again. The disease in his children and the thirty-five years of watching them deteriorate and die took a crushing psychological toll. He had not worked in forty years, but subsisted on welfare, veterans' benefits, and Social Security. The fact that he was still alive was something of a miracle.

All of this gained immediacy as we packed his belongings and went though his papers. We sat in the living room on the new couches he had purchased the year before, surrounded by the hundreds of books packed neatly onto shelves. The early spring night was unusually warm. Nineteen stories below, cars along the interstate belched and roared like a perpetual fire-breathing dragon. The Bronx itself entered through the living room windows as a soft, dirty, yellow glow.

"Look at this," I said.

Becky was trying to concentrate on her work. She was almost through the first year of her master's degree in pastoral theology. "What is it?" she answered absently.

"My aunt wrote a letter to Jerry Lewis."

"Why?"

"Because he did those muscular dystrophy telethons, and she thought he would help."

"When was it?"

"The early sixties."

As a matter of fact, she also wrote to President Kennedy, the mayor of New York, a congressman, and Senator Robert Kennedy. Her letters were pleading, desperate, angry, hopeless. She was in her early forties at the time.

In 1962, she was trying to find an institution willing to admit six-year-old Richard, who was also severely emotionally disturbed. "FOR THE LOVE OF HEAVEN," she wrote in capital letters to Jerry Lewis, "who will take him . . . PLEASE, MR. LEWIS, HELP ME. HELP MY CHILD."

A few months later she wrote to an expert on muscular dystrophy. Rage and frustration hung on every word.

You also speak of "giving guidance and assistance to the family" in your address. May I ask what that means? Oh yes, pardon me, I got "guidance" from the M.D.A.A. Social Service worker (Miss "Jones"), whose suggestion, after I told her that Richard was disturbed and was always attempting to "run away" and that Jonathan [Johnnie] who was just beginning to walk was not too steady on his feet, was that I "harness" them together as you would two wild animals. What humiliation! What indignity! When I told her that I thought possibly a nursery school or some facility similar might be a help, she told me to get one started in my neighborhood, and she further insulted me by asking me (as though I was

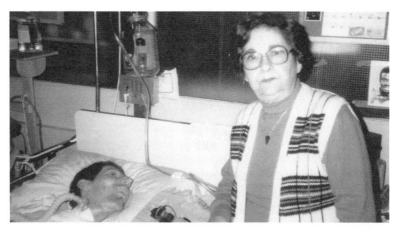

JOHNNIE AND AUNT MILLIE, AROUND 1988, GOLDWATER
MEMORIAL HOSPITAL.

*an idiot) if I planned on having more children and whether I knew about
contraception.*

A year later, while Uncle Sonny was breaking down and spending months in the VA hospital, she wrote to President Kennedy.

*All the anguish of a mother for her children, all of the anguish of a wife
whose husband is suffering from the frustration of not being able to help
his two children and himself; all of the anguish a human being is, and
has been suffering to see her family (for that matter, her life) disintegrat-
ing before her eyes . . . all these things and more cannot be conveyed on
paper. What are we to do? Please help us.*

A desperate woman,
Mildred Linet

Studying and Partying

And where was I during all this? Pretty much ignoring it. At the time
Uncle Sonny was breaking down and my aunt was writing impassioned
letters I was away at college. Their problems were background noise:
second hand gossip. I was deeply embroiled in the world of college—
studying and partying. By the time Richard died in February, 1969, I
was already overseas, teaching on Okinawa. How could I worry about

my aunt and uncle in the Bronx when I was busy planning my next trip to Hong Kong. I sent a sympathy card with the following warm sentiment.

Dear Aunt Millie and Uncle Sonny,
I was sorry to hear about Richard's death, but I guess it was expected.

Love, Fred

"That's because you were selfish and self-absorbed," Becky offered as we packed up his apartment.

"That's not fair," I shot back. "I was ten thousand miles from home. I wasn't there. I didn't see it every day. I didn't talk to them. I had only the vaguest idea of what was going on."

"You really didn't want to know," she said.

"Look, I did what I could. I visited him every summer and often sent letters. A lot of them are here," I said, referring to several files of correspondence my uncle had saved from an assortment of friends and relatives.

"How about this one?" I asked, proffering a post card I had forgotten about. "I sent this to Johnnie the day we got married in Copenhagen. He was often on my mind, but nothing was going to make him better."

Indeed, my uncle was crushed, my aunt was desperate, but in a sense it was even worse than that because if Uncle Sonny had been to hell and back, Aunt Millie had been to hell and back *twice;* her brother Eddie had suffered the same fate, dying at the age of eighteen in 1942.

We found a striking picture of Eddie in the apartment. A shock of straight hair standing on end, arms like sticks, chin resting on his curled hands, circular glasses on an intelligent face that seemed somehow resigned to his fate.

Eddie left a paper trail. We found a letter to the editor he had written in 1941. He was angry that the local newspapers were so critical of Mr. Roosevelt. Eddie must have been a liberal's liberal–against war, against the greed of Wall Street, sympathetic to immigrants, and a strong supporter of Roosevelt. "I think that [the editorial writers] should stop inferring that our president is a liar and an imbecile. And other such rotten sewage had better stop flowing from their pens."

He signed it, "Yours sincerely, A Disgusted Reader."

EDDIE, A DOOMED BOY, AROUND 1941.

Eddie also had a tender side, drawing a birthday card for his sister—my aunt—with the message, "Greetings, dear Kitty, to you on this your birthday. As cute as the Kitty is, it's not nearly as cute as you. I knew you'd like it best if I greeted you this way. Your loving brother, Eddie."

What a sweet boy—loving, bright, doomed. He might have been a doctor or a professor, or even a liberal newspaper columnist. But he had no chance. Neither did Richard. Neither did Johnnie. There is no cosmic justice; no Grand Design. Shit happens. Evil people thrive. Earthquakes kill thirty thousand praying in church. Life is arbitrary. Life is unfair. If god is the benevolent omnipotent entity, he sure has a funny way of showing it.

Once, long ago, my uncle said, "People tell me to see the silver lining. So many people have problems with their kids. The kids hate them, and they hate their kids. So many problems with kids rebelling and getting into trouble. They tell me I was spared all that, but it doesn't make the pain any less."

Exactly. Fabricated silver linings are just another version of *Zadig*. Richard and Johnnie could have grown up to be rotten kids, so their disease was really a blessing in disguise. But as Voltaire put it in verse,

From consolation you increase my pain.

7

johnnie, death, and god

Johnnie, there is peace for you, there is, there is!! This life has not been fair to you, and I'm sure that's why it so hard for you. But this life is not all! Ask God to give you peace, Johnnie, He is Shalom.

—Becky, 1988

On May 6, 2003, to our surprise, we actually got Uncle Sonny on the plane. "I have to have hope," he said about getting out of the Bronx nursing home. Yet faced with going to the unknown world of Colorado, he was fearful.

The morning of our departure, Uncle Sonny called a lawyer, who promptly called the nursing home administrator, who promptly called me. "You can't make him go against his will," said the lawyer.

The nursing home administrator, a tall, efficient, blonde woman, was on our side. She knew about his alcoholism and his battles with paranoia. She thought assisted living in Colorado with us nearby was a better alternative than a nursing home in the Bronx.

"Mr. Linet," she asked at his bedside, "did you call a lawyer this morning?"

"No."

"But I have a lawyer on the phone who says you did."

"Well, maybe I did."

An hour before our departure, we had a conference call with the lawyer in the administrator's office. "Mr. Linet," said the lawyer's tinny voice over the speaker, "what would you like to do: go to Colorado or return to your home?"

Uncle Sonny looked foggy and confused. "I'd like to go home," he said with a hard edge to his voice. "It's my *home.*"

The administrator and I exchanged glances. "I think that what he is trying to say is that if he could go back to his apartment he would, but his best option now is Colorado. Is that right, Uncle Sonny?"

"Mr. Linet," the administrator added, "we all understand your desire to go to your apartment, but I thought you were ready to try Colorado. Are you okay about going to Colorado now?"

My uncle hesitated. "Uh, yeah, well, okay."

So we went.

We fully expected him to get to the airport and refuse to get on the plane. Becky kept the small talk going constantly, which drove me a little crazy. At one point she tugged at my arm. "Talk to him about sports."

"He's okay, all right. We don't have to entertain him twenty-four hours a day."

"I know," she whispered, "but I want to keep him from thinking negative thoughts."

"Stop worrying," I insisted. "He's not drinking, and no one is confusing him now."

Nevertheless, Becky kept up the chatter. She talked to him about God on the plane. "If there is a God," she said, "He made such a beautiful world and made us capable of loving and enjoying nature." I didn't respond with my usual riposte—that besides creating this beautiful world, he created cancer. I didn't bring it up, of course, because we had been there and done that. I had long ago suggested we just record the conversation and then replay it whenever we got the urge to go over it again.

On the second leg of the flight, I showed him an article in *Scientific American* about the possibility of parallel universes. He read the first page and then said, "Imagine, there could be infinite universes and infinite versions of us, doing exactly the same thing."

He may have had dementia, but he was still interested in ideas; at eighty-three my uncle continued to have a sense of awe about the world and the universe around him.

Arrival

We arrived in Denver at 9:40 p.m. and immediately had a couple of minor setbacks. As Uncle Sonny tried to get into the back seat of the van, he smashed his shin, which became bruised and bloody. We stopped at a gas station for disinfectant, bandages, and a cup of coffee for him. Within moments I stepped on the brake, and he spilled the boiling coffee on his face and chest, crying out in pain. He had taken the cover off the coffee for the simple reason that he had never used a Styrofoam cup with a sipper hole for drinking in a moving vehicle. The next morning when he awoke at Garden Square Assisted Living, the nurse told us he lay on his back saying, "My family is killing me, my family is killing me."

Uncle Sonny Retreats from the Real World

Because Uncle Sonny had not lived in the real world for forty years, such things as Styrofoam cups were unknown to him. He had worked for fifteen years as a precision grinder. He ran for shop steward "to channel my grief" and was narrowly elected. "I changed things a lot," he wrote in a long handwritten letter he had sent to us in the late nineties as part of his therapy, "and saw to it that the workers got a break. I was reelected to a second 4-year term by a 3 to 1 majority. It was a tough job & the company made a concerted effort to break me by various psychological ploys—criticizing my work, complaining to the Business Agent about me taking up too much time on union business & writing grievances for the rank & file. It began to get to me & Richard & Johnnie were getting worse physically. Sometimes my grief would overcome me & I would punch out & sit in my car for a half hour. One morning I woke up & prayed for the mental & emotional strength to go to a dead end job with the prospects of watching my children waste away. I quit work in the afternoon & went to Kingsbridge Veterans Hospital. In short I had a nervous breakdown. . . . Millie had a terrible time of it & she used to take long walks with Richard in a wheelchair & Johnnie walking. . . . Millie could only come once a week to visit me as she had her hands full taking care of the kids. . . .

"After release from the hospital, I returned to work & was received happily by the guys & with a plethora of unresolved problems that

A YOUNG AND VIRILE UNCLE SONNY HUGS
BABY JOHNNIE, THE BRONX, 1959.

came up while I was gone. Soon I was up to my neck with union business. My problems with the company continued unabated.

"After 3 weeks on the job I had a relapse & again went to Kingsbridge Veterans Hospital where I stayed 5 months again. Again poor Millie could only visit me once a week or less . . . Altho I have total recall of the incidents of my life, I don't recall how Millie managed financially. Bernard the butcher supplied her with meat & we lived off savings. I guess by this time I realized that I couldn't work anymore & resolved to devote my life to making my children's life as happy as possible. I received social security disability & my veterans pension was raised. . . ."

As a result, he had enough money on which to live. But his world revolved around the children and doctors and summer camps for disabled kids. Unlike my parents who had a wide circle of friends, Millie and Uncle Sonny led a different kind of social life.

They lived for many years in the "projects," which was a euphemism for low-rent, low-class subsidized housing. Many struggling World War II veterans lived in the projects, which should have provided them with friends, but as my uncle wrote, "As the years sped by & the veterans who by now all had children moved to 4 room apartments & quite a few of them bought their own homes . . . we noticed a difference in their attitude toward us—we were sort of 'left out' as they were busy with their children and formulas & baby carriages. . . ."

The friends he did have all seemed to be somewhere between strange and tragic.

"Al," wrote my uncle, "was a wonderful black man and a dear friend . . . He & I cried together many times talking about the children. I remember visiting him in the hospital & we walked to the solarium (so I could smoke). It was only 15 feet but Al had a terrible time making it. He told me that he didn't think he would last the night. We walked back to his bed & I put my hand on his head & he turned to me, his eyes brimming with tears & said I was the best friend he ever had.

"He died that night & Katie, his wife, called to let me know when the funeral was scheduled. During the time I knew Al we both used to smoke and drink. Little known to me, he had joined Jehovah's Witnesses. It was a beautiful ceremony which I will always remember. Altho Al was functionally illiterate, he was one of the brightest men I've ever met. I guess we had a lot in common because we started working very young & had a tough life."

It seemed as if everyone my uncle knew in the Bronx had sad and empty lives. It was almost as if there was a "devil's cloud" hanging over them, blocking the sunlight and slowly draining the life from them all. We talk quite a bit in this book about the importance of having purpose and goals to give us a sense that we are achieving meaningful lives. And yet, countless millions of us exist in a kind of spiritual emptiness governed by inertia; there are no goals beyond the prosaic. Tomorrow will be the same as today.

One could say that people are responsible for themselves, and that their hopelessness is of their own making. And although that is a cruel overgeneralization, the fact remains that sometimes it's true. As we shall see, we often make decisions that we think will bring us happiness and satisfaction, when in reality those very decisions destroy us. At other times, bad luck or circumstances rob us of that sense of efficacy, the ability to take action in order to make things better.

Of all the people I've ever personally known, there has never been anyone more crushed by bad luck and circumstances than Johnnie. For him there was nothing—no hope, no sense of cosmic justice, and no one to blame but the mighty and impassive powers of the universe.

Glimpse of a Sad World

After Johnnie went permanently to Goldwater Memorial Hospital in 1978, my aunt and uncle's social interaction was limited to doctors, nurses, orderlies, psychiatrists, other patients, the patients' families, and, of course Johnnie.

I got a glimpse of this sad world of broken people every summer when we came to New York. Every patient was there for the rest of their life. Dozens of broken and diseased people lined the corridors and halls. On Johnnie's ward, a cool Hispanic kid in a western hat tooled around in his electric wheelchair. One woman had been there thirty-five years. She had contracted polio as a young mother and spent years in an iron lung. Eventually she was given a tracheotomy, and she too gained mobility through the wheelchair. Her husband was now retired and a permanent volunteer at the hospital. He raised the children and stayed loyal to her for decades.

We generally visited Johnnie twice during our annual two-week stay in New York. He usually greeted us with a big smile, the only physical movement he could make. We forced the small talk, told him about Germany and the kids, and talked about NASA, which was his passion. The whole experience of the hospital–the mangled bodies,

BECKY, PREGNANT WITH OUR FIRST CHILD MANDY, VISITS THE LINETS IN THE PROJECTS, SUMMER 1977.

the ruined lives, the hopelessness, and Johnnie reduced to bones—was breathtakingly poignant, and often led us to the ongoing debate of why bad things happen to good people.

"Do you want me to believe in god?" I would say to Becky. "Then god needs to explain to me whey he did this to Johnnie. God needs to do a big time miracle. When that boy walks out of that bed and puts on weight and is cured and is running through the streets, then I'll go to church. If god wants my soul, then he has to meet me on my terms. I need a miracle."

The visits to Johnnie were usually our last stop before flying back to Germany. The whole thing was emotionally and spiritually draining. We found it impossible to leave that place without thinking, "There but for the grace of God go I." At the end of the visit, we walk through the ward, down the corridor, into the elevator, out to the parking lot and into the car. Next comes the drive to Kennedy, drop off the rented car, check in, walk to the gate with the kids in tow, get a snack, fight the airport crowds, and finally collapse in a seat near a sign that reads "Flt 8764 Frankfurt, Germany."

It was not only a feeling of relief to be out of Goldwater Memorial Hospital for another year, and it was not only the relief of being away from the hopelessness, but creeping inside was the guilty and quietly euphoric feeling that I was not in one of those beds, that I did not breathe through a tube, that I was free and healthy and on my way back to Europe to a job where I could be productive and functioning, and finally that I had three healthy little daughters.

Of course the count-your-blessings emotion always faded as we got back to our lives; some kid in the school where I taught would be a discipline problem, or I would be tired of grading papers, or it would rain too much in Germany, and that odd negative-induced euphoria faded, and I would not be counting my blessings.

In the summer of 1988, about six months before Johnnie died, we brought the girls—ages ten, eight, and five—to visit. I was never more proud of them. Good grades or making the soccer team or getting a part in the school play paled before this. They understood exactly what was going on. They walked stoically through the hospital corridors, sidestepping wheelchair-bound people, easing past mangled bodies, making not a peep. They understood that these people were terribly sick; there was no pointing, no cringing, no callous comments.

At that time, Johnnie may have been the weakest and most helpless patient in the hospital, but he relished the visits, often committing them to memory. All he had was his mind, and as he lay there, he would remember . . . and remember . . . and remember. Because the girls were so short, they had to stand on a chair so Johnnie whose head was on the pillow, could look up at their faces. Each took their turn on the chair and made small talk. "How are you, Johnnie?" "Do you have any friends?" "It rains too much in Germany." "I'll be in seventh grade this year." "I'm seven years old and will be in third grade."

And then when it was over, we walked past the paralyzed people and the army of white coats, said goodbye to my aunt and uncle, and were soon on a plane back to Germany. We didn't talk much, the feeling of relief was quietly overwhelming.

But for Millie and Uncle Sonny, the misery never ended. The next day they were back in the hospital, and the day after that, and the day after that. They didn't socialize with friends, they didn't go out to

JOHNNIE, IN NEED OF A SHAVE, A YEAR BEFORE HIS DEATH.

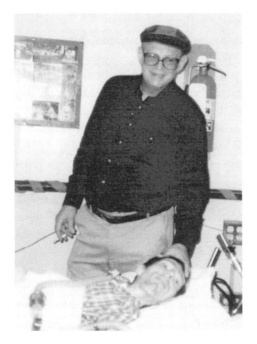

A BEEFED-UP UNCLE SONNY WITH HIS UBIQUITOUS CIGARETTE,
VISITS WITH JOHNNIE AROUND 1988.

dinner, didn't go on trips, didn't go to movies, didn't work, didn't have projects, didn't have careers, didn't have colleagues. They just went to the hospital every day to do what they could for Johnnie before he died.

During those first few years at Goldwater, when Johnnie was strong enough to sit in the wheelchair, they often asked if he would like to come home for a few days, especially around the holidays, but Johnnie always declined. "This is my home," he answered.

"He didn't want to torture himself," my uncle said. To go home for a few days, to feel what life could have been, to be reminded of what he had lost and what he could never have, would have indeed been a kind of poignant, bitter sweet agony.

Becky Writes to Johnnie

Shortly before Johnnie died in 1989, Becky sent him a letter. While my letters were basically small talk, hers cut to the existential core.

Dear Johnnie,

Happy birthday, dear friend! We are so hoping this gets to you on time . . . We surely wish we could spend this day with you! We would sing you a loud off-key happy birthday song. Put a silly hat on your head and toot those obnoxious horns all over the ward and make all the nurses mad. Wouldn't that be fun?!

We've enclosed a little present for you [an 8 x 10 family picture]. We hope you have room for it on your wall. And we hope it always reminds you of our love for you . . . There are so many things I want to say. Your folks, Johnnie, write that you have become obsessed with your illness and a fear has crept in. I truly understand how that could be. The physical discomfort and pain you must endure, surely must make concentrating on anything else very difficult. But my deepest concern for you, is for your emotional welfare. You, the inside of you, is the real you, and it hurts us all to see you in so much emotional pain.

Johnnie, I know I must seem like a broken record, always talking about God. But, Johnnie, He alone is where help can come at this point. I know it must be so difficult for you to believe that He exists because of your difficult life. But that's why Jesus died the death he did, his body ripped to ribbons and nailed to a cross so that we would know that God loves us.

Johnnie, Jesus has victory over death. He went before us, died and rose again. There is a part in the bible written to Hebrews (Jews like you) that says "Jesus himself became like men and shared our human nature. He did this so that through his death he might destroy the devil, who has the power over death, and in this way *set free those who are afraid of death.*

Johnnie, there is peace for you, there is, there is!! This life has not been fair to you, and I'm sure that's why it so hard for you. But *this* life is *not all!* Ask God to give you peace, Johnnie, He is *Shalom.*

If you want for me to write more about God, I will. For He is my peace and my life.

You are *ever* in our thoughts and especially on today, your b'day.

May the peace of God embrace you.

Your friends, Becky, Fred, Mandy, Ashlie and Melanie

The Only Hope for Johnnie Was Death

This was vintage Becky. Her message was probably the only one that could have brought him comfort. The message that god loves you and has a place for you in heaven is compelling for most people and certainly comforting for the dying. If Christianity is nothing more than an elaborate fabrication to allay our fear of death, then I say why not.

One of the reasons Christianity has been so successful was that it not only told us to not fear death, but, as psychologist, Ernest Becker wrote, *it required us to die in order to gain salvation*. Christianity, wrote Becker, "took creature consciousness," the concept that we are animals, and by implication mortal, ". . . and made it the very *condition* for his cosmic heroism."[1] Only by dying can we gain eternal salvation, so in that sense, death is not so bad. That is why martyrdom is not feared but desired. To die for Christ—or for that matter, for Allah—is the fastest route to heaven. We have to die eventually anyway, so why not do something of worth—even transcendence—and get to heaven a little faster. A martyr's death not only provides a sense of accomplishment, but earns them the holy grail of existence—eternal salvation. All of which will be discussed later.

The only hope for Johnnie for a better life was through death. He could not read a book, or toss a ball around, or play a violin, or even marry the girl next door. Not only was he denied the transcendent, he was denied the trivial. Thus for him, the only avenue to spirituality—to salvation—was god, and I can only hope that Becky's words brought him comfort. I suspect that at the end, Johnnie accepted death. "I feel a sense of impending doom," he joked with his father a week before he died. "He was at peace, really calm," my uncle said.

Morrie Talks to Johnnie

"That's what we're all looking for," Morrie said to Mitch Albom in *Tuesdays with Morrie*, as if he were talking about Johnnie. "A certain peace with the idea of dying." He went on:

> "If we know, in the end, that we can ultimately have that peace with dying, then we can finally do the really hard thing."
> Which is?
> "Make peace with the living."

Later in the book, he says to Mitch:

"... Everything that gets born, dies." He looked at me. "Do you accept that?"

Yes.

"All right," he whispered, "now here's the payoff ... As long as we can love each other, and remember the feeling of love we had, we can die without ever really going away. All the love you created is still there. All the memories are still there. You live on —in the hearts of everyone you have touched and nurtured while you were here.

"Death ends a life, not a relationship."[2]

Morrie is right to a point. The relationships we make in the here and now will be our legacy. Who we are, for better or for worse, will survive us. Ten years after you die, people you know will remember you. Remember that you were selfish, or loving, or overly ambitious, or mean-spirited, or kind, or stupid. The relationship goes on—but only to a point. To your grandchildren, you will be a much vaguer memory. To your great-grand children, you will not even be a name. Within two generations, we are forgotten. It's as if we didn't exist. And that is really one of the demons that haunts us.

The world will go on, and since there is no memory of us, for all intents and purposes—were we even here? The old philosophical saw comes to mind. *If a tree falls in the forest, and there is no one there to hear it, does it make a sound?* Similarly, if we lived our three score and ten years, but no one remembers—did we even exist? This is what really haunts us: did our individual existence count for something? Did we make a significant contribution to the scheme of creation? We certainly want to be remembered by our children and friends, but in our heart of hearts, we want to be remembered by eternity.

8

popcorn and free will

. . . free will, though it makes evil possible, is also the only thing that makes possible any love or goodness or joy worth having. A world of automata—of creatures that worked like machines— would hardly be worth creating.[1]

—C. S. Lewis, *Mere Christianity*

When Uncle Sonny arrived in Colorado in the spring of 2003 after forty years of relative isolation, it was as if he were seeing the world for the first time.

A Good Eye-Talian Meal

The first thing he noticed–after Styrofoam cups with sipping holes– was the sky. It was big and clear and blue, and often full of thick, puffy clouds. He spent hours looking at the clouds and the sunsets. He also noticed the birds and dogs.

"It must be the new hearing aid," he said. "I hear them all the time."

"Maybe it's because the Bronx was too noisy," I suggested.

But the mountains, they were something else again.

The first week he went on an assisted living excursion to a lake in the foothills, about forty miles from town, and marveled at the scenery. "It was so beautiful. I wish I could have taken it with me."

He also marveled at the food. He had never been a good eater.

65

His wife never cooked. They ate in bits and pieces and rarely ate out. Now he was discovering the world of dining. After a great meal at the Olive Garden he said, "Can you believe that I had to go all the way to Colorado to get a good Italian (pronounced 'Eye-Talian') meal?"

The next week we ate at Carrabas Italian Grill. He devoured the veal scaloppini. The food, he opined, was "just great," and again offered the observation, "Can you believe I had to go all the way to Colorado to get a good Eye-Talian meal."

But most of all he became addicted to Starbucks. "It's delicious coffee (pronounced 'cawfee')," he said over and over. "It's unbelievable. It's just the best cawfee." Many a time he would suck those mocha lattes through the sipper hole like the world's coolest yuppie.

Bruce Almighty

We also introduced him to movies. It may have been decades since my uncle had been to a theater. He shook his head and smiled at the gigantic bucket of popcorn at the gigantic price, and when the film was over, he said, "Oh, so there's not another movie?" hearkening back to the days of double features.

We saw *Bruce Almighty,* starring Jim Carey, in which God gives Bruce the power to be God. He laughed throughout the movie and thought Jim Carey was amazing, "a good looking guy who contorts his face."

After the film, Becky and I sat in the van in front of the theater, while Uncle Sonny sat on his walker smoking. I raised an interesting point from the movie. When God gave Bruce the power to be God, he imposed only one limitation: "You can't interfere with people's free will."

"So, god doesn't interfere with free will," I said, giving her an opening I knew she would take.

Becky shook her head and offered an amused smile. "That's what I've been trying to tell you for the last twenty-nine years."

"And I've been trying to tell *you* for twenty-nine years that we pay a horrible price for that free will."

Of course, we had been through the "free will" conversation many times, and I knew that if I brought it up, she would launch into it, and I would launch back, and it would fit neatly into this part of the book. Indeed, free will is a part of the paradigm, because if we as individuals do not have free will, then how can our actions be meaningful? How can our lives have any significance?

Why does god give us free will, which is the ability to take action without interference from Him? Becky and the church would answer thusly:

> We have free will so we can choose between good and evil. Of course, God wants us to choose good and to choose Him. Because God is all-powerful, He can make us do whatever He wants. But that would not be satisfying for God. He didn't create us to be manipulated. He created us with the dignity to be free as He is free. We can't be free if He controls us. Look at it this way: a man can't force a woman to love him. He can physically force her to have sex, or even force her to say, 'I love you,' but that's not real love, just coercion. Similarly, God could force us to worship Him, but that too is not real love. God wants us to choose Him and choose to live righteously and well.

I sigh. (I *always* sigh). "So the whole thing is about what *god* wants."

"*Fred*," she says, putting my name in italics. She *always* puts my name in italics. "Of course it's all about God . . . and His personal relationship with each one of us."

"Okay, but here's the point. Because god wants us to choose him, because he gives us the free will to choose him, and because he gives us the free will to do evil, he's willing to allow atrocities to take place without interfering. And why does he do that? Because he wants us to choose to love and worship him. It sounds incredibly selfish to me."

"But God doesn't want us to worship him. He doesn't need or want it. He doesn't need anything."

"So why do we always hear how he wants us to love him and have a relationship with him? He wants it. Isn't that right?"

Gotchya.

"Yes, he wants it, but not for His sake, for *our* sake, because it makes *us* happy."

"But doesn't it also make god happy? Is god even capable of being happy, or angry? Does he have human emotions?"

"Well, he is certainly capable of love, after all, He loves us. But God is not the feeling of love; God is the action of love. He does things for our sake. He *does* things for our good. He doesn't just *feel* things. So, yes, He wants us to worship Him, but it's more like He wants us to *choose* Him. And when we choose Him, we begin to know Him, we're in awe of Him, we're grateful for Him, and we're just amazed at Him, and that's worship. To say that He wants us to worship Him sounds like he's some egotistical maniac who wants everyone bowing down, but God is so much beyond that. Worship is for *our* benefit. It helps us reflect on God. It helps us listen to what He wants to say to us."

I looked out at Uncle Sonny, sitting on his walker, smoking and staring stolidly ahead. Becky's arguments, as usual, made sense, but . . . "coming back to the original question: if god loves us, how can he allow the ongoing brutality and suffering? Look, parents don't allow their children to commit atrocities. If you saw your child trying to gouge someone's eyes out, wouldn't you stop him? Of course you would. Freedom and free will only go so far. Children need guidance."

"And God gives us guidance. We know right from wrong. It's just that some of us choose wrong."

"You're changing the subject on me. The question is why doesn't god stop his children from raping and slaughtering, just like a real parent would?"

"Because if God prevented us from doing what we choose to do, we would not be free. We would just be puppets, and God did not create us to be puppets; He created us to be free, to *choose* to love Him."

"*Becky,*" I said shooting back with a verbal italic, "Remember when we were watching *Schindler's List* with the Williams, and in the midst of one of those horrible scenes, Brad blurted out, 'Where was God? Why didn't He do something?' It's a question that has no answer. How can a benevolent loving god stand by and watch such suffering?"

"It's not that He doesn't care; of course He cares. And it is terribly painful for Him, but it has to be that way because if He took away free will, then life as we know it couldn't possibly exist. If we can't think for ourselves, if we can't make choices and decisions, if we are not free to pray and communicate with God, then we cease to be people, we cease to be His children."

"Becky, do you realize what you're saying? You're saying that all the horrors and atrocities in the history of this world are the price we pay for free will. That because god wants us to choose good over evil, he allows tens of millions of people to die horrible deaths, and all those deaths inflict horrible grief on the loved ones, and it goes on and on for eternity. It's just too terrible a price to pay for free will."

Game. Set. Match.

Ah, if only it were so, but no matter how irrefutable my arguments, she never ran out of counter arguments, the result, I suppose, of a lifetime of reading Catholic theology.

"Fred. Is salvation worth it? Is living with God forever worth it? Yes, human suffering is terrible, but it is such a brief moment compared to eternity."

Now I was raising my voice—not in anger but exasperation. "But why even a brief moment of suffering? Why millennia of horrors? Why . . . "

Uncle Sonny was banging on the window. It had started to rain. I jumped out, folded his walker, put it in the back seat, and helped him into the front seat. We drove home in silence, each lost in thoughts about the meaning of it all.

The God Gene

The concept of free will has another dimension to it. It is entirely possible that our inclination to believe or not believe in god may be built into our genes. And if this is true, it raises a multitude of thorny questions. Recent evidence suggests that there is even a God-gene to explain why some are more spiritual than others. Geneticist, Dr. Dean Hamer, suggests that religious inclinations are at least partly "hardwired into our genes. Spirituality is one of our basic human inheritances. It is, in fact, an instinct."[2]

In other words, religion isn't as much a choice as a biologically based implant. Furthermore, according to Hamer, the God-gene implies that spirituality "doesn't result from outside influences." Although we would like to think otherwise, our children, he writes, "don't learn to be spiritual from their parents, teachers, priests, imams, ministers, or rabbis, nor from their culture or society . . . spirituality comes from within . . . It must be part of their genes." If we do, indeed, as Hamer wrote, have "a genetic predisposition for spiritual belief," then how can God blame us for not believing? And since God created life on earth, then He is the one who gave some of us the God-gene, leaving others unable to choose him. If genetics (via god) pull the spiritual strings, then it is out of our conscious—free will—control; and therefore, it would be terribly unfair to condemn an individual to eternal damnation.

9

some new characters on the spirituality spectrum arrive on the scene

What is the meaning of human life, or, for that matter of the life of any creature? To know an answer to this question means to be religious.[1]

—Albert Einstein, *Ideas and Opinions*

Around Memorial Day, three people passed through town, each of whom represented a different spot on what we might call the "Spirituality Spectrum."

Peter: Happy as a Clam

Peter and I had been teenagers together in the Bronx. Our neighborhood was basically Italian and Jewish. Peter was the latter. He generally had a smile on his face and was free of affectations. He became a dentist, moved to California, and retired at fifty-one.

When he passed through Colorado, he was sixty years old, a little paunchy, still smiling, and happy as a clam. He was on his way to Barcelona where he would embark on a twelve-day Mediterranean cruise, and then turn around and do it all again: twenty-four days of sumptuous meals and interesting sights. In between cruises, he played video games at home and poker in Las Vegas. He loved to chat with the people around the poker table. While others were focused intensely on their cards, Peter would make small talk. One could well imagine him, drill in hand, his patient's mouth full of cotton and suction devices, chatting-up a storm. "So who are you voting for?" he would ask. "Mmphhphhmmpsh." And Peter would keep right on talking.

He was traveling with his longtime girlfriend, a Korean woman named Eunjie, who was slim and cute and close to his age, although she looked much younger. Peter had gone through an interminable divorce, which had embroiled him in years of pressure from lawyers, courts, and judges. His three kids seemed close to him. He'd coached their soccer teams and put them through medical school.

Matzo, Circumcision, and Einstein: The Keys to Salvation

When the conversation turned to religion at breakfast, Peter and Becky got into it. Woe be unto the person who took Becky on in a conversation about What God Wants. Peter argued that as a Jew, he only had to do two things to satisfy the Jew's covenant with God: get circumcised and eat matzo at Passover. He pulled the passage out of the Old Testament that said as much.

"But if that's all you have to do," said Becky rifling the pages of the Bible, "then what is all this for?"

"It's a lot of stories and some rules, but for the Jews to have a covenant with God, it says right here, matzo and circumcision, that's all you have to do."

I kept out of the conversation for the most part, since the two of them were so intense, but I was able to jump in with, "But Peter, the covenant is clear: The Jews are chosen by god to be his special people and in return they must live by his law. Since circumcision is not something you choose to do, then you can be a rapist and murderer; but as long as you eat matzo, then you're okay? It doesn't make any sense."

"Fred," he said, "if I sell you a new Cadillac for ten cents, it may not make sense, but that's the way it is. Look, it says it right here." Then he would fold his arms and sit back with a satisfied smile, as if his argument was so irrefutable, there was nothing anyone could say.

Becky and Peter went on at great length, but the most interesting part of the discussion was how we got into it in the first place. We were talking about Uncle Sonny. I pointed out that although he is forgetful, he is still interested in things. "Just yesterday, we were sitting out in the yard, and he was talking about the immensity of the universe, wondering how Einstein was able to measure the speed of light. 'It's not like you can turn on a flashlight to see how fast the light goes across the room,' he had said."

This led Peter to tell us that Einstein had forced him to reconsider God. Peter, like so many Jews I knew, had little use for God. If the Jews did indeed have a covenant with God, many of us had long since abandoned it.

"I always thought that God and religion were for others," he said. "Fred, back in the Bronx, nobody we knew believed." He was right. We knew few Jews who were serious about their faith. Of course, the Catholic kids seemed to believe. They went to church, they crossed themselves, they had black hair and didn't seem as serious about school as the Jewish kids. You expected Catholic kids to be religious.

"I don't begrudge people their faith," Peter added. "If people are happy with it, it's okay with me. But I recently read that Einstein believed in God. Here's one of the greatest minds of all time, and if he believes in God, then maybe I should rethink the whole thing."

I don't know what Peter was thinking, but I saw little evidence of Einstein being a praying man. The closest thing Einstein came to spirituality was when he said:

The most beautiful experience we can have is the mysterious . . . It is the fundamental emotion which stands at the cradle of true art and true science. Whoever does not know it and can no longer wonder, no longer marvel, is as good as dead, and his eyes are dimmed. It is the experience of mystery—even if mixed with fear—that engendered religion.

In addition:

A knowledge of the existence of something we cannot penetrate, our perception of the profoundest reason and the most radiant beauty, which only in their most primitive forms are accessible to our minds—it is this knowledge and this emotion that constitute true religiosity; in this sense, and in this sense alone, I am a deeply religious man.

Okay, fair enough. But in the next sentence, Einstein showed his contempt for those who believe in a Supreme Being.

I cannot conceive of a God who rewards and punishes his creatures or has a will of the kind that we experience in ourselves. Neither can I nor would I want to conceive of an individual that survives his physical death; let feeble souls from fear or absurd egoism, cherish such thoughts.

For Albert Einstein, God is in the abstruse wonderment of the cosmos.

I am satisfied with the mystery of the eternity of life and with the awareness and a glimpse of the marvelous structure of the existing world, together with the devoted striving to comprehend a portion, be it ever so tiny, of the Reason that manifests itself in nature.

Einstein was clearly an atheist. God is for "feeble souls" lost in "absurd egoism." But the curious part of all this was Peter. He was not feasting on ambrosia. He was feasting on cruise food. He had no discernible spiritual purpose. He did not believe in God. He had no consuming projects. He hadn't worked in almost a decade. Peter was having a good time.

For some, life's a beach; for Peter, life's a cruise. And yet here we have Peter "rethinking" God. He may very well be misinterpreting Einstein, but I find it curious that someone like Peter could consider such a thing as God. As for me, even if Einstein was convinced of the existence of a Supreme Being, I would not be swayed. Einstein may have figured out the laws of space and time, but he was wrong on other issues. If Becky couldn't convince me, Einstein certainly couldn't.

Religion Is Just a Bunch of Fairy Tales

And neither could my old high school friend, Freddie, whom I visited when I was in New York, cleaning out my uncle's apartment.

"Religion," he announced, "is just a bunch of fairy tales."

Freddie had a full head of straight black hair without a shred of gray and was as sleek at sixty as when we were teenagers in the Bronx. He had attended private Catholic high school and private Catholic college, and although he recognized religion as a source of morality, he was contemptuous of the supernatural element.

"It's all bullshit," he said. "When we die, we're food for the worms."

Although I agreed with him, I found myself vaguely annoyed. "Do you think religion does any good?" I asked over a couple of beers at the Outback Steakhouse while we waited for our table.

"What good is it to believe in a bunch of stories? Religion causes so much misery and war. It makes people hate each other."

"But it comforts people," I offered. "It gives them hope . . ."

"But it's not true. They believe in nothing."

"But it's true to them, so if they believe it, then what's so bad?" (When a conversation is full of "buts," you just know the tension level is rising.)

Freddie is a scientist, a PhD in physics, and he had little patience with the supernatural. He was quick, confident, decisive, and argued aggressively.

"What's so bad?" he asked rhetorically. "You know how many people have died because of religion? That's what Osama Bin Laden is all about; and the Crusades, and Northern Ireland."

"But Freddie," I said slipping uncomfortably into the role of defending religion with yet another but. "It's not religion that caused those problems, but flawed men. People kill for all sorts of reasons."

"Right," he said. "And religion is one of them. Millions of people have died for god, which means that their stupid beliefs are responsible."

I knew what I wanted to say: that people sacrifice themselves and destroy others for their own personal gods, for their fabricated heroism and artificial defiance. They die for their holy missions. I wanted to say that religion is just one manifestation of spiritual purpose. But that was too much to spew out, and besides, the square plastic pager was lighting up announcing our table was ready.

As I drifted off to sleep that night in Freddie's little house just off the wharves on Long Island, it occurred to me that he and Peter were right about the dearth of religious people around us while we were growing up in New York. I did not have a single friend or relative who even remotely believed in God: not my parents, not my grandparents, not my sister, not my cousins, not Peter the retired dentist, not Freddie. Nobody. It was a spiritual wasteland, and I was one of them. Yet, I had just had a conversation in which I was on the other side. I was defending not the reality of god, but the reality of the importance to mankind of the belief in god and spirituality.

A Little Social Experiment

Two days after Peter and Eunjie left for their Mediterranean cruise, Melanie, my youngest daughter, returned for the summer after completing her sophomore year at the University of Wyoming. At age twenty, she was pretty, short, slight, sweet, kind, generous, quiet, loving, giving, and every inch a Christian.

Prior to our marriage, Becky and I had talked endlessly about how a relationship like ours could possibly work. How, for example, would we raise our kids? It was clear from the outset that since religion was paramount in her life and meaningless in mine, she would provide the Catholic upbringing. Becky assumed that taking them to church, exposing them to the faith, and most importantly, her influence, would result in three little Christian clones. I, of course, was the wild card. And I had my own assumptions. I assumed that just being who I am would influence their behavior, their psychological adjustment, and their spirituality. I had no plan to subvert Becky. If the kids ended up as little Christians, then so be it. But Dad's lack of spirituality would certainly have an effect. What that effect would be, I had no idea.

Now, almost thirty years later, the results are in on this little social experiment. And the results are resoundingly inconclusive. While Melanie is a Christian, middle daughter Ashlie is a confirmed atheist, and oldest daughter Mandy is religiously lukewarm.

Melanie Is the Real Deal

I'm not completely sure how one would define a "real" Christian. In Melanie's opinion, a Christian isn't just someone who has an inclination to do good, but is also someone who chooses the good when the bad choices are equally accessible. From my point of view, she is not only that, but is also naturally kind, honest, and empathetic; in other words, the Real Deal.

Melanie is dedicated to God and overwhelmed by His presence. Before most meals, she lowers her eyes to pray. She considers sexual promiscuity and premarital sex harmful to the dignity and happiness that God intended for men and women. When around me, Melanie, like Becky, avoids those annoying little phrases that people under the thrall of religion generally use with each other.

"God is so good."

"It's in God's hands."

"The Lord will provide" . . . and so on. But in her heart of hearts, she walks with God. One of my greatest fears is that she will become a nun. To marry God, to remove oneself from normal social intercourse, and to put on a habit, struck me as abnormal.

My first real sense of Melanie's Christian empathy came while traveling with the three girls in Bali in 1994 when Mel was eleven. We rented bikes and took off into the unknown. Bali was so exotic and beautiful that I figured whatever road we took would be interesting. We biked through what seemed to be a tropical rain forest—thick foliage, water buffalo, rice paddies, and bamboo shoots growing out of the water. We left early in the morning with backpacks full of bottled water, but within two hours, we had finished all the water and were buying more from kiosks along the way. At one of our many water stops, Melanie said to a wrinkled woman, "Do you have a bowl?"

"What for?" I asked.

"For the dogs," she said, motioning to the mangy dogs suffering in the intense heat. "They need water."

The next day, however, made me understand just how special she was.

Hovering on the beach around the tourist hotels were the ubiquitous peddlers. The police kept them from harassing hotel guests on the grounds, so they congregated on the public beach, assaulting westerners with Bali T-shirts, which when washed, shrunk to the size of postage stamps. They sold perfume, jewelry, postcards, silk pictures, and other assorted stuff. "Let me demonstrate how to bargain with these people," said the voice of experience to the girls.

Standing on the beach in the late afternoon sun, I was saying to the thin guy with bad teeth that I couldn't possibly pay ten dollars for a bottle of perfume and started walking away, knowing he would follow with a counter offer.

"How much you pay?" he asked.

"Two dollars."

He grinned and shook his head. I continued walking. "Okay, five dollah. Last price."

In the midst of this, one of the peddler-beggar women came over to us and handed Melanie a headband.

That was really strange.

"Why did she give you that?" I asked.

"I dunno," Melanie said.

Hmmm. "Well, there must be a reason. These people don't *give* things away. Did you buy it from her?"

"Not exactly."

"What does that mean?"

We were well-baked from the sun and salt water. The ocean lapped up against the beach and the late afternoon shadows were creeping along the sand. Peddlers were everywhere. The guy with bad teeth was getting annoyed because he had lost my attention. "Okay, four dollah," he implored.

"Well, I gave her some money," Melanie said uneasily.

"You *gave* her money? Well, how much?"

She shrugged. "I dunno"

"Melanie!"

"Maybe ten dollars."

I was momentarily annoyed. I was careful with money. I didn't give it away. I'd rather buy those T-shirts than just hand it over.

"Don't be angry, Dad," she said, reading my expression. "I just felt sorry for her."

Mel and Uncle Sonny

Knowing Mel as I do, it came as no surprise that she was happy to spend time with Uncle Sonny. She understood—empathized—with his life and his plight. Two years earlier she had written:

Dear Uncle Sonny,

This is Melanie. I am the youngest of Fred's children. I am thinking of you and wanted to write you a letter. How are you? I am doing very well. I am in my second semester of college. I am enjoying my classes. I am taking English composition, math, beginning acting, women's choir and a class called New Testament.

The dorm I live in is the tallest building in Wyoming! It is only 12 stories. That seems small compared to where you live.

Mandy is finishing up graduate school in Washington. Probably her boyfriend will propose to her soon. It is very exciting.

Ashlie has just moved to Texas. She is now a second Lieutenant in the Air Force and is beginning Intelligence training. We are all very proud of her.

I was very sad to hear about Millie. I hope there are people in your life who are helping you through your difficult times. I am definitely praying for you. I love you, Sonny.

Sincerely,
Melanie Singer

The first evening we visited Uncle Sonny, Melanie disappeared for about fifteen minutes. She was visiting with Hugh, a garrulous old man with garbled speech.

"So there you are," I said.

"Yup, he's quite a charmer, this guy is," Melanie said.

I pointed a finger at the ancient man in his electric scooter and said in mock anger. "You stay away from my daughter."

He laughed. "I've been told that many times."

Mel went over almost every day. She helped Uncle Sonny organize his photographs and took him to Starbucks where he raved about the coffee.

"It was great cawfee; just delicious, especially the mocha. *Chawklet* and *cawfee* are a great combination. It's just amazing."

Lieutenant Ashlie

The next day, Memorial Day, Ashlie arrived from Turkey where she was stationed as an Air Force second lieutenant in military intelligence. At the age of twenty-three, she was on the opposite side of the spirituality spectrum. If Melanie was a religious clone of Becky, then Ashlie resided with me on the atheist wing of the family.

Short, blonde, quick, bright, aggressive, confident, and a natural leader, she had dutifully gone to church with Becky and her two sisters as a child, but somewhere along the line concluded that it made no sense. She wasn't interested in being a Catholic and she wasn't interested in being Jewish; she simply didn't believe in God.

I liken that feeling to being gay. If I were offered ten million dollars to be a homosexual, I would lose the ten million dollars. Oh, I could go through the motions, really try to love men, think about it all the time, read gay literature, and so on; but I can't be what I'm not. Similarly, I cannot believe in god no matter how hard I try. Becky often says I should leave myself open to it; just consider it. Try it. Go on the assumption there is a God. Read the Bible and so on. But I can no more believe in god than I could become gay. If you offered me ten million dollars, I could go through the motions—pray, go to church, get on my knees, read the Bible—but in the end, in my heart of hearts, I would not believe any of it. And so it is with Ashlie.

The question that immediately comes to mind—that begs to be asked—is this: How can two children raised in the same home, with the same parents, in the same environment, molded by similar genes be so spiritually different? Since they came from the same environment, we could conclude that the mix of genes produced different children. Or did Ashlie identify more with me because of her personality? The answer, of course, is that we will never know why they are different; but the reality is simply that they are.

Ashlie was in Denver mainly to spend some time with her boyfriend Kevin, who was dark, handsome, broad-shouldered, well-muscled, a graduate of Notre Dame, and irony of delicious ironies—a practicing Catholic. He was a regular churchgoer, and he prayed with his rosary. He and Becky talked Catholic stuff together.

They had met in intelligence school eighteen months before; and while she opted for Turkey, he opted to be stationed in Denver. Their relationship consisted of a week here and a week there. They had no sustained time together, but equally important is that they had not discussed The Big Issue: religion.

How are you going to raise your kids?

Can you really love someone who doesn't believe in God?

Can you really love someone who *does* believe in God?

Are you not contemptuous of religious people?

Do you think Ashlie, who might be your wife, will burn in hell?

Do you think you can lead her back to the church?

And Ashlie, do you worry that he'll try to lead you back to the church?

I secretly chortled to myself. Ashlie and Kevin were faced with the same questions Becky and I had dealt with a generation earlier, with one exception: *they weren't dealing with it;* they never discussed the religious issue.

10

roaming around in the
past with ashlie

So one night on the retreat I went to the chapel and I just wanted
to have it out with God; but He wasn't there, and I thought there
is just no God here; there is no God in me.

—Ashlie

"Dad," Ashlie said, "you're making Melanie out to be a saint."

It was late March, 2006. Ashlie had just returned from a leadership conference in Washington in which she was generally rated higher than all the other men and women in their thirties and forties.

"I'm not making her out as a saint, Ashlie. It's just who she is."

This conversation was dripping with irony. For most of Melanie's life, we told her not to try to be like her big sisters. "Just be who you are; don't try to be anyone else." Now in an ironic twist, I found myself saying to Ashlie–just be who you are, you can't be Melanie.

Ashlie was just about to leave the house, jump in her car, and head back to the Air Force base in Denver. She was constantly coming and going, a perpetual motion machine, the quintessential little miss go-go. But as she moved her weekend bags to the door, she slowed up for a moment.

"Well, she does have her saintly moments."

"Like what?"

"I remember one day after we had returned to the States for my senior year, and I was feeling depressed and miserable. I was at a soccer game at night, and it was sooo cold, but I took off my warm-ups to show the coach I was ready to play. He never put me in."

She paused for a long moment, unusual for Ashlie who generally speaks with a fluid outpouring of words. "This was probably one of the low points of my life. It must have been well below freezing, but I wouldn't put my warm-ups on during the game, because, dammit, I was going to show the coach how dedicated I was. But it didn't matter, I never got in and sobbed all the way home. When I got in the house, I was shaking from the cold and crying hysterically. While Mom was calming me down, Mel snuck into the other room, found Megan's phone number, called her, and asked her to call me back to cheer me up. Megan didn't tell me until later that Mel was the one that called her. It was something I really needed."

On the spur of the moment I asked, "Do you ever talk to Melanie about religion?"

"Do you mean, do I try to talk her out of it?"

"Well, do you?"

"Of course not. Why would I want to do that?"

"Does she ever try to talk you into it?"

She shook her head. "I think she understands where I'm coming from. It's not going to happen."

After she left, I got to wondering about how in the world they could be so different. Why did Ashlie turn away from God? Was it my influence, or do we all have natural, genetic inclinations to accept or reject the spiritual? As the sunny winter day faded into twilight, I drifted off into the past to figure it out.

Hanau, Germany 1987

I'm sitting in my den, looking out onto a typical gloomy, dark, wet German day. It's Sunday morning. Becky is getting the kids ready for church and Sunday school, and I'm looking forward to three hours of peace. While they're away, I'll work on my lesson plans, grade papers, and get the week organized. I look with some frustration at the manuscript I've been working on. If only I were free to write full time; but, alas, a lesson on the Spanish-American War awaits.

My desk in front of a big window enables me to look out over the world from our house high on a hill. On one of those rare, clear days I can just about make out Frankfurt. Across the street, Herr Ackermann is working on a car in his garage. I note that the tape and scissors are missing. They are always missing. I gave everyone tape and scissors, but still they take mine. Of course, I keep spares hidden in a lower drawer, but I am more than mildly annoyed.

"Hey, Dad!" Ashlie bounces into the room. She is eight-years-old and about four feet tall. She wears a Sunday dress. Her blonde hair is curly, long, and freshly brushed. She wears ankle-length white socks and brown leather shoes with straps. She is in her Sunday best.

"Ready for church?" I ask.

"Yup," she says, sitting down on the couch under the TRY AGAIN sign and a wall full of family pictures. She motions to the computer on my desk. "Are you ever gonna learn how to use that thing?"

A friend got me the Apple IIc–a computer, printer, and monitor for about $500. The green wavy screen seems foreboding. I doubt it will be of much use, but when I have some time, I'll force myself to learn how to use it.

"Do you know why we're here, Ashlie?"

She nods. "You want to explore my spiritual roots." She looks eight but talks like a twenty-six-year-old. In the future, she will be an intelligence officer in the Air Force; today she is in the third grade.

"I thought this would be a good place to start." We hear Becky and the kids storming around upstairs. We'd better hurry; it's almost time to leave for church. Ashlie is squirming around in little girl fashion, in her little girl dress.

"So, at this point would you consider yourself religious, Ashlie? What does it feel like? What do you think about God?"

Her voice is tinny and high-pitched; somewhat nasal in tone. Her right leg kicks back and forth nervously. "Well, of course I believe in God, Dad. After all, I was raised going to church with Mom. That's the way things are–the grass is green, you go to school, you go to church. I never question it. I really do believe in God. I have no doubts."

It's raining steadily outside the window. The sky seems as dark as twilight. I lean back in my desk chair. "But what about me, Ashlie? Don't you ever wonder why I don't go to church?"

"Of course I wonder. I sometimes pray you will believe in God."

"But don't you wonder why I'm so removed from all that?"

"I don't understand why you don't believe since everyone else does. It's a matter of an entire community against you. So I naturally side with the community. Dad is the one who is wrong. On the other hand, you used to say, 'I want to believe in God.'"

"I said that? Really?"

"Yeah. You said it's just not something one can change, turn on and off. Either you believe or you don't. On those rare occasions when you would come to church with us and open the Bible I would think, oh maybe he'll start believing."

I laugh. "I was just bored and needed something to read."

Ashlie laughs with me, then her little face tightens. "What about you, Dad, didn't you ever believe?"

I start to say no, but then I remember. "There was one moment when I doubted my doubt."

"Really?"

I nod. "I was six years old, back in our little apartment in the Bronx. It was Christmas time and my grandfather had just died. Uncle Sonny's father. I don't remember being sad, but I must have felt something because I wrote a letter to him and to my other grandfather who was long gone. I clearly understood that death was permanent, that they were gone forever, and that I wanted to communicate with them."

"So, I guess you believed in God and Heaven and all that?"

"Sort of."

"What does that mean?"

"Well, I left the letter on the mantle, above where all the Christmas presents would be. And in the morning, the letter was gone, replaced by a Christmas present, a little red briefcase. I assumed that the letter had made its way to Heaven, and that God had given me the present."

"It's hard to believe Nana and Popa would do that."

"I know, I've often thought about it. At the time I didn't know what to think. Even at six I was very skeptical. For years I would ask them, 'Did you take the letter? Did you give me the briefcase?' and they always shrugged and said they knew nothing about it."

"Why did they do it?"

"Probably because I wanted so much to communicate with my dead grandfather that they wanted me to feel I had succeeded. Eventually I found the smoking gun, proving the whole thing a hoax. After the briefcase incident I wrote another letter to Heaven, telling God that I would be interested in getting a sports game and that I would reduce my television watching if He would be nice enough to send it. I figured I was on to something—write a letter, get a present. I put it on the mantle, it disappeared, but no more presents. Some years later, I found that second letter."

"Were you disappointed?"

"No, because I never really believed and had long ago concluded that my parents were behind it."

"Ashlie! We're going!" Becky calls as the rest of the troops, all freshly scrubbed in dresses and raincoats trundled down the basement stairs to the garage. Melanie is four, her platinum blonde hair is just starting to darken. Mandy is nine and urging everyone to hurry up. Her dark brown hair is straight, still a few years away from curling with puberty.

After they leave, I walk into the living room and look out over the miserable day through the huge picture window. This is a good time; small children with small problems.

I'd like to stay here in the past, but I have a date with Ashlie on a far away beach.

Okinawa, Japan 1995

We are walking by the ocean at Mission Beach, about twenty-five miles up the island from our house on a Marine base in Koza. Palm trees, blue skies, beautiful rock formations, and a gently lapping ocean surround us. It's mid-April. Ashlie is fifteen. Behind us up on the bluff is an old building used for Christian retreats. She is there with TEC– Teens Encounter Christ.

The warm sand on our bare feet feels wonderful. We are both wearing hats and sunglasses. "So, how do you feel about religion now that you're older?"

"Believe it or not, I'm still very religious. It's spring break, and I'm here to give my life to God—the food is terrible, and the building is crummy, but it's a very powerful experience."

"Even now?"

"Yeah, it's kind of in my nature that whatever I do, I really dedicate myself to it. I really did want to focus on religion and God. We have the best time at TEC—we always seem to be laughing or singing."

"But surely you have some doubts."

"Oh, definitely. The whole concept of the wine and bread turning to the blood and flesh of Christ was hard to believe. But still I prayed for people, prayed the Rosary."

"How do you feel at these retreats," I ask, motioning back to the Mission House. The sun feels like heaven. The wet sand at the water's edge cools our feet.

"The time I feel closest to God is when I'm singing at one of these retreats. Ironically, it was on a retreat that I turned around and said 'wait a minute.'"

"You mean you had a conversion in reverse?"

"Something like that. It was in that terrible year when we went back to the States."

I looked at the puffy, white clouds over the ocean and sighed. "We should have stayed here on Okinawa." At the end of Ashlie's junior year of high school we returned to the States, wrenching her from her established life on this semi-tropical Japanese island. Even for someone as strong as Ashlie, the move was utterly devastating.

"Are you telling me it was the move that turned you from God?"

Ashlie kicked at the sand. "I'm sure it would have happened anyway, but the move to the States was the catalyst."

"Maybe we should go there next," I suggest.

"I'd rather stay here."

"I know," I say with genuine regret. "But we can't change the past, we can only explore it."

Greeley, Colorado, March 1997

We're sitting in the stands at the Greeley Central High School football field watching Ashlie's soccer team play Greeley West. She is seventeen, a few months away from graduating. The night is dark and cold. Lights flood the field but it still feels dark. A scattering of parents and kids huddle on the bleacher seats. It's late in the game; Central is down two to one. Ashlie is on the sidelines, ready to play. We are annoyed that we are freezing in the stands, but the coach won't put her in.

It's been a terrible year for her. I walk down to the sidelines. The girls on the bench are cheering for their team. Ashlie is jogging in place to keep warm. We have been back in the States now for nine months, "Where were we?" I ask, continuing our conversation from the Okinawan beach.

"I can tell you where I am now," she says. "By this time in my senior year it was all over between me and God."

"What happened? What was it that pushed you over the edge?"

"Coming to the States really depressed me. I had to leave my best friends. I was going to be valedictorian on Okinawa, but here I'm number two; and even worse, the school refuses to recognize us at graduation. Back at Kubasaki High School, I would have been in the jazz choir for the second year, something I just loved to do. I would have graduated with my best friends instead of mere acquaintances." She pauses and motions to the game rushing past us. "On Okinawa I would have been captain of the soccer team, but here I hardly even get in the game."

"So, are you saying that being wrenched from your comfortable life on Okinawa is what turned you away from God?"

"It was a combination of things, Dad. I know for sure that when I was on Okinawa, I had no doubt at all about the existence of God, but the horrible move to the States seemed to take all emotion out of my life. It was easier for me not to feel. My entire world had been turned upside down, and I was no longer feeling the presence of God. I remember one day as I was training for the volleyball team, I was running around the track and tripped on my shoelaces—twice! But I wasn't embarrassed. I really didn't care if people were laughing. It made no difference to me. I was totally devoid of feeling. At that point, where I would normally feel God, He just wasn't there. Maybe I was angry at God. To me God was comfort, normalcy, security, and warmth. And that was gone."

"There must be more to it than that, Ashlie"

"I think the pivotal moment was on one of those religious retreats here in Colorado. They were pushing us to give our lives to God and I was going in the opposite direction, doubting His existence. We were all waiting for confession, and I opted not to go. Instead I stayed with the group and sang songs. Well, one of the things we do at retreats is write little notes to each other, and one of the kids who was thinking about becoming a priest, wrote me a note saying he could really see God in me when I sang. But my turned-on expression was not joy at God but just enjoyment of the music."

"So what's the point?"

"The point is that it made me realize that God is just something we put into everything—not the other way around. He saw God in me when it wasn't there. We see God in Creation, or say that God wants us to marry this or that person, and so on. But like the kid seeing God in me when it wasn't there, we see God everywhere because we want to.

"So one night on the retreat I went to the chapel, and I just wanted to have it out with God, but He wasn't there; and I thought there is just no God there; there is no God in me."

"Were you unhappy about that?"

"I was more than unhappy. It was demoralizing. I mean something I had put my heart and soul into for so many years just wasn't true. I remember sitting in calculus class feeling miserable because there was no God. I told Mom that I didn't want to go to church anymore, and she said, "Well, while you're under my roof you'll go. I kept going, but took myself emotionally out of it. I think Mom eventually realized I was serious. It was a very sad experience. Mom thought it was a phase, but it wasn't."

The noise level from the cheering fans goes up a notch as Central drives for the goal. I look up at Becky who is huddled in her coat and scarf wishing she were home. I feel no joy at Ashlie's words, and in a strange sort of way, wish she did believe.

"Do you think you could ever believe again? You're not even agnostic. Very few people admit to being an atheist. My mom was telling me last week that even my father said he believed in something."

"There are moments when I think I would like to believe in God, there are times when I'm tempted to go to church. I could be a reader, work with youth, I like the community aspect of it. In my heart I really want to believe, but in my head I can't."

I push her a little further. "Supposing there was irrefutable proof that God exists. How would you feel about that? Would you be religious again?"

"I don't think so. I don't think there is anything that would convince me it's true."

The soccer players shuffle around the ball on the far side of the field. In an ironic sort of way, I am saddened that she would so tightly close the door to ever believing again, and I tell her so.

"It's not as tight as you might think, Dad. I avoid church because it still exerts a pull on me."

"What does that mean? I thought you said nothing could convince you."

"It's not that I could be convinced, but it still has an emotional effect. Look at it this way: A piece of paper is naturally straight, but if you roll it up into a tube, it will eventually take that shape. When I stopped being religious, I was unraveling the paper, but every time I got near a church I would feel the paper roll back up. Just being near church evoked a lot of emotion in me. Sometimes I'd get a lump in my throat, but I knew it wasn't real, not true." She wrapped her arms around herself to keep warm. "If you are married for thirty years and then you get a divorce, there is still a huge emotional attachment. It's like I had been married to this person for so long and had been betrayed and didn't want anything to do with him, yet the emotional pull would still be there. I don't want the emotional connection to overwhelm my logic." And at that moment, she did indeed open the door, just a crack.

"I just refuse to give in to emotion, and when I get near church I feel that emotion. Maybe another ten years down the road I'll be able to open that door a little bit so then I'll know that I'm looking at it from a totally logical perspective."

I put my arm around her. "I'm sorry I dragged you back to the States before you graduated. I never realized how crushing it was for you."

"Go Rachel, go, go . . ." she shouted as a teammate was moving with the ball. Ashlie had always been a star, especially academically. Teacher after teacher would come over to me to say how spirited she was on the track team, or what an asset she was in choir, or that she was getting another academic award. I became a little uncomfortable with it. Perhaps, like the Jews, she is too successful in the secular world to worry about the hereafter. People who struggle need God more than those who don't.

Or is it all caused by the God gene?

11

do things happen
for a reason?

Before the year is out, Jesus will have your soul!
—Alan, 1975, Erlensee, Germany

Early in June, Uncle Sonny and I went on the senior center trip to the Blackhawk casinos in the mountains. He played the slots. "I love the sound of the coins dropping," he said.

UNCLE SONNY PLAYING THE SLOTS AT BLACKHAWK.

He settled in at the dollar slots with a cup of coffee and a pack of cigarettes while I found a bench outside to read Po Bronson's recent bestseller, *What Should I Do with My Life? The True Story of People Who Answered the Ultimate Question*. It was about people searching for their true calling. Since I was in the midst of writing a book about "What People Really Want," it seemed like a book I should read. The opening paragraph was right on target.

> We are all writing the story of our life. We want to know what it's "about," what are its themes and which theme is on the rise. We demand of it something deeper, or richer, or more substantive. We want to know where we're headed—not to spoil our own ending by ruining the surprise, but we want to ensure that when the ending comes, it won't be shallow. We will have done something. We will not have squandered our time here.[1]

The first chapter asked, "Do things happen for a reason?" Voltaire dealt with that question centuries ago with *Zadig*, and later in his masterpiece *Candide*. Life is arbitrary. *Whatever is, is.* Earthquakes kill innocent people.

If things *do* happen for a reason, then we are in the realm of supernatural forces, and we might as well just chuck reason and read our horoscopes. If things happen for a reason, then there must be a Master Planner, and by implication we human beings exist for a purpose in Creation. The problem is that we continually try to put the square peg in the round hole—to find logical explanations for arbitrariness and injustice.

Alan Comes to Town

Uncle Sonny came out forty dollars ahead on that day, but seemed preoccupied on the bus ride home. He occasionally looked out the window at the mountain scenery, but most of the time he stared forward, blinking wildly, which meant he was ruminating on something negative. I tried to read a few more chapters about "People Who Answered the Ultimate Question," but drifted back to that first chapter about "Do things Happen For a Reason?" I've been told any number of times that the reason I married Becky was because God was giving me a chance to be exposed to Him. Why else would two people with such differing religious views get married? Well, there are other reasons why people get married—like shared values, mutual respect, similar body types, same level of self-esteem and similar education levels —none of which has to do with fate or destiny or god.

Alan would disagree. Just the week before, Alan had retired to Wyoming after thirty-five years as an elementary school counselor in an American school in Germany. Alan was part of a prayer group Becky had been involved in when we were going together in 1975. He had the look of an old time preacher, the quintessential Puritan—thin, intense, and certain, a thin beard framing his pale face. Alan was and is a fired-up Christian, and I'm sure he wondered at the time what Becky was doing with the likes of me.

Back then, before any of us were married, we were sitting in a German *gasthous* discussing Alan's relationship with Debbie, a teacher in his school, who, he told us, was the only girl in the world for him. They had met only eight months earlier and quickly fell in love.

"Do you mean to say," I said, "that there is not another single girl in the entire world whom you could marry."

"That's exactly what I mean. Debbie is the only one for me."

"But there must be tens of thousands of girls who are the right age and attractiveness and so on. It's just a matter of who you happen to meet."

"No," said Alan, his eyes flashing. "There aren't thousands, only one. It was meant to be. It's what God wants."

Statements like that really push my buttons. "How can you possibly know what God wants?"

Alan's jaw tightened. I suspect we were out to dinner together so he could get ammunition to counsel Becky against, well, yoking herself to an unbeliever. But somehow the conversation had turned to his love life instead. "It's obvious that God wants us to get married," Alan said. "The fact that we both came to the same school at the same time. We both are Christians. We instinctively knew right from the first moment. It was just meant to be."

I pointed out that all couples meet by coincidence. Becky and I were both in the same school at the same time. "Does God want *us* to get married?"

Alan hesitated. He wanted to give a resounding, No! He wanted to save Becky from making a huge mistake. But discretion being the better part of valor, he opted for, "He might."

"But why would god want someone like me to marry someone like her?"

"Maybe He wants Becky to bring you to Jesus," said Alan, warming to the subject.

Now he was just pissing me off. "And maybe there is nothing supernatural about it at all. Maybe we just met by chance. Besides, I'm not going to Jesus. I don't believe in Jesus. I don't believe in miracles. I'm Jewish and intend to stay that way."

Now Alan was raising his voice and pointing at me. "And I'm going to tell you right now that before the year is out, Jesus will have your soul!"

However, on December 31, 1975, I was Jesus-free and remain so to this day. And in spite of what Alan thought at the time, our marriage, which was certainly not made in heaven, is alive and well.

Why Would God Care about Me?

"You can't put that in the book," Becky said with finality.

"Why not? Because I mention Alan?"

"Of course. You can't talk about people we know like that."

"But it happened just that way."

"It doesn't matter."

"Okay, I'll change his name."

"Don't be silly, everyone will recognize Alan."

"So I'll make him a big guy." *Late in May, a former friend of Becky's from Germany, Big Mike, rumbled into town. He was six feet tall and six feet wide.*

Becky shook her head. "Besides, I don't agree with you. Maybe our marriage *was* God's plan."

Of course, I knew where she was going with this. "It was the only way god could get to me."

She nodded. "It certainly would help explain us."

I shook my head. "But why would god care about me?"

"Because he wants you to come to the truth. He wants everyone to find Him."

"So why doesn't he arrange to have every nonbeliever marry a believer?"

"Because," she said thoughtfully, "God knows that not everyone can be reached through a marriage. All roads lead to Rome, but there are many different roads."

"Well, in any case, that's what Alan said almost thirty years ago. But if there is a god, and we have free will, then god is breaking his own rule by interfering in my life."

"No, God didn't force us to get married, it's just that he might have put us in a position to meet and let nature take its course."

"You're sounding more and more like Alan every minute. We would all like to think that god has an individual plan for us. When people say things happen for a reason, what they really mean is that god is pulling the strings."

"But Fred, things *do* happen for a reason. How else would you explain that night you were in the singles bar."

Do You Come Here Often?

She was right, of course. That night at Barney Googles was an extraordinary life-changing event. If I was going to believe in Divine Intervention, this would come pretty close.

Early in May, 1968, when I was twenty-four and life was new, I was offered a teaching job on Okinawa and was given just two days to respond.

I wanted to go overseas—wanted my life to go in new directions, wanted adventure, and certainly wanted to get out of New York. But Okinawa? I didn't even know where it was. A map in a World War II book showed it was south of Japan, sixty-seven miles long and three to five miles wide. It was on the other side of the world, which was good. It was Japanese, which was good. It was semi-tropical with palm trees and tropical rains, which was good. It was different and exotic, which was very, very good. But what would it be like? What would the reality be? It was a military base. I didn't know what to do. My dad provided the decisive argument. "You'll be on an island with a bunch of soldiers and at the mercy of the local commander. For a swinger like you, that might be bad."

On Friday morning, swinger that I was, I mailed the letter turning down the job.

That night, I went to Barney Googles, an East Side singles bar, with a couple of friends and was reminded of everything I wanted to escape from—crowded, smoky bars where I would make artificial small talk to get a phone number to get a date. The night was going as usual—I was feeling cramped, uncomfortable, and overstimulated. The perfumes and colognes competed with the smoke. The incredibly loud music made it impossible to carry on a conversation. "SO WHAT DID YOU SAY YOUR NAME IS? DO YOU COME HERE OFTEN? WHAT'S YOUR MAJOR?

I wasn't very good at artificial small talk. What I wanted to say in those crowded bars was, I REALLY DON'T CARE WHAT YOUR MAJOR IS, CAN WE DISPENSE WITH THE SMALL TALK AND GO OUT NEXT WEEK? MAYBE WE'LL FALL IN LOVE. IF NOT, MAYBE WE CAN MAKE OUT. I'VE GOT TO GET OUT OF HERE. THERE IS A WHOLE WORLD TO SEE. I'M TWENTY-FOUR AND LIFE IS PASSING ME BY. WHAT DID YOU SAY YOUR NAME IS?

I went to the men's room, wondering if I had made a mistake. Whatever Okinawa was, it wasn't this. Standing next to me at the urinals were two sailors. "Man," one said to the other, "I wish I was back on Okinawa."

***

Becky would say it was God interfering in my life. After all, consider the odds against so many variables coming together in this time and place. I had rejected the job offer just hours earlier. This was a decision upon which my subsequent life would be based. I was in Barney Googles along with a shipload of sailors on shore leave who had been on Okinawa. I was in the men's room at the precise moment that one of them mentioned Okinawa. Call it a crossroads moment.

If I had waited another thirty seconds before going to the men's room, the ripples traveling outward at the speed of life might have negated Becky, Melanie, Ashlie, Mandy, Colorado, and in effect everything I lived through since that night. Uncle Sonny would never have come to Colorado. This book wouldn't exist. I would not be sitting at this computer in Colorado at this very moment. You would not be reading this book.

***

"Excuse me," I said to the sailors, "I heard you mention Okinawa. I just got a job there and was wondering how you liked it."

"Greatest place in the world."

"Beautiful beaches and palm trees."

"The girls are unbelievable."

They went on and on and on.

I asked the opinions of other sailors at the bar who had the same ship insignia on their arms.

"Loved it."

"Would go back in a heartbeat."

"Best kept secret in the world."

I beat a path to the exit. If half of what they said was true, Okinawa would be great. The smoke, the beer, the deafening music, and the inane small talk were replaced by the outside noises of cars, horns, and the general hum of the city. Inside or out, New York was loud and exhausting. I wanted out. I wanted palm trees and beaches and fishing villages. There wasn't much to keep me in the city. My parents would survive. The tough inner city school where I taught would muddle through without me. My roach-infested Manhattan apartment would have another tenant. And my Jewish girlfriend in Brooklyn, well, she would have to wait another year until I sowed my wild oats.

On Monday I called Washington and told them to disregard the letter. One hundred days later, at three o'clock in the morning, I stepped off the plane into the steaming humidity of Okinawa and stayed overseas for twenty-eight years.

12

uncle sonny contemplates the universe or how can we go on if we don't believe in god?

Man positively needs general ideas and convictions that will give a meaning to his life and enable him to find a place for himself in the universe. He can stand the most incredible hardships when he is convinced that they make sense; he is crushed when, on top of all his misfortunes, he has to admit that he is taking part in a "tale told by an idiot."[1]

—Karl G. Jung, *Man and His Symbols*

70, 000,000,000,000,000,000,000
70 sextillion—the number of estimated stars in the universe[2]

—Australian National University in Sydney

It seemed a good idea to take Uncle Sonny along on whatever errands we were running. He was interested in doing just about anything, so one day I took him to Kinko's to run off a photograph. It was an 8 x 10 black-and-white of my three-year-old self sitting on my grandmother's lap. I didn't look too happy, and I wasn't. Grandma smelled unpleasant and would smother me in kisses and say *shane kindele*, and all I wanted to do was escape.

My uncle sat on his walker in the sun in front of Kinko's, wearing his usual New York Yankees baseball cap. His face as always, an inscrutable, unchanging mask. Puffing on a cigarette, he looked up at the sun, and his mind drifted out to the stars. "Life on earth," he stated with a certain finality. "We are just the right distance from the sun. If we were closer or farther away, life would be impossible." He paused for a moment and added, "It's all so big. Alpha Centauri, the nearest star, is four light years from earth."

According to Einstein's definition, Uncle Sonny was a religious man because he was in awe of creation. The immensity of the universe, the possibility of life on other planets, and the development of life on earth were subjects he often raised. His mind may have been fried from alcohol, but he still maintained a genuine sense of wonder.

Since this is a book about who we are, what motivates us, the meaning of our personal lives, the significance of our existence as a species, and how all this relates to religion, then the nature of the universe must eventually be part of the discussion. And since Uncle Sonny brought it up, this is as good a time as any to elaborate.

The Size of the Universe Negates God

For me, the size of the universe negates god; for Becky, it confirms Him.

Just how big is the universe? We don't know for sure, but here are a few numbers. Our own Milky Way galaxy has around one hundred billion stars. "Near" our galaxy are other galaxies, some of which have over a trillion stars, and they combine together to form a cluster of galaxies. This cluster in turn, combines with other clusters to form a cluster of clusters. And this cluster of clusters of galaxies is part of a conglomerate of other clusters of clusters. We have now identified around one hundred billion galaxies.

Something called the star registry will name a star after you for a fee. But why not a galaxy? Why not seventeen galaxies? Yes, we could name seventeen galaxies for each of the six billion people now living. How many stars is that? Approximately one trillion, seven hundred billion stars for each person now living. And there is surely much more out there that we haven't yet identified.

We talk of light years and parsecs. We can travel at the speed of light, 186,000 miles per second for millions of years and not even begin to find the end. "End" is for finite minds. So is "beginning." So is "now."

In spite of the immensity of creation, the entire life span of the universe might be nothing more than a passing moment. We pretty much accept the Big Bang theory, which tells us that the universe was condensed into a small ball, exploded outward, and continues to expand. It will eventually slow down and contract back into that dense ball and explode out again, creating infinite incarnations of the universe.

Even worse, something called "string theory" suggests that there may be multiple parallel universes and as many as seven more dimensions. The more we learn, the smaller we become.

"If god created the earth," I said to Becky on many occasions, "and he wanted us to be the center of his attention, then why did he create *tens of billions of galaxies and many trillions* of stars? What does any of that have to do with us and his interest in us and his love for us and all that other stuff?"

"He created it for us to appreciate and discover. He created the wonders of nature and the beauty of the world for us and gave us the capacity to recognize it and to simply love the beauty of it. The mountains, the flowers, the animals—all of nature is a wonder."

"But why do we need one hundred billion galaxies?"

"We don't *need* them, but we do appreciate the wonder of it all. You're always in wonder of it yourself."

"But that's not the point. The point is that if we are the center of god's attention, why do we need so much? How about a few thousand stars. Why do we need trillions and trillions?"

Becky smiled, knowing exactly what she would answer. "God made the universe so vast as a testimony to his grandeur. We wouldn't be impressed by a handful of stars. Only God could create something so awesome."

"But he created it all for nothing. What good is it? What is it used for? It's nice that we can look up at the sky and be awed, but for me it's demoralizing."

"Fred, that's ridiculous. How can you be demoralized by something so grand?"

"Because it reminds me we are alone in the universe. Forget about *Star Trek* and those ridiculous aliens with ridged foreheads. It's so big, and we are alone in it. We're the anomaly. We are the one in a trillion chance happening. If we are the only intelligent life, then that means we are a freak accident. It means the universe doesn't exist to support life. It doesn't exist for anything, at least anything we can understand. The universe is there. We're an aberration in it. And that's demoralizing."

Becky shook her head. "But you should feel just the opposite. God created all that and made us special. We are unique. We are the center of God's attention. You should be joyful, not demoralized."

"How can I be joyful about being alone in the universe and being utterly insignificant? You've got to be kidding."

Answers on the Radio

Six weeks later, in the middle of traffic, I heard another explanation for the immensity of the universe. As I waited to make a left turn, conservative radio talk show host Dennis Prager, a religious Jew, said something like this: "So why are there billions of galaxies? Why is it necessary? Are the stars necessary for our existence?"

I waited impatiently for the traffic to pass, made my turn, pulled over to the side, and furiously scribbled some notes.

Dennis was talking to Stephen Barr, author of *Modern Physics and Ancient Faith,* and I wondered if they would come up with a satisfactory explanation.

They didn't. At least for me.

So what did they have to say? Barr said—like Becky—that the infinity of the universe is there to show us or illustrate the infinity of God.

Okay, fair enough. God is showing us how incredible he is.

If the universe was only a million miles across, Professor Barr argued, then according to the physical laws, it could only last a few seconds. Therefore, God had to create the billions of galaxies.

Okay, we can accept that too, but since god created the physical laws of the universe, he could have created a million-mile universe that worked.

Professor Barr pointed out that we need a large number of stars to have life on some. Fair enough, but again like a broken record, god could have created one single planet—us—and put life on it. Or is god, as Rabbi Kushner said, not as omnipotent as we thought?

If We Don't Believe in God, Then How Can We Go On?

Professor Barr also had an answer to my lament about our minuteness and insignificance. He points out that there is no reason to equate size with importance. Both large and small objects can be important. Besides, he said, size is relative. We tend to think of the earth as a piece of cosmic dust, miniscule in comparison to the rest of the universe. And yet, in terms of relative size, our planet is in the middle of creation. The earth is larger than an atom in the same proportion that the universe is larger than earth, so in that regard, our planet is at the midpoint in the size of creation.[3]

That's an interesting perspective, but does little to console me because the numbers are still incomprehensible, and the vastness of the universe tells me that there can't be a god. I know I will never understand creation, or the universe, or the distances. Our minuteness implies no Ultimate Meanings. And this raises another one of those huge existential questions: *How is it possible for us, as individuals, to take life seriously in the absence of a supreme being?* How is it possible to pursue one's interests, to fall in love, to have children, to embroil oneself in a career, or for that matter, to care if our team gets to the Super Bowl, when we are nothing more than cosmic dust? Why should we be concerned about what we do if we are, as Voltaire said, atoms on a ball of mud, or as Ernest Becker put it, a biological accident germinated on a hot-house planet? If we cognitively recognize our minuteness and insignificance, and if we see ourselves lost in the incomprehensible vastness of time and space and dimensions, then how can life be challenging, interesting or meaningful? If we don't believe in god, if we don't believe that we exist for some cosmic purpose, then how can we exist at all, and how can we vigorously pursue life surrounded by one hundred billion galaxies and billions of years on each side of us, not to mention eleven possible dimensions and multiple parallel universes?

Brief Is the Season of a Man's Delight

I have an answer to that long-winded question, but as it turns out, there is nothing new under the sun, and the ancient Greeks beat me to it by around 2,500 years. I was, at that moment, teaching about the Greeks in my Western Civilization class at a local university. The textbook had this to say about a poem written by Pindar (518-438 BC). "Although life is essentially tragic—triumphs are short-lived, misfortunes are many, and ultimately death overtakes us all—man must still demonstrate his worth by striving for excellence."[4]

He who wins of a sudden, some noble prize
In the rich years of youth
Is raised high with hope; his manhood takes wings.
He has in his heart what is better than wealth.
But brief is the season of man's delight.
Soon it falls to the ground;
Some dire decision uproots it.
Thing of a day! such is man: a shadow in a dream.
Yet when God-given splendour visits him
A bright radiance plays over him, and how sweet is life.[5]

The point is this: although we are transient, minute beings–and we know it–the pleasures of success and significance are still sweet. *We are genetically programmed to pursue life,* we are *psychologically required* to feel what we do is important. We want the respect of others, we want love, we want satisfaction from accomplishments. We are competitive, curious, and emotion-driven. If we are falling in love, or angry at the driver who cuts us off, or embarrassed by saying something stupid, we are feeling these emotions *regardless of the fact that it won't matter in a hundred years or a thousand or a million or a billion.* At that brief moment in our life span, what we do and what we think and how we feel all matter to us; and, as individuals, they matter very much. We all want to be *significant to the moment,* even if we know in our heart of hearts that the moment is fleeting, that all life is fleeting, that we are nothing more than a "shadow in a dream," and that time and space gobble us up.

We may be just "a thing of a day," but that day is vital. It may be lost in the vast and incomprehensible sweep of time and space, but the moment is all we have, and we hunger to make the best of it. In addition we "know" that if we make that moment important, we have gained a piece of immortality. The moment is now, but immortality is forever.

We All Want Our Lives to Matter

"I don't really disagree with what you're saying," Becky said, "and Christianity wouldn't disagree with what you're saying. The church would say that everything we do on earth matters. After all, our choices here on earth either help us grow closer to God or grow further away from Him."

"Okay, but what about the point that without god, existence would have no meaning? Christians can't understand how people can be happy, productive, and functioning without god."

"I'm still agreeing with you. I think there is an instinctive feeling that this life does matter. We don't have to talk ourselves into it. We feel it. I don't doubt that we're wired to feel that reality is important, but for a Christian, our life on earth is not only important, but has a depth that sometimes is almost frightening. That's why people become Mother Theresas, because in some kind of a conversion moment, they see how desperately important everything is, that they have to withdraw from all frivolousness and only do things that matter. Because you only have one life to do what really matters. Mother Theresa saw that the minutes of her life were a treasure or a commodity that was so priceless that she could not waste one part of it anymore with something that just doesn't matter."

"Like your sorority," I said.

Becky's mother and grandmother had belonged to the same sorority in college. But in her junior year, she quit the sorority and depledged.

"There was a war going on in Vietnam. Civil rights was a big issue, yet the sorority was worried about the next dance. It was meaningless, and I just couldn't waste my time."

In a sense, Becky and I are coming to the same conclusion from different angles. For the Christian, activities are meaningful because God gave them life, and they have a duty to use it wisely and well. From my point of view, we are in a hurry—sometimes a frenzy—to make our lives meaningful before death overtakes us. In either case, we recognize that our time here is limited, leaving us only one brief moment to make it important. The Christian wants to honor God by living well. The rest of us, lost in space and time, want to know that our brief lives were worthy.

Either way we are psychologically programmed to want to be significant to the moment.

Life Is an End unto Itself

Talk show host Dennis Prager would not agree with me. Prager is a deeply religious Jew whose secular opinions I admire, respect, and—perhaps most importantly—agree with. Yet he cannot envision life without God. Prager wrote:

I also know that faith in God is necessary in order for life to have ultimate meaning, that without the Creator, there is no ultimate purpose to the universe, let alone our lives.[6]

And yet I function well without Ultimate Meanings. I love my wife and three daughters. That the girls exist is amazing and wonderful and awe-inspiring. That they are of my flesh is breathtaking; but I can love them without having any supernatural premises. There is no Ultimate Meaning, but my psychological underpinnings are imperatives mandating that I feel life strongly, take it seriously, want to do well in it, want respect and accomplishment, want love, want justice. In other words, life is important; *life is an end unto itself.*

If I had my way god would exist. Who wouldn't want to know for certain that human life has a cosmic purpose and that our individual lives have some kind of eternal worth? Who does not want to believe in an eternal afterlife? I wish it were so.

Later in that article Dennis nailed it.

Humanists are so committed to faith in humanity and to denying God's existence that they refuse to confront the built-in need people have for the transcendent and that more than people are needed for inner peace and happiness.

Yes, we have a built-in need for the transcendent, but as we shall soon see, god is only one manifestation of that need. We also turn to other supernatural helpers, to wars, revolutions and mass movements, and to worshipping false gods like Lenin or Hitler or Mao or Stalin or Hussein or Manson.

Dennis is right—transcendence is useful for inner peace and happiness—but it is also the foundation of human evil.

These Men Are Brilliant, Yet They Believe in God

The encounter with Prager and later reading Professor Barr's book, left me in a kind of awe: *these men are brilliant, yet they believe in god.* I can understand believing in the morality of religion, but how could such intelligent men believe in a benevolent supreme being in the face of the arbitrariness of life and the horrible brutality of human history? In my younger days, I was convinced that religious people were naive peasants, but Becky long ago cured me of that misconception. I now understand that religion has nothing to do with IQ or intellectual sophistication, but everything to do with our need to be important to the universe, something we shall discuss later.

13

uncle sonny and
the little old ladies

What's wrong with being number two?

—Morrie Schwartz, *Tuesdays with Morrie*

The point of the last chapter is that *we are psychologically programmed to want to be significant to the moment.* The here and now is important to us, even if we know that everything will be lost to the vastness of time and space. As it turns out, a couple of examples of this came, not from the ancient Greeks or from brilliant professors, but from Uncle Sonny and a bunch of very old ladies.

An Isolated, Monotonous, Stultifying Life

Uncle Sonny was somewhat inscrutable. We didn't always know what he was thinking. As a matter of fact, *he* didn't always know what he was thinking. He spent a lot of time sitting on his walker out on the front porch of Garden Square, legs crossed, wearing a New York Yankees baseball cap, smoking, and looking out at the scenery. He generally stared straight ahead as if he were studying something in front of him. He never held a book or newspaper. He watched plenty of television, and most of the time was agreeable enough to make small talk, but his days of reading were over.

During those long, lost years when his children were dying, he had taken solace in the printed word. Life had nothing to offer, but when he opened a book he could be in another time, another place. For the hours he immersed himself in books, he was not agonizing, but he also was not living in the real world. During the week we packed the apartment, I went though his books. There were hundreds of them, mostly hard cover, mostly nonfiction. We found six more large boxes of books in the storage bin. He had read them all, and many, many others.

But now, he just sat and stared and ruminated. He was polite when people spoke to him, but completely uninterested in making small talk or making friends, and he never participated in the activities. "I'm really shy," he said. "I don't know how to make conversation."

That's why I was surprised when on an afternoon early in June, he suggested we go downtown to the senior center to shoot some pool. This was something of a revolution. For at least two decades, we had been encouraging him and my aunt to get out of the apartment and go somewhere—join an organization, interact with other people, go on a trip, *do something*. But their defeat and demoralization had become an all-encompassing psychological inertia. They were incapable of ordering a pizza, or going out to dinner with friends, or going to a movie, or cooking a meal. Consequently, they lived this isolated, monotonous, stultifying life, year after year after year.

When Johnnie was alive he had been the focus of their attention, but in the fourteen years since his death, as they edged from late middle age to aged, they became increasingly negative. When my uncle wanted to go to Atlantic City to play the slots, Aunt Millie would bitterly refuse to let him go. "How can I stay here by myself?" she whined. She refused to leave the apartment. My uncle complained that he was "in a prison."

Uncle Sonny's bitterness was more cerebral. He may indeed have had total recall as he claimed. He remembered the names of army buddies from sixty years ago. He could recount incidents in detail. And he seemed to dwell on the negative. Something someone said fifteen years ago bounced around his brain like a pinball, hitting all those raw nerves. He didn't forget, and he rarely forgave. The combination of his continual rumination on the slights and selfishness and perceived wrongs of the past, combined with alcohol, sent him into violent rages. The last couple of years, with my aunt gone, he was often out of his mind with a visceral drunken bitterness at his life and the people around him. Thus, the fact that he actually came to Colorado was amazing. And the fact that he said, "Let's go down to the senior center" to do something, and to do something with me, who had been one of the focuses of his hatred, was in a sense, a whole new world.

Shooting Pool with Uncle Sonny

The senior center was roomy and pleasant, with a half dozen shuffleboard courts and eight pool tables. The hint of a smile crossed his face, a complete change from the tight jaw.

We were sitting at the senior center drinking coffee from Styrofoam cups when an energetic, well-groomed elderly woman with dyed brown hair came up to make conversation about his walker, a pick-up line perhaps for the very old. She was chatty and friendly and at times touched his arm. She was in the assisted living place across the street, and she encouraged him to get in touch with her. Finally, unable to resist, I said, "Are you making a pass at my uncle?"

She smiled. "Well, of course I am." And then to him, "By the way, what's your name?"

Without missing a beat he said, "Leonardo."

Leonardo?

"Oh, what a nice name," she said.

You've got to be kidding me, I thought. *Leonardo?*

"Why did you tell her your name was Leonardo?" I asked, as we headed for the pool table.

"Why not? After all, I'm called Lenny, and that's pretty close." He had an assortment of names. His real name was Bernie. Lenny was a derivative of Linet, and Sonny was a nickname his father gave him based on the old Al Jolson song, "Climb Upon My Knee, Sonny Boy."

As it turns out, he had been giving out false names since his army days. As he fornicated his way through England and France, he rarely gave the girls his real name. "Probably to avoid paternity problems," Becky suggested. Indeed, he and the other GIs were ordered one day in England to line-up in formation as a young woman walked through the ranks trying to identify a man who had "raped" her. The word among the guys was to avoid eye contact. She might identify the wrong guy—or for that matter the right one.

Meanwhile, "Leonardo" and I shot three games of pool.

I stood there chalking my cue and studying the table. I was a very occasional pool player and not very good, but it felt so familiar. Not so familiar was the old man across the table who was holding his cue and studying the table and calling his shots, "Seven ball in the side," he intoned in his strong New York baritone. He probably hadn't played for decades, but there he was calling shots, picking up the bridge for a hard shot, as he put it, "almost on instinct."

He didn't have much need for his walker which he pushed out of the way as he circled the table and lined-up his shots. He seemed to genuinely enjoy it; and so did I. We were equally bad, but we both played to win. In the greater scheme of the universe, this pool game was meaningless, and yet, it was meaningful enough in the here and now.

A Golf Game for Old Ladies

Two days later, with temperatures in the mid-eighties, we went out to the front patio to sit on the rocking chairs at Garden Square and found Joe, the recreation director, organizing a golf game for eight old ladies. He kept up the chatter, joking with the women, and we watched as each one took her turn hitting golf balls into a hole twenty feet away. Some had hunched backs, some carried oxygen containers attached to their noses, others took their turns with their walkers close by.

One by one they hobbled up, gripped the clubs, took careful aim, hit the balls, and watched the result. They really aimed, really tried, really took it seriously. Here we have another activity that is utterly meaningless and soon forgotten, yet even these ancient, bent women with oxygen tubes in their noses, like Uncle Sonny at the pool table, want to succeed.

What's Wrong with Being Number Two?

Morrie would disagree that competition is a good thing. Mitch Albom relates the following anecdote:

It is 1979, a basketball game in the Brandeis gym. The team is doing well, and the student section begins to chant, "We're number one! We're number one!" Morrie is sitting nearby. He is puzzled by the cheer. At one point, in the midst of "We're number one!" he rises and yells, "What's wrong with being number two?"

The students look at him. They stop chanting. He sits down, smiling and triumphant.[1]

In Morrie's world competition is bad. We should cooperate, not compete. We should love each other, not try to outdo each other. Perhaps there is a parallel universe somewhere where that is the case. But in this world, for better or for worse, we are naturally competitive beings who derive pleasure from winning. From the pool table to the blackjack table, from the ancient Greeks to the ancient ladies hitting golf balls, to the corporate board rooms, to the kids cheering "we're number one," we all love to win. What's wrong with being number two? Nothing really, it's certainly better than being number three. But number one is better. The desire to win, achieving that *God-given splendor* is part of our mental make-up. It allows us to take life seriously in spite of the fact that we are "a shadow in a dream."

14

uncle sonny deals with the big question: who am i?

In the last few years—common people, poor people, uneducated people, powerless people, as well as the more affluent—are beginning to ask themselves the basic existential questions: "Who am I?" and "What is my human potential?"[1]

—William Glasser, *The Identity Society*

If this is a book about The Most Important Questions, then "Who am I?" is among them. The question implies dissatisfaction and uncertainty: "I don't like who I am and/or I don't know who I'm supposed to be. I'm trying to find myself." It's not only that we want to know who we are, but also we want to know that who we are is *worthwhile*.

Most people of the past never considered such questions. They knew who they were. "I'm a farmer." "I'm a wife." "I'm a carpenter." "I'm a Christian." They could not conceive of change, opportunity, or improvement. They had no lofty goals like meeting their "human potential." The only hope for change was in the afterlife. Today, as psychiatrist and author William Glasser pointed out, we worry, sometimes to the point of obsession, about who we are. We have the luxury of being able to wonder what our purpose in life is and if we are achieving that purpose. Unfortunately, the more we think about it, the less satisfied we seem to be, as I learned while accompanying Uncle Sonny on his monthly gambling trip to Blackhawk.

SPIRITUALLY DYSFUNCTIONAL

What Should I Do with My Life?

The pinball-like popping of hundreds of slot machines and the jangling of dropping coins surrounded us. We got some coffee and settled in on the dollar slots. He put a few dollar coins in the machine and a hundred coins jangled out. A few coins later, twenty-five coins clattered into the metal basket. His usual impassive expression was replaced by smile after smile. He was having a great time. I quickly lost ten dollars and went for a walk through the town, finally finding a gazebo next to an artificial river where a bronze statue of a miner panned for gold. The day was typically beautiful for Colorado—hot, bone dry, and a sky so blue it seemed to be painted. This to me was heaven—peace, quiet, a babbling brook, a beautiful day, and a good book to read.

I read a few more chapters in *What Should I Do with My Life: The True Story of People Who Answered the Ultimate Question.*

Each chapter had a subtitle. "Working with What's Already There." "Stimulation/Intensity VS. Significance/Fulfillment." "The Need to Impress People on Their Terms."

Tim, a lawyer, had "neglected his potential." In high school, he had been a six-foot-seven-inch "skinny freak" who "wore black fingernail polish and Goth clothes and long hair . . ."[2]

Tim was terribly dissatisfied. "Po," he told the author, "I honestly believe in my heart that I'm capable of great things. But the life's draining out of me. Hell, it's being sucked out of me. If I don't do something *soon*—but I'm such a shit. Why haven't I done something? I should have done something long ago."

Noah had held sixteen jobs in eight years. "He never stayed anywhere long enough to move up the ladder—everything was entry level."

Bret, who had "sensitive" brown eyes, had tried college, driven a newspaper delivery truck, gone from florist delivery boy to store manager, spent a year in a baby wipes plant, and worked for ConAgra, where the temperatures climbed to 120 degrees at night. He eventually got a job in the Clinton administration.

In the chapter titled, "Ashley on Planet Hug," Ashley "a scrawny Irish redhead," who suffered from anorexia, seemed to have had it all. "I was blessed," she said. "I went to a preeminent law school, the best film school, my parents didn't beat me. I have an incredible sense I should have accomplished something. When people say I'm talented, it makes me feel worse. The blessing has become a curse."

Like many of the others in the book, she drifted from job to job, trying to find her place. She had a degree from the film school at the University of Southern California and worked a few years in Hollywood. Looking for more meaning, she became a speechwriter in the Clinton administration and had friends in the White House, but after sixty speeches it grew old; she quit the job and stopped eating. Unemployed, without a car and without a phone, she finally found her way to St. Agate's church, where "strangers are *always* greeted with a warm hug." Father Ken and the congregation "rescued her."

The chapters were surfeited with pseudo-psychoanalysis. "She gave herself permission to dream." "Most of his life had been spent avoiding rejection and then getting vengeance for the times he suffered rejection." "I've got to get over my inferiority complex." "I don't feel worthy of God's love, or anyone else's for that matter."

I closed the book and absently watched the water running down the artificial waterfall.

The people in this book were dissatisfied professionals looking for something . . . but for what? They seemed to be unfocused, drifting without purpose. They had no raging talents, no intense desires, no lifetime goals. They only knew they were dissatisfied. These stories were not about people struggling to achieve a particular objective; they were not about people who knew what they wanted, only about people who didn't know what they wanted. Like my uncle.

A Life of Fragments

As a young man, Uncle Sonny drifted. He never had a plan, never asked, "Who am I?" never committed to a career.

Before the war, he had worked as a grocery packer, theater usher, and salesman. After the war, he went to college for two years and then helped his father in the Linet Sign Painting Company. He worked for a while repairing lamps. He flirted with podiatry. The VA sent him to dental technician school, but the only job he could get was errand boy. He tried switching to interior decorating, but the VA declined. He visited every dentist's office on the Grand Concourse selling a new concept in dental drills—ones that splashed water to ease the pain.

UNCLE SONNY, AROUND AGE TWENTY, AS A THEATER USHER NEXT
TO THE VERY TALL BARKER, 1939.

In the early fifties, he latched on to a moneymaking scheme—a luncheonette napkin holder that answered questions. Customers in restaurants put pennies into the machine, asked it yes or no questions, and got answers. "TURN PENNIES INTO DOLLARS," said the flyer, which I found among his papers.

I have a clear memory of accompanying him as he made the rounds of luncheonettes, emptying the machines of pennies. At the age of nine, I found the whole business quite fascinating. What I couldn't understand was how the machine could read my mind. I would think of a question like, "Will I find a million dollars?" drop in a penny and the machine answers, "Time will tell." Ask the machine, "Am I a Martian?" and the machine answers, "It's certainly possible."

My uncle's working life was one of fragments, not finished pieces. If he had had a career, if he'd had a purpose beyond his children, he could have fallen back on that. But he had none of those things. His life was empty—no children, no career, no projects, no hobbies, no hopes, no future. *Life happened to him; he didn't make life happen.*

As I walked back through the streets of Blackhawk to pick up my uncle for lunch, I was vaguely annoyed at the Bronson book. I was looking for inspired stories of tenacity. I wanted to read about people with vision who would not be deterred from their dreams. I was looking for the people who never gave up, for people who knew their calling and ached to actualize it. Where are the people who hung in there decade after decade, never giving up, finding it impossible to give up, because they never lost their focus? Where are those people?

The people in the Bronson book were nothing like that. They seemed unable to find any sense of purpose. They were educated, in some cases privileged. They went to good schools. But instead of taking advantage of their talents and opportunities, they drifted with no genuine sense of meaning or passion. These are the kinds of people who fall prey to demagogues, cult leaders, and hopeless causes, as we shall see in Part 2.

"That's a little judgmental," Becky said after reading my comments. "You seem to dismiss the people in Bronson's book because they don't share your strengths of tenacity and perseverance."

"It's not that I dismiss them. I understand that there are huge numbers of people who never find their calling. But I find it hard to be sympathetic to those who have every opportunity, but instead endlessly drift. They have nothing to complain about."

"I don't think they're complaining," Becky said. "In their own way they're asking the ultimate questions. They are struggling to find out what it means to be a person and specifically this human person that they are. How do they live out this person? For the Christian, the answer to the question, Who am I? is: 'I am a person loved by God, born for a purpose of goodness.' This is deeply satisfying. Of course, there are a lot of details to fill in, but when one feels that God is at their side, there is a sense of peace.

"These people are searching for their places in eternity. They are struggling to find what it means to be a human being. God fills *both* the now and eternity.

"Fred, God is not offended by those who are still wandering and confused. In fact, it is precisely those times of confusion and questioning that we are often most open to His voice. God can use those times for good. Christian anthropology would say that the human person is constituted to ask *why* so that God can answer."

"But the problem, Becky, is that so many dissatisfied people don't ask why, don't turn to god but turn to false gods. They dedicate their lives to destructive holy missions. They kill innocent people for gods like Charles Manson. They blow themselves up in crowded markets for their transcendent causes. They worship deities like Hitler and Mao and the concept of communism. They . . ."

"Okay," Becky said, " it's true. And terribly sad. People make flawed choices. But God is still there lovingly, patiently waiting for us."

Uncle Sonny on "Planet Hug"

This idea of false gods and holy missions will be explored in Part 2. But let us now return to the blackjack table in Blackhawk.

After lunch, Uncle Sonny and I played blackjack at the three- to five-dollar tables. Sitting next to us was the same guy who had been there the month before. He had a memorable face—large, bulbous nose, thinning hair, and a cauliflower ear. "He looks like a fighter," said Uncle Sonny. "He looks like Jake LaMotta."

So there he was again, nursing three-dollar bets and making lewd comments to the female dealer.

"What an empty life," Uncle Sonny said, missing the irony.

As we rode home on the bus, I drifted off into a writing fantasy, imagining another chapter in *What Should I Do With My Life?* I called it:

COLORADO SUCKS BIG TIME:
EATING AT RED LOBSTER VERSUS GETTING DRUNK ALONE IN THE BRONX

I found Uncle Sonny in a rocking chair at the Garden Square Assisted Living. His smoldering, sensitive blue eyes stared forward as he

UNCLE SONNY WITH HIS SMOLDERING, SENSITIVE BLUE EYES.

120

contemplated cloud formations. His blue jeans were full of food stains accumulated over the past week.

"I need to give myself permission to be happy," he said in a clear baritone.

"Why haven't you done that before," I asked.

He rubbed the three-day growth of gray stubble on his angular chin. "I dunno."

He seemed confused.

"You need to do what's right for you," I suggested reluctantly.

"Then I'll go back to the Bronx."

"Why?"

"Because I'd be free there. I can smoke and drink myself into a stupor. I can punch my neighbor, Steve, the one-eyed man, in the face. I can phone my nephew and curse him out."

I could see the hurt in his eyes. "What's wrong with staying in Colorado? The sky is blue. You get to suck up a venti latte mocha frappuccino every day."

"I don't feel like I deserve it."

"You need to forgive yourself."

Sonny looked confused. "Just think, I had to come all the way to Colorado to get a good Eye-Talian meal."

"What does that have to do with your purpose in life?"

"I have no purpose in life. That's the trouble. I never have. I drifted from job to job, from school to school. Never focused, never stuck with anything. A career could have been therapeutic for me when the children where sick."

"It's not too late, Sonny," I said. "It's okay to give yourself permission to dream."

"Did you know that Alpha Centauri is four light years from Earth?"

I wasn't sure what to say, so I fell back on one of those therapeutic lines from the sixties. "Sonny, you've got to stop punishing yourself."

"I could really go for a grande coconut mocha frappuccino with whipped cream."

"How about a big hug?" I suggested.

Sonny looked a little embarrassed and lowered his eyes. "I'd really like that."

Something tapped my arm.

An envelope. "It's for the driver," said the huge guy sitting behind me on the bus. "Put a tip in the envelope."

The white haired woman across the aisle was staring at me, amused.

I had been talking to myself in hushed whispers.

I Floated Like a Feather

On a warm day, late in October, sitting in Starbucks sipping frappuccinos, my uncle opened another mental file. Smiling wistfully, he said, *Arbiet macht liebe suss.*

"What?" I said absently, staring at a huge Starbucks cookie, and wondering if I should pay $1.65 for it.

"My father used to say that. *Work makes life sweet.* He was a wonderful man, my father. He worked so hard; he loved to work. But me, I never accomplished anything in my life. I floated like a feather, never landing anywhere."

PART 2

THE QUEST FOR IMMORTALITY

Wrongfully do men lament the flight of time . . .
Let your work be such that after death you become
an image of immortality.

—Leonardo Da Vinci

15

a brief history of
modern spirituality

The birth of America and the coming of the French Revolution
marked the entrance of nobodies onto the stage of history. The
revolutions of the twentieth century are a reaction against history
made by common people.[1]

—Eric Hoffer, *Truth Imagined*

It is now time for the camera to fade back from Starbucks in order to
dig into the human psyche.

In Part 2, we shall be dealing with existential psychology, with
death and immortality, and with man's place in creation. These are
heavy-duty ideas, but easily accessible to all of us. We'll skim over
Freud and Nietzsche, make a stop in a Nazi concentration camp, take
a different look at the American Revolution, analyze Hitler and Charles
Manson, peruse the touchy-feely sixties, and take a peek at eternity.
We will visit hippies and hipsters and Chinese coolies. We'll talk about
the masks we wear and why we wear them. And most importantly, we
will consider the implications of spirituality run amok.

Up to this point we have taken a glimpse of a spiritually dysfunctional marriage. Although Becky and I have been facing off theologi-
cally for over thirty years, we have managed to survive. However,
those suffering from a malaise of the spirit represent another form of
the spiritually dysfunctional. When people in an existential funk connect with their artificially created religions, they become psychologi-

cally dependent on them, and the result is often a world of unnecessary suffering.

Consider this statement by E.O. Wilson from his Pulitzer Prizewinning, *On Human Nature*: "It is one of the universals of social behavior, taking recognizable form in every society from hunter-gatherer bands to socialist republics. Its rudiments go back at least to . . . Neanderthal Man . . . Since that time . . . man has produced on the order of 100 thousand . . . .[2]

The "it" in Wilson's statement is *religion*. Over the centuries, there may have been a hundred thousand recognizable religions, but there were many more that were not so obvious. We have come to the point in human history where secular religions compete with traditional ones. Because we are naturally and profoundly spiritual beings, when one form of religion declines, another rises to take its place. *If nature abhors a vacuum, then human nature abhors a spiritual vacuum.*

New Roads to Salvation

Historically in the Western world, we gained salvation through Christianity. If God personally loves us and has a particular purpose for us, then we can be assured that our existence has meaning in creation. But over the centuries, Christianity has taken its share of hits. The Protestant Reformation, starting in 1517, splintered Christianity into hundreds of bickering and competing sects. A quarter of a century later, Nikolas Copernicus provided mathematical proof that the Earth was not the center of the universe, as the church had believed for over fifteen hundred years. In the next century, after perfecting the telescope, Galileo made a number of startling discoveries about the cosmos, all of which refuted the church's traditional vision.

In the late seventeenth century, Isaac Newton figured out the physical or natural laws of the universe, convincing man that, if he put his mind to it, he could figure out the natural laws of *everything*–politics, economics, human behavior, and so on. The result of this confidence was the European Enlightenment of the eighteenth century, which was an explosion of inquiry into both the social and hard sciences. One of the casualties of that intellectual juggernaut was the church, which was not only proved wrong, but to its detractors, was made to seem irrelevant or even worse, harmful.

By 1789, the people of the West were not only ready for more secular pursuits, but for secular religions as well. This secular spirituality was provided by two revolutions that took place almost simultaneously. The Industrial Revolution transformed the world economically, socially, and eventually politically, when socialism and then Marxism captured people's imaginations. Adherents of Marxism became convinced that this was the idea that would transform the world into a workers' utopia, and they therefore pursued it with religious fervor.

Secular spirituality was also unleashed in 1789 by the French Revolution. We associate it with the masses rising up, storming the Bastille, lopping off the heads of tens of thousands of arrogant nobles, and ushering in a new era of liberty. But it was more than that. "The French Revolution," wrote the oft-quoted Frenchman Alexis de Tocqueville, "was . . . a political revolution, which . . . resembled a religious one. It had every peculiar and characteristic feature of a religious movement; it not only spread to foreign countries, but it was carried thither by preaching and by propaganda."

In addition, wrote de Toqueville, the Revolution "became a kind of new religion in itself–a religion, imperfect it is true, without a God, without worship, without a future life, but which nevertheless, like Islam, poured forth its soldiers, its apostles and its martyrs over the face of the earth."[3]

A Beautiful, Sacred Moment

The French Revolution ushered in an era of secular spiritual movements in which love of country (nationalism) on the one hand, and love of liberating causes on the other, became new gods. Dedicating oneself to the political uprising, overthrowing the tyranny, gaining one's freedom, or being uplifted by association with one's ethnic group became an idea whose time had come, not only because the movements were emancipating but also because they were *empowering*. For the first time in the Western world, masses of common men came to believe that it was within their power to affect events.

Most uprisings of the past were insurrections by desperate people, but the concept of planning a political upheaval and gaining a sense of purpose from it became commonplace in the nineteenth century. When common people join together, as they did in these revolutions, they made a dent in life–and the feeling was exhilarating. Because there was so much psychological benefit from fighting the good fight, the sense of purpose derived from these uprisings, conspiracies, and unifying identities took on a transcendent quality. It was as if the particular political uprising was the most important event in creation. These movements provided camaraderie, direction, and meaning; they were empowering and uplifting. As a result, the nineteenth century was characterized by multiple revolutions in Spain's South American colonies and Spain itself, as well as in Italy, Sicily, Greece, Russia, France, Belgium, Poland, and others. National identity and ethnic loyalties grew increasingly intense throughout the century, culminating in the nationalistic fervor of World War I.

By 1914, love of country or love of one's ethnic group had become a potent spiritual force. Bosnians, Serbians, Germans, Magyars, Croats, Russians, Hungarians, and others reveled in mythical past glories, sanctified themselves, and demonized others. It's no wonder that when World War I broke out, the capitals of Europe exploded in joyous fervor. The war was described as "a beautiful . . . sacred movement," satisfying an "ethical yearning."[4] In France, crowds sang the Marseilles, while "thousands of men eager to fight would jostle one another outside recruiting offices, waiting to join up."[5] A German newspaper announced that, "It is a joy to be alive. We wished so much for this hour."[6]

Wild Dogs Braying at the Stars

The sacred new god of World War I turned out to be horrifying and disillusioning. Millions of eager young men who went marching off to war were plowed under. By 1930, Jose Ortega y Gasset recognized the "terrible spiritual dilemma in which the world's great youth find themselves." People are free, he wrote, but "they feel empty."[7]

He noted "the immense spectacle of uncountable human beings wandering lost through the labyrinth of themselves because they have nothing to which to give themselves. . . . A life which is 'expendable' [i.e. insignificant] is a greater negation of existence than death."[8]

And how do people overcome this existential dread? His answer, over seventy years ago, was to find a spiritually uplifting cause. "To live is to have something definite to do, a mission to fulfill." The less we dedicate our lives "to something," he wrote, the less meaning our lives have.[9] And then—perhaps with Hitler, Mussolini, and Stalin in mind–he issued this warning: "Soon a cry will go up from around the planet, rising like the howl of an innumerable pack of wild dogs braying at the stars, crying for someone or something to take command and impose a [holy?] mission."[10]

The secular religions of war and nationalism came to full fruition in the twentieth century. Risking death for one's country or ethnic group was an emotionally gripping and psychologically exhilarating experience. They not only loved their country, they *worshipped* it. And yet, with the next generation, Europe saw an even more intense flowering of spiritual nationalism in the worshipping of a god, Adolf Hitler, and the conviction that the German people were superior. In addition, the vision of two generations of Russians filing past the embalmed and sacred body of Vladimir Ilyich Ulianov, otherwise known as Lenin, who brought communism to Russia, and the sight of almost one billion Chinese worshipfully waving Mao's little red book, only serves to underline how spiritually dysfunctional secular religion can be.

Spiritual Emptiness Today

Where are we now in the early twenty-first century? Churches are full and religious book and music industries are booming. Obviously, God is alive and well, but so is the need for secular spirituality. As former Senator John Edwards said in December 2005, "There is a hunger in America, a hunger for a sense of national community, a hunger for something big and important and inspirational that they can be involved in."[11]

In his 2000 book, *The American Paradox: Spiritual Hunger in an Age of Plenty*, David G. Myers argues that we seem to have it all yet are uneasy. Myers's paradox is that the more peace and prosperity we have, the less content we are, and the more our society seems to be unraveling. Since 1960:[12]

- the divorce rate has doubled
- teen suicide has tripled
- recorded violent crime quadrupled
- the prison population quintupled
- illegitimate births have increased sixfold
- the number of children living with only one parent rose from less than one-tenth to more than one-quarter

- some estimates put the incidence of depression in the year 2000 at ten times what it was after World War 11
- homicides are 50 percent more frequent today than in 1950
- homicides by fourteen- to seventeen-year-olds are around double what they were in 1984.

Why should social indicators decline in a time of relative peace and plenty? Why do we seem to be in the midst of a national malaise? Myers's answer is that we suffer from what he calls a "spiritual hunger." We have the vague feeling that something is missing from our lives. Former tennis great Chris Evert Lloyd said the following to her husband at the height of her success: "We get into a rut. We play tennis, we go to a movie, we watch TV, but I keep saying, 'John, there has to be more.'"[13]

Chris Evert had run out of challenges. Life was good, but life was easy. What was the "more" that she wanted? Challenge? Excitement? Struggle? Something she could sink her teeth into? Something that required effort? Perhaps a greater sense of purpose. The American Dream used to be *opportunity*. We were free to work towards the dream of a better life, but now that we have reached an unprecedented level of affluence, there still seems to be something missing.

"We have placed too much hope in politics and social reform," said Aleksandr Solzhenitsyn, "only to find out that we were being deprived of our most precious possession: our spiritual life."[14] In 1994, pollster George Gallup concluded, "One of two dominant trends in society today [along with a search for deeper, more meaningful relationships] is the search for spiritual moorings . . . Surveys document the movement of people who are searching for meaning in life."[15] Between 1994 and 1998, Gallup found that the number of Americans who want to "experience spiritual growth" increased from 54 percent to 82 percent.[16] Historian David McCullough said of the American people, "They really want to be stirred in their spirit. That's when we are at our best."[17] *But it's also when we are at our worst.* Hitler stirred people's spirits. So did Charles Manson. So did World War I, which raised the spirits of millions of young men who have been moldering in their graves for almost a century. When our spirits stir, people die.

Like Chris Evert, we want more. We need something exciting to get our blood boiling. Evidently, for some of us, living the good life with its freedom, opportunity, and consumer goods is not spiritually satisfying.

In Part 2 we will look at the many and varied ways we attempt to find spiritual purpose without god. Sometimes it's productive, sometimes destructive. Sometimes it's completely out of control. It has resulted in wonderful cultural achievements on the one hand, and atrocities on the other. It has changed the course of history, for better and for worse.

16

what do people want?

In order to understand spirituality run amok, we need to understand what is most important to people in this brief and transient life. And for that we turn again to Morrie in our evening reading. "Once you get your fingers on the important questions," he said, "you can't turn away from them."[1]

And what are the important questions?

"As I see it," said Morrie, "they have to do with love, responsibility, spirituality, awareness. And if I were healthy today, those would still be my issues. They should have been all along."

These may be "important questions," but they are not The Most Important Questions. Love, of course, is vitally important. If people love us, and we love them back, then we gain confirmation of our existence and confirmation that we are meaningful. But love doesn't do it all. It sounds good coming from Morrie, but down beneath the surface—in *the existential core*—is where we find the answers. In our heart of hearts, deep in our psyches and our souls, what do we want from life? We know we are mortal. We know our time is limited. As we go through life, day by day, year by year, *what do people want?*

Answering this question will take us closer to understanding the spiritually dysfunctional.

Pleasure or Power

Start with Freud. He gave us "the pleasure principle," which, as he wrote, "dominates the operation of the mental apparatus from the start." And what brings us pleasure? Sex. "... sexual (genital) love ... affords ... the strongest experiences of satisfaction ... [and provides] the prototype of all happiness."[2]

The great German philosopher, Friedrich Nietzsche, a contemporary of Freud, argued that people only hunger for power. "The love of power," he wrote, "is the demon of men. Let them have everything–health, food, a place to live, entertainment–they are and remain unhappy and low spirited: for the demon waits and waits and will be satisfied. Take everything from them and satisfy this and they are almost happy ..."[3]

One of Freud's younger contemporaries, Alfred Adler, picked up on the theme of power. Because we are born as helpless infants, he wrote, we spend the rest of our lives compensating for that helplessness by trying to gain power or superiority. "For Adler," wrote Christopher F. Monte, "in contrast to Freud, the basic striving of life is not to achieve pleasure, nor final rest; the fundamental urge is to achieve 'superiority,' to achieve, that is, a sense of competence and fulfillment."[4] Because as infants we do not like the feelings of helplessness and inferiority, our life's goal is to become superior, in control, in power; but it is all a facade to hide our real feelings of inadequacy and inferiority.

Another of the great German psychiatrists of the early twentieth century, Karen Horney, tells us that those who cannot overcome the isolation, hostility, anxiety, and helplessness of childhood, (neurotics) become consumed by these negative feelings, until they "pervade the entire personality, as a malignant tumor pervades the whole organic tissue."[5] So what do these neurotic adults want? Like Nietzsche and Adler, Horney says *power*. "The neurotic striving for power ... is born out of anxiety, a hatred and feelings of inferiority. To put it categorically, the normal striving for power is born of strength, the neurotic of weakness."[6] The individual who is dissatisfied with himself, creates an "illusory" or "fictitious" self. In other words, a mask. If I don't like who I am, I'll fool everyone–especially myself–into thinking I'm someone else, someone better. "As long as his image remains real to him and is intact, he can feel significant, superior, and harmonious, in spite of the illusory nature of those feelings."[7]

Self-Esteem

How about self-esteem? That's one we can all agree on. Just about anyone living on Planet Earth knows it's important and feels it on a personal level. This has been another popular subject of psychologists during the last generation. Psychologist Nathaniel Branden put it thusly:

> There is no value-judgment more important to man—no factor more decisive in his psychological development and motivation— than the estimate he passes on himself. . . . The nature of his self-evaluation has profound effects on a man's thinking processes, emotions, desires, values and goals. *It is the single most significant key to his behavior.* [Emphasis mine][8]

The desire for self-esteem, says Branden, is "an urgent imperative" of "life and death importance." Those who feel they do not have self-esteem *"fake* it." They create "the illusions of self-esteem—condemning themselves to chronic psychological fraud—moved by the desperate sense that to face the universe without self-esteem is to stand naked, disarmed, delivered to destruction."[9]

The person desiring self-esteem will distort reality and create a fictitious self in order to convince himself and the rest of the world that he is worthy of respect. Because this faking of self-esteem is so existentially vital, the pursuit of it can become religious in its intensity. But this "religion" is a form of spiritual dysfunction that is often self-destructive, harmful to others, counterproductive, and irrational, something we shall discuss later.

Touchy-Feely Time

Post war psychology, most notably ideas associated with the "human potential" movement of the sixties, focused not on power, but on *personal fulfillment*, or in the words of the leading light of the time, psychologist Abraham Maslow, "self-actualization." Living in a secure world with full bellies and full wallets, the sixties' gurus upped the ante. What we really want is some higher form of psychological gratification. Maslow's hierarchy of needs became a trendy guide to what we all should aspire.

According to Maslow, once our physical and security needs are met, and we have love, acceptance, and self-esteem, we are then in a position to ascend to the pinnacle where we are "self-actualized," which enables us to rise above ourselves to where we help others become self-actualized and achieve their human potential.

Self-actualized people have reached the summit of wisdom, perception, and psychological health. Because they have strong self-esteem, they are free of affectation and therefore have no need to hide behind those ego-inflating masks. They have no need to earn the world's respect because they respect themselves. They have no ego needs and therefore can focus on their own genuine interests and the world beyond themselves. The self-actualized have a sense of humor, are creative, and have a fresh way of looking at the world. They appreciate and get pleasure from the world around them and are empathetic and sympathetic to the plight of others.[10]

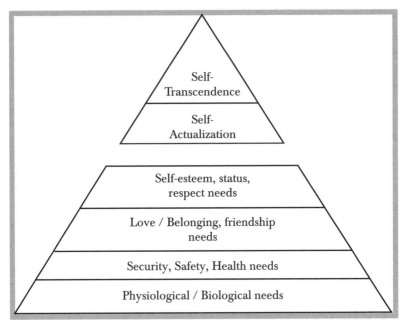

MASLOW'S HIERARCHY OF NEEDS

Maslow, of course, has described the psychologically healthy person. While this is fine, and certainly a worthy goal, I would like to suggest that Maslow is wrong in arguing that what we all want is the psychological health at the top of the hierarchy of needs. Although it would be great to be self-actualized, it's not something we consciously work towards, and it is so lofty a goal that few of us can ever hope to achieve it. We do not *naturally* strive for it. But we do naturally strive for something far greater. The pinnacle of our psychological/existential needs is spiritual. But more on that later.

Another of the sixties' gurus, William Glasser, tells us that people want roles, not goals. They want a fulfilling identity. They want to know who they are and what their function is in society. The implication is that being a good person has a higher moral value than working for something as prosaic and selfish as profit.[11] In the touchy-feely sixties, money is out and meaning is in. Goals are out and roles are in. Work is out, love is in.[12] We want to know who we are, and the sixties' gurus tell us who we should be–cooperative, non-competitive, loving creatures who pursue their genuine interests, improve their talents, and reject the competitive hierarchical world.

This is Morrie's world.

It's also the world of the seekers in the Po Bronson book. Growing-up in a society that promises the holy grail of self-actualization, they feel cheated and disoriented because they haven't found it.

Meaning and Purpose in the Nazi Death Camps

Viktor Frankl, who survived years in Nazi concentration camps, also came to a conclusion about what people want. Those who survived the camps had particular traits. They had something to look forward to. They had purpose in their future. They had goals to achieve.

> The prisoner who had lost faith in the future–his future–was doomed. With his loss of belief in the future, he also lost his spiritual hold; he let himself decline and became subject to mental and physical decay.[13]

When a prisoner lost all hope, he was as good as dead. "No entreaties, no blows, no threats had any effect. He just lay there, hardly moving," wrote Frankl.

"He simply gave up. There he remained, lying in his own excreta, and nothing bothered him any more."

Out in the real world, said Frankl, people also give up. They feel helpless and hopeless. They are powerless to improve their lives. They are the living dead. Life is pointless. So what do these people want? What should the psychiatrist suggest? In order to function and be happy, we must have something important to do. Frankl argues that it's not power, we crave, nor identity, nor the mountaintop of self-transcendence, but *purpose and meaning.*

Frankl quotes Nietzsche who said, "He who has a *why* to live for can bear with almost any *how.*" In other words, if we have goals, purpose, and an important reason to live, we can endure any hardship life throws at us. But when we reach a point where life has no hope, no purpose, no goals, no projects–in effect no worthwhile future–then life is over. "Woe to him who saw no more sense in his life, no aim, no purpose, and therefore no point in carrying on. He was soon lost."[14]

Frankl concluded that the "primary force" in human motivation is "man's search for meaning," which was the title of his first book. "That is why," he wrote, "I speak of a *will to meaning* in contrast to the pleasure principle [or, as we could also term it, the *will to pleasure*] on which Freudian psychoanalysis is centered, as well as in contrast to the *will to power* stressed by Adlerian psychology."[15]

Frankl comes closer than any of the others to pinpointing What We Really Want. Meaning is far more important to us than mere psychological health. But why do we want meaning? And what could possibly be more important than meaning? Don't despair, we are getting closer to the top of this psychological/existential stairway, and closer to the answers; but since our attempts to gain meaning through "fictitious selves" is so important, we will first examine the many and varied psychological machinations we engage in to make ourselves better than we are.

17

image boosting

Nature has eased every lot with egotism; there is no worker so slowly, nor any swain so homely, but some delusion of grandeur will come to comfort and sustain him.[1]
—Will and Ariel Durant, *A Dual Autobiography*

Perhaps the most pervasive fictitious self has been mankind's attempt to place ourselves at the center of creation. As individuals and as a species, we have a burning need to believe that we are important here on earth and have a special place in the cosmos.

We Are All the Chosen People

Until Copernicus and Galileo burst our bubble in the sixteenth and seventeenth centuries, we believed mankind was the center of the universe. Going one step below mankind, we find that almost every group, ethnicity, tribe, or nation has believed that they were either the focal point of existence or were at least the best people on earth. Many groups have referred to themselves simply as "the people," implying that the rest of humanity was somehow something less. Ancient Egyptians and North American Arapaho Indians called themselves, "the People." The Hebrews were the "Chosen People." Catholics know for sure that only the chosen will be saved. Lutherans believe that only a select few have been predetermined for Heaven. Ancient Greeks and

Chinese considered all others to be barbarians. The Chinese referred to themselves as "the Middle Kingdom," meaning they were at the center of the world.

As a species, we make ourselves the center of the universe. As a nation, culture, or subculture, we see ourselves as the normal standard upon which all others are based (ethnocentrism). As the center of God's attention, we are obviously important and have a meaningful place in the cosmos. *But as individuals, we have doubts.* We are never quite sure if we are making it, and as a result, we create a multiplicity of masks to elevate ourselves.

I have on my desk a book called *Beneath the Mask* by F. Monte Christopher, which attempts to summarize the main currents of psychological thought.[2] The implication of the title is that we construct artificial personalities to improve our images. We engage in a multiplicity of psychological devices and machinations to fool ourselves and the rest of the world into thinking we are somehow different, somehow better.

Coolies and Hipsters

Consider the Chinese coolie. In the 1930s, while traveling in China, historian–philosopher, Will Durant, sat in a rickshaw pulled by a coolie. At first he was embarrassed to be carried in such a manner, but soon realized that the coolies felt no shame. On the contrary, Durant wrote, "They are happy to be among the chosen. Privately they console themselves with their varied superiority to us, who do not know Chinese."[3]

Durant understood the psychological forces at work. "Nature has eased every lot with egotism; there is no worker so lowly, nor any swain so homely, but some delusion of grandeur will come to comfort and sustain him." To varying degrees, we all want to believe we are "among the chosen."

Another example of subconscious image boosting is the "hipster." Psychotherapist Sheldon Kopp played that role in the late 1940s.

What mattered to "us" was to be hip. In the main, "us" were the bright but unhappy, out-of-it kids, who neither played ball nor pleased their families. Hip was being in the know, cool, street-wise, a sophisticated primitive whose rebellion was aimed, not at saving society, but at escaping from it.[4]

But the real focus of the Hipster identity was not so much escape as *elevation*. The Hipster was cool, detached, removed from square society. Sounding like Durant's coolies, he wrote, "We saw ourselves as alienated, and yet more privileged than those trapped in the square world." But in retrospect, Kopp realizes that their real motivation was to emphasize how morally superior, smarter, and more perceptive they were compared to their parents and to mainstream society.

This seeming freedom of the Hipster must be seen within the context of his being cool. There is a hidden self-containment in his unwillingness to be upset or thrown off balance by any of the concerns or norms of niceness and normality that bind the squares. Our impassivity gave us the untested illusion of magical om- nipotence. We robbed the squares of their power by making them uneasy while we ourselves remained passive and unruffled. In our own eyes, we were an elite, in the know, digging where it was really at.[5]

Your Vanity Peeps Out through Every Hole in Your Robe

We find this kind of thing in all times and places. On a sunny day in ancient Athens, 2,500 years ago, a young man in a tattered toga got up to speak. Among his listeners was Socrates, who had little patience with affectations. "Young man of Athens," said Socrates, "your vanity peeps out through every hole in your robe." In other words, the young man was a phony—he was playacting poverty to add sincerity to his plea.

Long before Socrates, the Old Testament advised, "One man pre- tends to be rich, yet has nothing; another pretends to be poor, yet has great wealth."

We do a whole lot of pretending to make ourselves better. A study on smoking revealed that "Young people who smoke are trying to be older; and older people who smoke are trying to be younger." Smok- ers feel more confident and virile when they puff. They feel cooler, tougher, sexier and more sophisticated.

Some people try to seem smarter in order to gain respect. Men in particular love to dispense information to impress those around them. Linguistics professor Deborah Tannen calls it "report talk."[6] Yet others try to be dumb. I've seen any number of bright kids who purposely do badly in school to gain peer acceptance.

Changing one's name is an effective way to become someone else— someone better. A sixty-three-year-old man named Winfred Eugene Holly, described by UPI as "a bearded, winkly-eyed man," officially changed his name to Santa Claus. He receives thousands of letters from kids and loves what he does. Another Santa wannabe is Leroy Scholtz, who tried to change his name to Santa Christopher Claus. He has a head of white hair, a bushy white beard, and a crinkly, friendly smile. Scholtz had been St. Nick for twenty-five years and claimed he had lost his former identity. Lost? More to the point, he gave it away.

Then we find Rick, who has run in more than fifty marathons and solidified the image by officially changing his name to Rick Marathon. In a television interview he admitted that running was his life, his love, his mistress, and his religion.

People who join cults invariably take on new names. One of the appeals of cults is that they provide dissatisfied people with the opportunity to be born again, to shed their old, worthless selves like a snake sheds its skin, and to replace them with new and more meaningful self-images. Susan Atkins, a follower of Charles Manson, was given the name Sadie Mae Glutz. Testifying at the Manson trial she explained, "In order for me to be completely free in my mind, I had to be able to completely forget the past. The easiest way to do this, change identity, is by doing so with a name."[7]

Sixties' radical, Susan Stern, went though a series of identity switches to find a satisfactory self. In her memoirs, *With The Weathermen,* she tells us that she grew up "thinking I was stupid and ugly . . . lonely and envious of people . . . to whom friends and grades came so easily." She was unhappy in her marriage, "became nervous and morbid," and "went on long crying jags."[8]

With the sixties counterculture raging around her, she transformed herself into a hippie.

> I threw most of my clothes into a valise, and went to the Ave. and bought myself a long skirt and an old blouse several sizes too

large for me . . . I got my ears pierced and wore long, dangling vividly colored earrings. I let my hair curl naturally. I went without make-up. I gave up shoes and underpants.

Two years later the shoes and underpants came back as she slipped into the identity of women's liberation.

Off came the sloppy jeans and on went the mini-skirt and knee-high boots . . . I was a new Susan Stern, and, honey, when I walked, I threw my back my head, and moved with determination . . . people looked at me and God damn it, when I talked, they listened, finally they listened.

She drifted into other identities—topless dancer and protester—finally finding her place with the Weather Underground, the most radical of the sixties groups. She embraced it with such intensity that "my family, my past all faded into dreary insignificance. For the first time in my life that I could remember, I was happy." She was happy because she had left her failed self behind and had donned the mask of significance, respect, and meaning.

Keeping the squares off balance, gaining a new identity, acting smart or dumb, rich or poor, strong or weak, and just about anything else one can imagine, makes us feel we are better than we are. But what we really want is more than a brief ego buzz, which will be discussed in Chapter 20, after we take a brief diversion to see what Melanie has to say.

18

i will not be anything other than what i am

> Most people do not live up to the standards put on them by this world. There is no shame in this. Perhaps not many people see the value that is you. That should not matter. I will not be anything other than what I am. To do so would be to dishonor my parents.
>
> —Melanie

It's easy enough to write dispassionately about Freud and Nietzsche, and about coolies and hippies, but it is quite another thing to look at the people around us, most notably at my daughter Melanie, who at twenty-one had no doubts about eternity, but was still wrestling with the question of who she was here on earth.

Bludgeoned by Her Intensity

Being introspective and analytical, Melanie filled volumes of journals trying to understand her place in the world. During the second week in June, after a visit to Starbucks with Uncle Sonny, I found Melanie's diary in the living room. I opened it. I closed it. There is plenty of debate about whether or not parents should intrude on their children's privacy. I opened it. I closed it and tossed it on the table. Kids sometimes need to be saved from themselves. What in the world did she write about day after day? I felt terribly guilty, but I worried about Melanie. I opened it at random and was bludgeoned by her intensity.

Will it matter in the long run? Will it matter that in college I was fun and pretty and popular? It seems so utterly important, so essential to my current happiness. I look at my parents. My mom was not particularly happy in college. My dad was not by any means popular. Neither are athletic or very good-looking or especially fun, but I look at them in awe. They have three well-adjusted children. They have had fulfilling careers . . . and they still love each other. I can see the admiration my dad holds for my mom when he looks at her. After so many years, my mom still loves my dad. Despite his quirky ways, and lack of romance, she loves the goodness inside him that only she understands. She sees the depth of his constantly searching soul and his unconditional love for his three awkward daughters.

Most people do not live up to the standards put on them by this world. There is no shame in this. Perhaps not many people see the value that is you. That should not matter. I will not be anything other than what I am. To do so would be to dishonor my parents.

Melanie's premise was only partially correct, but her conclusion was the right one. It's not that we don't live up to the world's expectations, but that *we do not live up to our own expectations.* Until we are satisfied with our place, role, and function in the world, we can never be fully content. Her conclusion, "I will not be anything other than what I am," implies that she is still fighting a war within herself. On the one hand, she is expressing dissatisfaction with herself; on the other, she is saying–*refusing*–to wear a mask, to fake self-esteem, to try on false identities, to fabricate a sense of purpose, to create an illusory or fictitious persona. Like all of us, she wants that Adlerian sense of "competence and fulfillment," but she will get it by being who she is. And it was clear that Mel was a Christian.

June 30, 2002

What a wonderful God I have. He always provides. I need only trust him. My heart is so joyful when I think of Him! What a sweet Lord He is. He wants so much to spoil his little ones. If He could He would shower us with gifts and surprises and He would play with us all day. Of course, if we are to be worthy to enter Heaven we must overcome evil and pursue holiness no matter how tiring and difficult. You may wonder what brought on this joyful outpouring. I was just thinking how God has provided for me. I feel very alienated from my good friends. I don't really fit in with them anymore, but God has given me so many wonderful people to fill the gap . . . God is good. I love Him very much right now.

Another time she wrote:

My King,
My love. I come to you now with only a desire to express my love for you. I adore you, not just because you have given me more than I could ever deserve, but because you fill an emptiness in me than no one can fill; you light a fire in me that makes me feel alive and you bring a peace to me that at times seems to flow in me like a boundless river.

God the Surrogate Parent

Her place in eternity was secure, but her place on earth was not.

Life and love and pain are such a mystery. Can't the God who under-stands these forces see that I am doing the best I can? What does He want from me? Where am I supposed to be? What am I supposed to be doing?"

Melanie is asking the fundamental questions: Who am I? How can I make my life meaningful? Even if we are secure and comforted by god, we still want significance here on earth.

Melanie wrote something else, which I believe, is one of the reasons man created god.

What is it You do? How do You work? Lord, I want to love you as I used to. It is hard for me now. I don't know what to pray. I don't know whether you will help me or if I am to help myself. I suppose you would want me to feel successful and proud of myself. Therefore, you challenge me to take the initiative and get things done myself. You know that I need this confidence, but what if I fail? Lord, my sweet love, I feel overwhelmed and I feel the tasks ahead of me are too hard to bear. All I want to do is climb into your daddy-sized lap and feel warm and sure. I want to hear your heart beating steady and strong; each beat strengthening my confidence and resolve to succeed. How fortunate I am to know the love of a father. Even the years before I could retain memories, I soaked in the love of my earthly father as he rocked me in our old rocking chair, singing soft and holding me close. This is how I can understand the love of my Heavenly Father. Lord, I may never experience your love as others have, but I have had a taste of it with my earthly father.

"God," I often said to Becky, "is a surrogate parent." When we are children, our parents are all-knowing, all-powerful beings, quite similar to gods. They protect us, love us, provide for us, set guidelines, and so on. We want their love and approval. The most comforting and secure place we will ever inhabit is in the arms of our parents. As adults we create gods to provide that same overwhelming security. We want to be loved and cared for by omnipotent beings, and as a result, we create god to take the place of our parents. The words of a Christian song come to mind.

I cast all my cares upon you.
I place all of my burdens, down at your feet.
And anytime, I don't know, what to do,
I just cast all my cares upon you.

When life is hard, when the burdens of work and family overwhelm, how many of us would like to rest, to fall into the arms of a loving and powerful person who would care for us and relieve us of life's uncertainties. We want to be children again, we want a father to love and protect us. We created god as a surrogate father.

Becky, of course, has a different explanation.

"God created us to have a need to love our parents and be cared for so that when the time came, we would need and love Him. We didn't create God as a surrogate parent, he makes us psychologically dependent on our parents so we will be open to depending on and choosing Him."

I always thought that people without strong fathers, or with absent fathers, or emotionally distant fathers would turn to god as adults to compensate for that gap in their childhoods. On the other hand, children with loving fathers might be so attached to them that they create god to continue the good feelings. Either way, many of us choose god. So how do we account for those who do not choose god? I rocked all the kids in the rocking chair, but I had a special song for Melanie, which I sang to her every night at bedtime. Did she choose God because I was so comforting to her? Or because of Becky's influence? I rocked Ashlie, the atheist, too. Or is it all genetic? Are we programmed at birth to be good, or bad, or honest, or evil, or Republicans, or religious? And if, as the evidence suggests, genes are responsible for much of our behavior, then why would god program some people to be destructive psychopaths? And—to add yet another question—if the genes pull the behavioral strings, then isn't free will at least somewhat negated? And since free will is the reason we are given as to why god allows evil, and we learn that it's not really free will since god gave us our genetic endowment which limits our ability to make choices, then the whole free-will argument as an explanation for human suffering goes down the tubes.

Sisterhood Is Sounding Better and Better

The problem, which sometimes keeps me up at nights, is that if Melanie is really is true to herself, then Christianity might lead her to a convent.

After breaking up with a boyfriend she wrote:

> *Oh, well, only one relationship will ever work out in my life and he will be my husband or else I will be a nun. I've not really been liking guys much lately, so sisterhood is sounding better and better. To be a nun would be to go against everything I've ever known. I always imagined I would get married and have beautiful children. I'm afraid that if I become a nun I would disappear from the world I've always known. Won't I miss the intimate sexual relationship with a man someday? How can I leave behind my friends whom I love more dearly than life? My heart is so torn.*

It had often seemed to me that many nuns were escaping from life. Yes, of course they are dedicated to god and are good Christians, and so on, but—like in cults—they are free from decision making, free from the burdens of job and family. Life is uncomplicated, controlled, orderly, and simple. Psychologist Erich Fromm suggests that many people do not want freedom, they want to escape *from* freedom.[1] Freedom puts them out there in the competitive world where they have to fend for themselves. In the bosom of a cult or a convent, they are free from freedom and the possibilities of failure.

Melanie may not have been sure yet of who she was, but she certainly filled volumes trying to figure it out.

Preening for Eternity

If we could all answer the question, "What do people want?" with Melanie's answer, *I will not be anything other than what I am,* the world would be a far better place. Unfortunately, most people say the opposite: *I want to be different than who I am; I need to fabricate masks; I need to fake it; I prefer illusion to reality; I must be different; different is better.* But on a deeper and more significant level, when we are polishing our images, we are really preening for eternity, as we'll discuss in the next chapter.

(And by the way, Melanie, what exactly did you mean by "quirky"?)

After reading this chapter, Melanie wrote:

What is a young woman to think when her father reads her diary, her sanctuary that she has turned to for so many years; a place that feels more like home than her long-time home in Colorado? In that sanctuary, no one will criticize my spelling or handwriting. No spell-check will highlight my many errors.

So then, how can I possibly be comfortable letting this part of me be put out for just anyone to see? I should have been furious. I should have shed tears and refused to let my private thoughts be put into his "little project." Yet I felt none of these things and I have learned enough about life to not depend on the "shoulds."

Somehow, I know my journal entries will not be shocking or cosmically mysterious to anyone. They are things that everyone has felt or understands. I guess it gives me happiness that I might, in a small way, become a part of the people who read my thoughts. (I know what you are thinking, Dad, a quest for immortality, right? It could be.) The fact is that somehow I don't mind, and maybe at some level I was always writing for more than myself.

19

immortality projects

I don't want to become immortal through my work; I want to become immortal through not dying.

—Woody Allen

. . . History is the saga of men and women working out their Atman [immortality] projects on one another . . . creating thereby kings and gods and heroes on the one hand, and strewing recklessly the corpses of Auschwitz and Gulag and Wounded Knee on the other.[1]

—Ken Wilber, *Up From Eden*

Finally, we get to the top of our existential needs.

It's not a pyramid but a series of building blocks. Self-esteem, power, family, purpose, goals, sex, love, respect, acceptance, identity, and importance provide our lives with meaning. The masks we wear are designed to improve our images in order to acquire that meaning.

This is normal and expected, but the psychological gymnastics we go through are merely tributaries originating in the ocean that represents our greatest need. And what is this need? A few years ago, I would have answered *significance*. Earlier incarnations of this book were called "The Quest for Significance." On the cover of the book proposal was a medieval knight in full armor sitting high on a stallion, lance upturned. It seemed that in any hierarchy of psychological needs, power, self-esteem, importance, meaning, and identity are simply means to gaining significance. The Holy Grail of life is the attempt to justify one's existence, to know that our individual lives are worthy.

But the quest for significance is *not* the pinnacle of our psychological/ existential needs. Ratcheting it up one more level, we can say that the reason we want significance is to gain immortality; beyond that there is no higher level.

But what does immortality mean? It means that we want to not die. Since this is not an option, the next best thing is knowing that our individual lives count for something in the greater Scheme of Creation. If we are satisfied that our lives added something to the cosmos, then we have gained immortality. What do people really want? *Meaning. Significance. Salvation. Eternity. Immortality.* The rest is in the details.

Secular Salvation

Many of us gain salvation through our mainstream churches and synagogues; but as we have already noted, in the past few centuries, we have increasingly found secular roads to eternity. While worshipping Hitler or "the cause" could be quite exhilarating, most people in most times achieved their sense of worth through everyday affairs, what Sören Kierkegaard called *tranquilizing on the trivial.* Earning a living, making friends, sexual conquests, marrying the man of one's dreams, buying a better house, getting a promotion, or making the company bowling team are among the subplots of our lives that give us a sense of direction and accomplishment.

Our lives are low-key immortality projects. *An immortality project is the ongoing task that justifies one's existence.*[2] It requires effort, action, and perhaps struggle. The *process* of carrying out the project is the action that gives us the sense that our lives are moving in a worthwhile direction. It's a project—something one works toward over a period of time. One does not necessarily have to finish it for it to have the desired effect.

In a sense, all of our lives are *general* immortality projects. Every success, every pay check, every problem solved helps us gain that immortality. When we accomplish our everyday goals, we are busy succeeding at life, which means that when we leave this life, we can die content, knowing that we added something to the cosmos and that our lives were worthwhile. This general immortality project is gradual and lacks intensity. We make our way to eternity one step at a time. We use the little subplots of our lives to build an edifice to cosmic significance. Every positive action takes us closer–getting that big contract, having the support of good friends, a pat on the back, putting a bumper sticker on our car that reads "I'm the parent of an honor student at Central High School" all add to our sense or worthiness. The hunger for cosmic significance is subliminal and unarticulated. We are driven to it, we are moving toward it, without consciously recognizing it. Yet it is always there, floating just ahead of us, the holy grail of existence.

Some of our immortality projects are *specific* and focused. They can be tasks of any duration, as long as we consider them important and they require an ongoing effort. Specific immortality projects come in all sizes, shapes, and levels of intensity. What they have in common is *dedication,* and *the exertion of effort.* Dedication to a candidate during a political campaign, working for years to reach the Olympics as a figure skater, working for a decade to write a book, or raising money to help fund a youth center would all be considered immortality projects, even though they are finite in duration.

The Hunger for Transcendence

But some people are not satisfied with the trivial and the finite. They hunger for the transcendent and the infinite. They want to change the world. Because they are incapable of changing themselves, they attempt to change–and sometimes destroy–the society around them. The new chapter they write in their life stories is dramatic, exciting, compelling, and often destructive. These are the people who latch on to some project or purpose they perceive to be more important than life itself.

"This power," wrote psychologist, Erich Fromm, "can be a person, an institution, God, the nation, conscience, or a psychic compulsion."[3] It manifests itself as fanatical dedication to an ideology, a politician, a general, a lifestyle, a war, a political movement, or a love object. "If I join the Nazi party, I'll be part of the huge and noble struggle to resurrect Germany from defeat and humiliation." "If I become a hippie and reject middle class values, I'm passing myself off as different and better than everyone else." "If I marry that person, my life will be transformed." "If I follow that guru, I will be among the chosen people to proselytize for the truth." Or as Alan Harrington put it, "I am making a deeper impression on the cosmos because I know this famous person. When the ark sails I will be on it."[4] When a weak person associates himself with powerful forces, he becomes powerful.

"Psychic compulsions" are almost by definition, *religious* in nature. Organized religion like Christianity, cults like the Krishnas or the Moonies, social struggles like the civil rights movement, mass movements like fascism and communism, wars, revolutions, and liberation movements all have great appeal because *they have a spiritual or revivalist quality.*[5]

They give people a sense of being on the winning side of something historically important. Accomplishing the objective becomes a consuming religious experience. The follower is focused as never before because for the first time in his life he has genuine purpose. By associating oneself with a cause of cosmic importance, the individual, says Fromm, is:

saved from doubt of what the meaning of his life is or who 'he' is. The questions are answered by the relationship to the power to which he has attached himself. The meaning of his life and the identity of his self are determined by the greater whole into which the self has submerged.[6]

In other words, an individual who has doubts about his worthiness can allay those doubts and gain certainty by associating himself with people and projects that give him strength, identity, support, purpose, meaning, direction, and sometimes transcendence. The great purpose to which he attaches himself is his road to salvation. "By participating in this hugely important event, project or person," he thinks, "I will have done something of great worth with my life, and have therefore earned a place in creation."

Holy Missions

When people and groups become convinced that their cause is vitally important to mankind or society (and most importantly, to themselves) and because of the religious/transcendent nature of the causes, the movements could be called *holy missions,* a subset of immortality projects.[7] And because people on holy missions believe their place in eternity is on the line, they become almost psychopathic, caring not a whit for the lives of those who get in their way. They are motivated–

not by love of mankind, nor by love of self (narcissism), nor even by hatred of the enemy–but by self-doubt and the quest for salvation. They are driven by their own existential fears. "Faith in a holy cause," wrote Eric Hoffer, "is to a considerable extent a substitute for the lost faith in ourselves."[8] Fanatical dedication to a holy mission originates more from existential necessity than from political exigency. People on holy missions are spiritually dysfunctional fanatics who worship false and destructive gods.

Consider the example of Oklahoma City bomber, Tim McVeigh. Dr. Jeffrey M. Schwartz, a neuropsychiatrist at UCLA, explained his actions thusly: "The grandiosity that McVeigh exhibited–that by his act he would bring down the government–shows how badly the hero ethos can go wrong when it is not grounded in a strict moral code. Narcissism is what allows you to get evil acts from seemingly ordinary people."[9]

McVeigh certainly wanted to be hero, but he was not motivated by narcissism. He didn't love himself. On the contrary, he was *unsure* about himself. He was *afraid* that his life would be meaningless. By lashing out at the "evil" government, he wrote a new chapter in his life. By blowing up the Murrah building, he assured himself of a meaningful life, gained immortality, and earned a place in the cosmos. McVeigh's existential fear resulted in the deaths of 168 people.

Religious Conversions

The initial attachment to a holy mission is like a religious conversion, because when an individual links to a person, cause, or project that seems to transcend everyday existence, he immediately moves into another psychological/spiritual dimension. It is also the moment when he becomes spiritually dysfunctional because his sudden conversion becomes a psychological prop that he must maintain at all costs. To give it up means to give up on a life of significance and worth.

The conversion seems to happen suddenly, although the individual had been unconsciously looking for something to save him from his self-perceived, ineffectual self. When he "converts" to the cause, he is lifted from the morass of his self-doubts and is magically elevated to the heavenly narcotic illusion of transcendent importance. Thus, in the context of this discussion, religious conversion is defined as *the moment when an individual recognizes the immortality project that will bring him salvation.*

Scales Fell from His Eyes

The classic example of a religious conversion was Saul on the road to Damascus. Saul was a Jew who persecuted the very first Christians. The New Testament tells us that as he walked to Damascus, "a light from the sky suddenly flashed about him. He fell to the ground and at the same time he heard a voice saying, 'Saul, Saul, why do you persecute me?' 'Who are you, sir?' he asked. The voice answered, 'I am Jesus, the one you are persecuting. Get up and go into the city, where you will be told what to do . . .'" After three days of blindness, ". . . something like scales fell from his eyes and he regained his sight," but even more importantly, he gained a holy mission to convert the gentiles to Christianity. When the scales fell from his eyes, he saw the truth and the purpose of his life was now clear.

History has its share of sudden realizations of "the truth" and the concomitant recognition of one's destiny. Late in the fourth century, one Aurelius Augustinus, overwhelmed by his lust for women, became overwhelmed by the sudden realization of his life's mission. While speaking to a student, he heard a child's voice chanting, "Take up and read; Take up and read." Tearfully, he interpreted this as a command from God, opened the Bible at random, and read about St. Paul. "No further would I read: nor needed I: for instantly at the end of this sentence, by a light as it were of serenity infused into my heart, all the darkness of doubt vanished away." He went on to write *The City of God* and was canonized as St. Augustine.[10]

The great seventeenth-century mathematician and philosopher, René Descartes, who was immortalized by his statement, "I think, therefore I am," also had an epiphany. In a series of dreams, he was overcome by a "dazzling light" and a thunder and lightning storm in his room, which convinced him he would be able to get answers to his questions. He emerged from the experience with a goal to unify knowledge through reasoning and the exactness of mathematics.[11]

Dazzled by a Thousand Sparkling Lights

Then we find the eighteenth-century philosopher, Jean Jacques Rousseau, in a French forest in 1749 reading a newspaper as he walks. Rousseau was a strange character. While others rode on horses or in carriages, he preferred to walk. He loved nature and hated the cities with their phony sophistication and atheism. He disliked the company of people. When "obliged to speak," he wrote in his memoirs, "I infallibly say something stupid."

Rousseau was a wandering soul–lost, depressed, vague, murky, bitter, angry, and at odds with everyone. He succeeded in alienating every friend he ever had. He wallowed in self-pity and craved sympathy. He had delusions of grandeur and saw a conspiracy behind every tree. He felt persecuted, unloved, and unappreciated. But he had his immortality project.

On one of his solitary walks in the woods, his nose in a newspaper, he came across word of an essay contest and was immediately overcome by a blinding realization of his destiny. "All at once," he tells us. "I felt myself dazzled by a thousand sparkling lights. Crowds of vivid ideas thronged into my mind with a force and confusion that threw me into unspeakable agitation; I felt my head whirling in a giddiness like that of intoxication. A violent palpitation oppressed me."

He fell to the ground, passed out, and awoke, wet with tears and with a clear vision. "Ah, if ever I could have written a quarter of what I saw and felt under that tree, with what clarity I could have brought out all the contradiction of our social system!"[12]

Rousseau's sudden recognition of an absolute truth was clearly a religious conversion. He had seen the burning bush and knew what had to be done. The scales had fallen from his eyes, and he was off on a holy mission to spread the gospel that "God makes all things good, man meddles with them and they become evil." It was an immortality project that actually brought him immortality.

Hitler Falls to His Knees in Rapturous Enthusiasm

Another religious convert who gained immortality was Adolf Hitler. Hitler was not always a strutting Nazi. Until August 1914, he was a purposeless, drifting failure. As a young man, Hitler had harbored a fervent desire to be an artist, but was repeatedly denied entrance to the European art academies. Angry and frustrated, he seemed to give up on life. He drifted around Munich, a homeless waif seemingly bereft of hope. He spent many nights sleeping on park benches and soon found himself in homes for the utterly destitute. He had no money, no job, no prospects, no present, and no future. For a while he begged on the streets.

Here we have an amazing phenomena. The man who was to become the greatest mover and shaker of the twentieth century was a totally defeated park bench bum. What resurrected him from failure and despair? The holy mission of war. When World War 1 erupted, Hitler experienced a religious conversion. "I am not ashamed to say," he wrote in *Mein Kampf,* "that overcome from rapturous enthusiasm, I fell to my knees and thanked Heaven from an overflowing heart for granting me the good fortune of being allowed to live at this time." Why was he so energized? Because his life suddenly had a purpose. Biographer John Toland wrote that for Hitler, "There was no more room for doubt; he knew for the first time in his life exactly where he was going and why."[13]

The war gave him identity, direction, transcendence, and success.

War was Hitler's fairy godmother bringing him the good news that life had meaning. It was his glass slipper. His Prince Charming. His savior. His salvation. His immortality project. Just as Cinderella was transformed from ragamuffin to queen, Hitler morphed from street waif to soldier to the Chancellor of Germany. Twenty years later, Hitler, *der Fuhrer,* would do exactly the same thing for the people of Germany—resurrect them from failure and lead them on an energizing holy mission.

Something Clicked in My Brain

Kurt G. W. Ludecke, an early supporter of Hitler who later broke away from the Nazis, spoke of *der Fuhrer* in religious terms. "His appeal to German manhood was like a call to arms, the gospel he preached a sacred truth. He seemed another Luther." Like so many pilgrims in search of meaning and purpose, Ludecke describes himself as "weary of disgust and disillusionment, a wanderer seeking a cause; a patriot without a channel for his patriotism, a yearner after the heroic without a hero." Hitler became his hero, his god, and his purpose. "The intensity of the man, the passion of his sincerity seemed to flow from him into me. I experienced an exaltation that could be likened only to religious conversion." After hearing Hitler speak, he wrote, "I knew my search was ended. I had found myself, my leader, and my cause."[14]

Arthur Koestler, a journalist and writer in Germany, explains how the scales fell from his eyes in 1931. The religion he converted to was communism. Koestler was concerned about the rise of Nazism and after reading some political tracts by communists, he wrote:

Something had clicked in my brain which shook me like a mental explosion. To say that one had 'seen the light' is a poor description of the mental rapture which only the convert knows (regardless of what faith he has been converted to). The new light seems to pour from all directions across the skull; the whole universe falls into pattern like the stray pieces of a jigsaw puzzle assembled by magic at one stroke. There is now an answer to every question, doubts and conflicts are a matter of the tortured past–a past already remote, when one had lived in dismal ignorance in the tasteless, colorless world of those who *don't know*. Nothing henceforth can disturb the converts inner peace and serenity–except the occasional fear of losing faith again, losing thereby what alone makes life worth living, and falling back into the outer darkness, where there is wailing and gnashing of teeth.[15]

Koestler was "born again" with an exhilarating sense of purpose. His newfound faith made his "life worth living." His only fear, which is typical of people who psychologically fuse with their immortality projects, was that he might lose this new faith which would leave him in "the outer darkness," adrift in a deteriorating world.

Koestler eventually became disenchanted with communism; his god was false. But religious converts are often loath to give up their holy missions because to lose their cause is to lose their reasons to exist. Once they "see the light," their destinies are assured. The past becomes meaningless and the future glows with the promise of transcendence and cosmic significance. They become fanatical adherents to their respective causes, and as a result, they are extremely dangerous.

These religious conversions have a lot in common–a sudden and blinding realization of a vitally important truth, recognition of one's purpose in life, certainty, references to lights, falling to the ground, religious allusions like *gospel, faith, preach, rapture, sacred truth, serenity,* and *inner peace*, and excitement about the new world they are entering as contrasted to the drab meaninglessness of the old one they are leaving behind.

The True Believer

Over fifty years ago, Eric Hoffer brilliantly defined the characteristics of those who are irresistibly and fanatically drawn to mass movements.

The True Believer is an unhappy and dissatisfied person who is looking for success and meaning by joining a cause that is bigger than life itself. "Their innermost craving is for a new life—a rebirth—or, failing this, a chance to acquire new elements of pride, confidence, hope, a sense of purpose, and worth . . ." And how do they gain this rebirth? "By an identification with a holy cause . . . If they join the movement as full converts they are reborn to a new life in its close knit, collective body . . ."[16]

Holy missions are therefore extraordinarily powerful. They are pure emotion. They don't have to make sense. They don't have to be real. They are often in the realm of fantasy. But for the convert, they hold out the promise of salvation. "In [man's] anxiety to escape from the utter futility and meaningless existence," wrote John H. Hallowell in 1950, "he is tempted to give up his most priceless heritage—his freedom—to any man who even promises deliverance from insecurity. He is tempted to put his faith in the most absurd doctrine, to submit his will to the most brutal dictator, if only in such a way he can find that for which he longs with all the passion of his being—a meaningful existence, a life worth living, a life worth dying to preserve."[17]

But it is more than even a meaningful existence that the true believer craves, because if he gains satisfaction in *this* life, he has gained admission to the next one. When these inadequate and unsettled individuals have a religious conversion to their holy missions, they rewrite their life scripts. They change identities. They transform from impotence to omnipotence. They become heroic. They have hugely important goals and joyfully pursue them. They kill and destroy anyone or anything that gets in their way, sacrificing others on the alter of their personal salvation. There is nothing more dangerous, selfish, and spiritually dysfunctional in this world than a recent convert to a holy mission. They are happy because they have suddenly found the cause that will justify their lives, but there is often hell to pay for the rest of us.

20

heroism

Heroism transmutes the fear of death into the security of self-per-
petuation, so much so that people can cheerfully face up to
death and even court it under some ideologies.[1]
—Ernest Becker, *The Denial of Death*

Fascism, now and always, believes in holiness and in heroism.[2]
—Benito Mussolini

Psychologists have long noted that we tend to see our lives as a story
being played out one day at a time. Like all stories we want our lives
to make sense and to progress successfully from one subplot to another. It also needs a main plot, a general direction in which the story
proceeds. And it needs to make sense. Why does this story exist?
What's the point? If we conclude that the plot is in chaos, or is dull, or
that the story has no point, we can become frantic. After all, the book
does not go on forever. Our time is limited. There is a final chapter.
And what if we come to that final chapter and conclude the story is
meaningless, that our life is a tale told by an idiot, signifying nothing?
What if we come to these conclusions in the *early* chapters of our
lives? The result is fear and sometimes desperation. We feel compelled by our existential uncertainty to rewrite our life scripts—add
more chapters, change the characters, fabricate masks, create plot
twists, dream up surprise endings, fake self-esteem, and create "illusory" or "fictitious" selves—in order to bring drama, excitement, and
importance to the story of our lives.

Unfortunatly, these new chapters sometimes take the form of personal holy missions. The key ingredients of holy missions are *defiance and heroism*. Going with the flow requires little effort or courage; going against the grain requires both. Going against the greater forces in our lives clarifies our identity and gives us a sense of accomplishment because we have exerted effort to achieve a goal.

The Universal Story

There is, I believe, a universal story upon which all compelling life stories are based–heroically overcoming obstacles to achieve one's objective. It can be as obvious as a knight questing for the Holy Grail or as subtle as a character overcoming a personality flaw. Mysteries involve finding out whodunnit or getting the person who did it. Romances almost always involve overcoming problems standing in the way of the love affair. The Bible, fairy tales, children's stories, Greek epics, and modern drama all revolve around this universal plot. The Hebrews escape from Egypt and make their way to the promised land. Ulysses spends years on an odyssey to return to Penelope. The prince searches for Cinderella. Scarlet O'Hara and Rhett Butler face obstacles to their relationship.

One of the most satisfying human stories is rising from humiliation to heroism. Rudolph the Red-Nosed Reindeer and Dumbo, the elephant, changed from laughed-at fools to respected heroes. When my kids were young, we read them a children's book called *Clumsy Clyde the Cowboy*. Clyde was a klutz. He did everything wrong. He constantly fell off his horse. Everyone laughed at Clyde. One day he ingeniously stopped some bad guys. Everyone cheered and "no one ever called him Clumsy Clyde again."

Because the role of hero is so extraordinarily fulfilling, those in an existential funk *create a dramatic story in which they can play a heroic role in overcoming obstacles*. They find authorities to defy, enemies to defeat, and devils to destroy. They re-write their life scripts. They reinvent themselves. *They fabricate heroism.*

Consider the case of Joe Mauk, a highly decorated Vietnam veteran.[3] Mauk has eleven Purple Hearts for wounds he suffered in Vietnam. He has both the Silver and Bronze Stars for bravery and was a prisoner of war for almost two-and-a-half years. Mauk frequently speaks to military groups and in school classrooms. According to a newspaper article about him, Mauk's "stories have stirred awe in Colorado schoolchildren and brought tears to the eyes of adults." The trouble is that none of this is true. Mauk is a fraud. He made the whole thing up. According to army records, he was never in Vietnam, was not a prisoner of war, did not win any medals, was not a member of the Special Forces, and was not a master sergeant.

Mauk is not the only hero wannabe. The Navy SEALs have identified over four thousand men who fraudulently claim to be members. There are thousands of phony members of the Army Special Forces, and at least seven hundred fabricated prisoners of war. Even prominent men who are successful in other areas of life have created this heroic military persona. Historian Joseph Ellis, who won the Pulitzer Prize in 2001 for *Founding Brothers,* repeatedly lied to his students at Mount Holyoke College about his Vietnam experience. A Los Angeles superior court judge was fired in August 2001 for falsely claiming he fought in Vietnam and worked for the CIA in Laos.

Why do they do it? Most frauds are perpetrated for money, but in these cases the payoff is in psychological pleasure. They aren't satisfied with who they are, so they transform themselves into something better—a hero. While most of us look forward to the accomplishments that will gain us significance and worth, these men gain their heroism by reinventing themselves. They rewrite their life scripts.

Screaming for Glory

So how does one become a hero in his own life's story short of becoming a true believer or fabricating a heroic past? He adopts a *defiant* pose against the larger forces in his life. When we say, "I disagree," we become courageous and independent. From the two-year-old screaming "no" to everything in order to feel he has an effect on life, to the rebellious adolescent defying his parents, going against the grain produces feelings of strength and effectiveness. Defiance against those in power has a heroic quality. Defying our parents, our teachers, and our society's conventions takes courage and effort and makes us feel satisfied. To fight the good fight—against the odds—provides a feeling of satisfaction that sometimes harbors on euphoria. "I've done something worthy. I've been in a struggle, I'm hurt, I'm battered and bleeding, but I fought well and I feel good. Because I have suffered, I have earned a place in eternity. I *deserve* a place in eternity."

Unfortunately, when people try to rewrite their life stories from failure or farce to defiant heroism, they often cut a destructive path. Ernest Becker believes that the desire for heroism can be "a blind drivenness that burns people up . . . a screaming for glory as uncritical and reflexive as the howling dog."[4] When discontented people discover their paths to meaning and eternal purpose, logic and reason are crushed under the gravity of their holy missions, and they will let nothing stand in their way. When a person is screaming for glory, the rest of us are in danger.

People trying to rewrite their life scripts into a defiant, heroic odyssey have been and continue to be one of the most powerful and destructive forces in human history. Disaffected individuals who become religious converts to their causes are impossible to reason with because they have subconsciously concluded that if their lives on earth are heroic, they will have earned a place in the cosmos. Once they link up with their reason-to-be, they become religious fanatics who are drugged with spiritual intensity. They are out of control. They have broken through into a psychological dimension that is beyond the pale of reason. Becker put it thusly:

> I don't think one can be a hero in any real elevating sense without some transcendental referent like being a hero for God, or for the creative powers of the universe. The most exacted type of heroism involves feeling that one has lived to some purpose that transcends one. This is why religion gives the individuals the validation that nothing else gives him.[5]

American Taliban

The most potent immortality project, then, is to combine mainstream religion with defiance and heroism. Consider the case of John Walker Lindh whose spiritual journey led him from the affluent suburbs of California to the wretched caves of Afghanistan in 2001.

Lindh was evidently unhappy and insecure and was trying to find his place in the world. At the age of fourteen he tried on the black identity. Haunting hip-hop websites and using the Internet name "doodoo," he passed himself off as black. "Our blackness," he wrote, "should not make white people hate us."[6]

Walker was looking for a clearly identifiable, out-of-the-mainstream group to provide him with identity and acceptance. "I've seen Walker's type before," wrote African American columnist, Clarence Page. "Black street culture, a byproduct of historical exclusion and oppression, has long offered an attractive alternative for rebels [i.e., defiant heroes] against mainstream society."[7] It also offers an attractive alternative for pilgrims searching for their place in the universe.

Lindh was such a pilgrim. He tried the Black Muslims, but eventually made his way to Islam, which he embraced with fanatical intensity. He grew a beard, dressed in flowing robes, and changed his name to Suleyman al-Faris and then to Abdul Hamid. He went to Yemen to study and memorize all 6,666 sentences in the Koran, slept on a rope in his teacher's home, and eventually took up arms against Americans in Afghanistan.

Some have argued that Lindh was looking for spiritual truth, or enlightenment, or he wanted to "find himself." But what he really wanted was to *lose* himself and to be reborn with a new identity, a new life script, and new sense of spiritual purpose. His embracing of Islam provided it all–spirituality, identity, heroism, defiance, purpose, suffering (that gave him the feeling of having worked for that purpose), acceptance, camaraderie, a demonized enemy, certainty, guidelines for life, an apocalyptic vision, and a holy mission/immortality project to worship. He not only rewrote his life script, but he changed identities. He didn't like John Walker Lindh, so he became Suleyman al-Faris. His fanaticism was really a crying out for salvation. It was not a quest for enlightenment; it was a quest for significance. He was motivated by existential dread. He wanted to gain happiness through absolute truth. He wanted to touch transcendence to insure his place in eternity. He is a classic example of someone who is spiritually dysfunctional.

The End of the World Is Coming and I Can't Wait

All of this plays out in religious cults. People join them to find a spiritual intensity that had been lacking in their lives. As we saw earlier, cults give dissatisfied people the opportunity to be born again with a new identity. But even more importantly, they get to rewrite their life scripts into one of heroism and significance. For example, when publishing heiress Patricia Hearst was kidnapped by the Symbionese

Liberation Army, she joined their heroic struggle and changed her name to the more exotic "Tanya." New name, new person, new sense of purpose.

Along with a new identity, the cult member becomes part of a heroic movement to transform the world. Cults, almost by definition, create an apocalyptic fantasy from which they will emerge as the chosen people. Disciples come to believe that there is some Grand Scheme to history or Creation, and that they alone are earmarked for greatness. Up ahead is a Judgment Day when the meek shall inherit the earth. Instead of living as nonentities, they are among the elite of the universe.

Charles Manson formulated a bizarre plan called "Helter Skelter," designed to start a racial war from which he and his followers would survive to lead a new order. Jim Jones, who led over nine hundred of his spiritual progeny to suicide in 1978, told his followers of a "divine revelation" that warned of a "total annihilation of this country and other parts of the world."[8] Jones advised that "the only survivors will be those people who are hidden in the caves that I have been shown in a vision." He and his followers would survive to "begin a truly ideal society." David Koresh, whose Branch Davidian cult went down in flames in Waco, Texas, in 1993, convinced his followers he had the power to open the so-called Seven Seals in the Bible's Book of Revelations, which would result in a series of catastrophic events leading to the end of the world. His followers, of course, would rise from the ashes to become the inheritors of the earth. In *Cults in America*, Willa Appel summarized the heroic appeal of these groups when she pointed out that, "Members were told that their lives had a very real and very important significance: they had been chosen to save the world."[9]

The cult takes a purposeless individual and says, "Alone you were nothing, but in the bosom of this group you are taken care of, you are loved, you are special. You are a new person. Leave your old, failed self behind and be reborn as a member of the elite. The leader loves you. His strength is your strength. Together we can change the world. Come join us." The cult transforms individually powerless people into the *chosen people*. The appeal is irresistible, but all they really gain is a temporary high. The guru is a charlatan. The apocalypse never comes. The movement inevitably dies, and they are either destroyed or back to square one—alone, disillusioned, failed, and wondering if they will ever find meaning in life.

Many of the people discussed in this chapter are examples of spirituality run amok. It is more than dysfunctional; it is destructive both to the worshippers of the fabricated gods and holy missions, and to the people around them. The bombs at the Murrah building, the flames at Waco, and the murders ordered by Manson were atrocities caused by secular religions and the false heroics they embraced.

The Artifice of Eternity

Arguing that heroism is psychologically self-serving sounds cynical and is bound to meet with resistance. Every single hero in the world's bloody history would insist he is sincere and only acting for God or country or for the good of "the people." The hero has absolutely convinced himself that his courage is motivated by altruism, that he was driven to it by evil forces who must be defeated. For how could the hero possibly believe he is a fabrication, or to put it another way, that he is a fictional character in his own life story? Edward O. Wilson, the Pulitzer Prize-winning author of *On Human Nature*, attributes false heroics to the hunger for salvation. "Lives of the most towering heroism," Wilson concluded,

> are paid out in the expectation of great reward, not the least of which is a belief in personal immortality. When poets speak of happy acquiescence in death, they do not mean death at all, but apotheosis, or nirvana; they revert to what Yeats called the artifice of eternity.[10]

Wilson, Yeats, and I seem to agree that many heroic deeds are false, that the ulterior motive for heroism is the "great reward" of recognition in this world and immortality in the next. The "apotheosis" Wilson referred to is the process of turning a human being into a god; it's the act of glorifying and deifying the hero. The hero performs his deeds, not primarily to help others, but for his own immortal soul.

There are, of course, genuine acts of heroism. In times of war, heroism is a common occurrence. The man who makes an instant decision to fall on a grenade to save his comrades is a hero. He doesn't even live long enough to gain any recognition.

In the early 1990s, Franklin Simon confronted a man who was attacking his own sixty-three-year-old mother. The son raised a sawed-off rifle, pointed it at Simon, and said, "I'm going to blow your head off." He pulled the trigger, but Simon knocked it away in time, after which he led the woman away. Simon, who had already risked his life, subdued the attacker again when he threatened a passer-by.

Genuine heroes take extraordinary risks with little or no promise of rewards. Johtje and Aart Vos, a Dutch couple, are among a handful of Europeans who hid Jews from their Nazi occupiers during World War II. Why did they do it? Gay Block and Malka Drucker interviewed 105 Europeans who had risked their lives to hide the Jews. They found that these very brave people considered their actions merely a normal thing to do. "We didn't think about it," said Johtje Vos. "You started off storing a suitcase for a friend, and before you know it, you were in over your head. We did what any human being would have done."

Of course, very few human beings would have had the courage to risk certain death. These 105 heroes were very special people. They came from all economic backgrounds. They tended to be individualistic people who were not "constrained by the expectations of the group (who) were better able to act on their own." They tended to have a history of doing good deeds. They never planned to be rescuers. It just happened.

A cynic might argue that these acts only seem genuine and altruistic, and that the "heroes" gained some kind of psychological or self-congratulatory payback. They were performing for god, or it made them feel good about themselves. Perhaps it fit some image they wanted to project. Perhaps, but I would prefer to call them what they are—heroes.

Unfortunately, real heroes are few and far between. Many heroes create their own heroism and are looking for existential returns on their investment.

The intertwining relationship between heroism and immortality was evident to the Greek poet Homer almost three thousand years ago. In the *Iliad,* when Hector faces certain death in his fight with Achilles, he announces to the world and to posterity,

> *So now I meet my doom. Let me at least sell my life*
> *dearly and have a not inglorious end, after some feat*
> *of arms that shall come to the ears of generations*
> *still unborn.*[11]

A Poignant and Tragic Irony

There is a poignant and tragic irony to human life. In our fervent and often frenzied quest to make our lives worthy, we find many ways to destroy others. Defiance and heroism may make us feel good, but our pursuit of immortality leaves in its wake, as Ken Wilber pointed out in the epigraph of Chapter 19, "the corpses of Auschwitz and Gulag and Wounded Knee." The world would be a far better place if we could all be satisfied tranquilizing on the trivial. Unfortunately, war and revolution have a far greater existential appeal, as we shall see in the next chapter.

21

the holy missions of war and revolution

War is one of the constants of history, and has not diminished with civilization or democracy. In the last 3,421 years of recorded history only 268 have seen no war.[1]

—Will and Ariel Durant, *The Lessons of History*

Wars and revolutions are generally the most satisfying and dramatic holy missions, and it's not hard to see why. They have all the elements required for spiritual purpose—heroism, defiance, meaning, purpose, camaraderie, and identity all wrapped-up in a transcendent cause. Ernest Becker nailed the concept when he wrote:

> It begins to look as though modern man cannot find his heroism in everyday life anymore, as men did in traditional societies just by doing their daily duty of raising children, working and worshipping. He needs revolutions and wars and "continuing" revolutions to last when the revolutions and wars end. That is the price modern man pays for the eclipse of the sacred dimension.[2]

Becker is saying that since we gave up God as a means to salvation and because working our way through life in the traditional sense is no longer spiritually satisfying, we are turning to wars and revolutions to find a higher sense of purpose. And because it feels so good, we *create* wars and revolutions where there is really no need for them.

Or to put it another way, we invent enemies and obstacles in order to add heroic chapters to the story of our lives.

American Revolutionaries—Failures in Everyday Life

There are, of course, many justifiable revolutions—overtaxed, brutal-ized, and starving people reaching the point of desperation rise up against their oppressors. These are not so much revolutions as insur-rections. The Jews in the Warsaw ghetto fighting back against the Na-zis was certainly genuine. Similarly, war is sometimes unavoidable—call it irreconcilable differences, or defending one's homeland. How-ever, since around 1776, the concept of fighting the good fight has become a popular psychological tool for gaining salvation.

Take, for example, the American Revolution. The words them-selves conjure up images of muskets and redcoats, *taxation without rep-resentation,* the Boston massacre and the Boston Tea Party. We think of George Washington at Valley Forge and Thomas Jefferson writing the Declaration of Independence. But a closer examination reveals that something else was going on—some of the fomenters of the Revolu-tion, I would suggest, were motivated more by existential fears than by unfair taxes.

Patrick Henry, an early rabble-rouser of the American Revolu-tion, had failed at storekeeping and tobacco farming. After a short period of studying, he squeaked through his bar exam and became a lawyer. He was a complete unknown when he stood up in court and became a defiant hero by declaring that the King of England "degen-erates into a tyrant and forfeits all right to his subjects' obedience." The vast majority of colonists at that time did not agree with Henry and considered themselves loyal to the king. But his stance was heroic, and the attention he gained encouraged him to continue on the radical path, transforming him from an obscure failure into a pa-triot fighting for "the holy cause of liberty." By publicly condemning the king and urging revolution with his cry, "give me liberty or give me death!" he rewrote his life script. But what he really meant by his defiant rant was "Give me a sense of purpose or I'll die from insignifi-cance." For Henry, the "holy cause of liberty" was a religious crusade to give his life meaning.

The most successful colonial patriot/rabble-rouser was Sam Adams; but until he discovered his role as a revolutionary, his life had been a dead end. After graduating from Harvard, he failed at his first job at a counting house and was so lax and irresponsible (and possibly corrupt) as a tax collector that he was soon fired. He squandered his father's inheritance and took handouts from friends and relatives. It was customary to speak of "poor Adams as a failure."[3] But as a revolutionary agitator he was extraordinary. His dedication was consuming. He was the organizing genius who channeled the unruly street gangs of Boston into acts of violence against the British. He arranged to smash the presses of colonial newspapers loyal to the British and had the editors beaten up and run out of town. At forty, he was a drifting ne'er-do-well. At forty-one, he was a revolutionary, a patriot, a fighter for noble causes, a person of worth, notoriety, and purpose.

Colonial Patriot Benjamin Rush said of Adams, "He once acknowledged to me that the independence of the United States . . . had been the first wish of his heart . . . He said to me if it were revealed to him that 999 Americans out of 1000 should perish in a war for liberation, he would vote for that war, rather than see his country enslaved." This is the kind of statement we regularly hear from zealots. What Adams really meant was, "I don't care how many people have to die in order for me to pursue my artificial and defiant heroism. It's the only way my life can have meaning."

Perhaps the best example of rewriting a life script was another colonial patriot, Thomas Paine, who completely reinvented himself. Actually, he wasn't an American but an Englishman who arrived in the colonies at the eleventh hour, in late 1774. In England he had been a failure, unable to work steadily or successfully as a staymaker (corsets), tax collector, English teacher, tobacconist, and grocer. After his last failure, at the age of thirty-seven, he sold his furniture, divorced his wife, and set sail for the new world where he hoped to get a fresh start.

In England, he had never shown any interest or concern about the colonies and had evinced no political philosophy, but after landing in America, he sniffed the pungent air of revolution and became intoxicated. Within a year he took up the cause with unbridled fervor. "The sun never shined on a cause of greater worth," he wrote. Not to be outdone by Patrick Henry, Paine spiked his words with endless exclamation points, firing them like darts at the reader. "Oh, ye that love mankind! Ye that dare oppose not only the tyranny, but the tyrant, stand forth! Every spot of the old world is overrun by oppression! Freedom hath been hunted round the globe." His pamphlet, *Common Sense,* convinced many undecided colonists to join the cause.

His attempt at reinventing himself by adding a heroic chapter to his failed life succeeded, and no one ever called him Clumsy Clyde again. He transformed himself into a freedom fighter of world renown and then went on to gain immortality as an admirable historic figure. When the French revolution broke out in 1789, he couldn't resist getting involved and sailed into the storm with the self-important comment that, "Where freedom is not, there is my country." What he really meant was, "Where freedom is not, there is my immortality project. There is my opportunity to gain distinction here on earth and salvation in eternity."

They Were Not Patriots, They Were Pilgrims

The colonial patriots are certainly not in the same category as terrorists who kill innocents, but they wanted the revolution first and foremost to save their eternal souls. They sent people to their deaths because their cause gave their lives meaning. We call them patriots and celebrate their courage and success, but they were not patriots; they were spiritually dysfunctional *pilgrims.* They were lost souls wandering in the desert in search of immortality. They did not fight the revolution so much as worship it. It was their false god. It was their holy mission. It was their salvation.

Remember that salvation means living a worthwhile life so one can die content in knowing his one shot at existence was a good one, and that he has added something to creation. Remember also that these men were failures in everyday life. They were generally in their late thirties and were already thinking that they would never achieve success. They embraced the revolution to infuse their lives with meaning and success, which would carry them into eternity.

Of course, if Patrick Henry, Sam Adams, and Thomas Paine could read this chapter, they would roundly reject every syllable. They would argue that they were motivated by the purest of intentions, that their revolutionary fervor was precipitated by the tyrannical injustices perpetrated by the King.

But they would be wrong.

Followers of heroic holy missions are always–in their own minds–sincere. They must believe in their cause because to do otherwise, to doubt for a minute its worthiness and transcendence would mean that their road to a meaningful life and immortality is a false one.

There is always a rationalization for their actions, always a justification, always some demonized enemy that must be destroyed for the good of humanity. In their own minds, their intentions are honorable and their actions noble, otherwise the fabrication crumbles along with their salvation. And I can think of no better example than the radical student movement of the sixties.

The Weathermen: Any Means Necessary

A news report on August 22, 2003, which I read out in the backyard while Uncle Sonny smoked, provides an equally dramatic example of the destructive and often irrational nature of the spiritually dysfunctional. The 1960s' radical, Kathy Boudin, was finally paroled after twenty-two years in prison.

In 1981, Boudin was involved in a robbery that left a security guard and two police officers dead. At the time of her capture, she was already on the run for a 1970 explosion that accidentally killed three of her cohorts.[4] Boudin was a member of the Weather Underground, the most intense and violent of the 1960s' leftist groups. The Weathermen were convinced that the United States was a vile country–inherently racist, greedy, materialistic, and unequal–in which capitalism enriched the few and exploited the many. And they, along with their so-called idealistic generation, were going to change all that.

Because their cause was noble and unselfish, "any means necessary," (a favorite phrase of leftist radicals), was justified.

The radical sixties was a classic holy mission. Liberating the downtrodden, bringing down the corrupt and capitalist American government, fighting against racism, war, and unfairness was inspiring, noble, and spiritually intense. By declaring war against "the establishment," the radical students were rewriting their life scripts.

At her parole hearing in August, 2001, Boudin explained that self-doubt had led her into the radical life. "The very identity of being underground gave me a certain moral identity. I kind of saw myself as Joan of Arc."[5] It couldn't be clearer than that. She wanted Joan of Arc's heroism and defiance. She wanted a holy mission. She wanted a transcendent cause linked to God. Destroying evil "Amerika" was her chosen cause.

Susan Stern, whom we discussed earlier, was also in the Weather Underground. She had undergone a number of identity switches including hippie and women's libber in order to gain esteem and respect, but when she discovered the Weathermen, it was even more intense than a religious conversion because she *psychologically fused* with the movement and lost all sense of who she was.

> There was only one reality in my life. Weathermen. I fell in love with the concept. My white knight materialized into a vision of world-wide liberation. I ceased to think of Susan Stern as a woman; I saw myself as a revolutionary tool. Impetuously and compulsively, I flung myself at the feet of the revolution and debauched in its whirlwind for the next few years . . . my family, my past all faded into dreary insignificance. For the first time in my life that I could remember, I was happy.[6]

Here is a young woman who personifies the spiritually dysfunctional. Her identity switches were attempts at rewriting her life script by creating a new and heroic persona. Her compulsive embracing of the Weathermen was purely spiritual. She saw the light and was transformed. Just as a religious convert might fall to the ground and worship at the feet of Jesus, she flung herself "at the feet of the revolution." Just as Christians fuse with the body of Christ by taking communion, she ceased to be Susan Stern, but psychologically and spiritually grafted herself to the movement. In a sense she *became* the revolution. Just as a nun marries God, Susan Stern wedded and welded herself to transcendence. The "white knight" that saved her was the fantasy holy mission, which she called a "vision of world-wide liberation." She was happy for the first time in her life because she had purpose. She was happy because she replaced her failed past with a vibrant and exciting present.

But the intensity she felt for her cause simply wasn't warranted. America in the sixties wasn't paradise, but it was hardly a repressive tyranny in need of revolution. The holy mission of "world-wide liberation" was a grandiose, self-inflating fantasy. Susan Stern was the peasant going off on a Crusade. She was Sam Adams at the Boston

Tea Party. She was Paul on the road to Damascus. She was Hitler falling to his knees in "rapturous enthusiasm." She was Kathy Boudin and Joan of Arc. She was every holy warrior finding gratification in defiant heroism. She could have been speaking for all of them, and the millions of others who thirst and burn (and sometimes die) for distinction when she said of her commitment to the Weathermen: "Standing up there on that platform . . . I felt that I had finally connected with my own personal destiny; that I had a place, a function in life." And she could have added, "I had a place in eternity."

Trampled Underfoot

Wars and revolutions will never go away because they provide a dramatic and transcendent spiritual quest. The Western world has long believed that education, science, reason, secularism, and prosperity would eventually negate the emotional, irrational, and destructive need for war. But emotion generally defeats reason in the minds of men. Prosperity does not necessarily make us happy, education does not guarantee rationality, and secularism does not motivate like spirituality. When men are caught in the emotional vortex of a nationalistic holy mission in which they glimpse eternity—science, logic, and reason are trampled underfoot.

22

feasting on ambrosia: good immortality projects

This is the true joy of life, the being used for a purpose recognized by yourself as a mighty one; the being thoroughly worn out before you are thrown on the scrap heap; the being a force of Nature instead of a feverish little clod of ailment and grieving, complaining that the world will not devote itself to making you happy.

—George Bernard Shaw

Part 2 has focused on spiritually dysfunctional individuals who, driven by religious intensity, fabricate heroism and holy missions and who are often harmful to themselves and others. But is there such a thing as a *good* immortality project? The answer is, yes, of course, and they are easy to spot.

Ascending to Zeus

The historian/philosopher Will Durant described the pleasure of good immortality projects thusly: "The secret to significance and content is to have a task which consumes all one's energies, lifts the individual out of himself, and makes human life a little richer than before."

People consumed by creative and challenging tasks seem to be the happiest and most fully alive. Michelangelo could almost feel a sculpture bursting from the stone. Norman Rockwell had an unfinished painting on his easel when he died. Thomas Edison was a tireless worker who produced a mind-boggling 3.5 million pages of notebooks and letters and 1,093 patents.

History has its share of these people, and it is no coincidence that their drive and addiction to their chosen fields made them part of history. Perhaps the clearest statement of this creative love was the ancient astronomer Ptolemy: "Mortal as I am, I know that I am born for a day, but when I follow the serried multitude of the stars in their circular course, my feet no longer touch the earth; I ascend to Zeus himself to feast me on ambrosia, the food of the gods.[1]

Another example is Albert Schweitzer—a theologian, philosopher, physician, and music scholar—who dedicated his life to missionary work in Africa. "To observe him at work at his hospital in Lambarene," wrote Norman Cousins, "was to see human purpose bordering on the supernatural."[2] His task was all-consuming, monumental, and never-ending. "The essence of Dr. Schweitzer," wrote Cousins, "was purpose and creativity."

Will Durant, who was producing huge volumes right up to his death at the age of ninety-six, was also the essence of purpose and creativity. He was probably describing himself when he defined his "ideal character" thusly:

> What he has above all is will. Not wills, but will; not a medley of ambition and desires canceling one another in unreconciled hostility, but a unity of aim, an order and perspective and hierarchy of purpose, molded in his character by some persistent and dominating design. His will is disciplined; . . . he produces work, not fragments or "impressions;" and he is so absorbed in his effort that he never thinks what comments it will evoke . . . He dies never doubting that life was a boon, and only sorry that he must leave the game to younger players.[3]

This is spiritual purpose; this is what an immortality project was meant to be. This is what the sixties gurus called self-actualization. It is the opposite of fabricated; it is genuine. People like Durant and Schweitzer do not need to rewrite their life scripts because the story is already satisfying. It is not something everyone can possess, but those who have it are feasting on ambrosia.

A Miniature Circus

Must one have a raging talent to ascend to Zeus? No, only a raging interest. Consider Howard Tibbals. At the age of seven, Howard watched a huge circus roll into town. Fascinated by the logistics of putting the whole thing up and then taking it down, he decided to build his own circus. For fifty years he has carved, painted, and purchased almost a million pieces for his own miniature 1930s-style circus. Authentic down to the tiniest detail, it includes 15,000 stakes, five miles of rigging cord, 6,000 knives, forks, and spoons, and 7,000 individual folding chairs. During his high school summers, Tibbals would hitch rides to catch-up with a circus in Columbus, Ohio, and would spend all day sneaking around taking pictures.

"I never quit," he said. "If I'm building a circus wagon, I go to sleep looking at photographs of old wagons. I keep them on the nightstand beside me. Everything I see I wonder, 'Where can I use this?'"

Some would say that Howard Tibbals is one-dimensional. I would say he is feasting on ambrosia.

Flow

It could reasonably be argued that Tibbals, Schweitzer, Durant, and others were not worrying about immortality. They weren't on a quest for significance. Eternity had nothing whatever to do with their intensity. They pursued their earthly projects for one simple reason—they loved what they were doing. While it's true that they had a genuine love of their projects, and it's also true that we can't get into their heads, it's a good guess that they also had a sense that they were each fulfilling their life's purpose.

During one of those trips with Uncle Sonny to Blackhawk, I came across this very concept in a new book by Charles Murray.

I left my uncle at the slots with a pack of cigarettes, a cup of coffee, and a cup full of quarters (he was in heaven) and headed through town to my favorite reading spot in the gazebo by the brook. It was already March, approaching my uncle's one-year anniversary in Colorado. The weather was extraordinary—close to seventy degrees with a blue-painted sky. If one had placed a bet in the casinos that a cloud would roll by, one would have lost that bet.

Murray's book, *Human Accomplishment: The Pursuit of Excellence in the Arts and Sciences, 800 BC to 1950,* explained why Western Europe has had such an amazing outpouring of talented and creative people during the last six hundred years. The book was about people with purpose who loved what they did and who immersed themselves in projects for the pure pleasure of it. Those who are engrossed by a challenging and stimulating project achieve something called *flow*, described by Murray as "what happens when one is fully engaged in an activity—the kind of absorption that leads one to lose track of time and of everything else that is going on around them. Flow is human enjoyment in its most meaningful form. You are not saying to yourself, 'How enjoyable this is,' but are completely involved in the actual experience of enjoyment."[4]

Murray suggests that religious people have an easier time pursuing these great purposes than agnostics or atheists. "Devotion to a human cause," he wrote, "whether social justice, the environment, the search for truth, or an abstract humanism, is by its nature less compelling than devotion to God."[5] *But*—I would suggest that Murray is wrong for this reason: If we make our purpose god-*like*, if our devotion to the project is as gratifying as our devotion to God, and if we are feasting on ambrosia in the process, then it becomes god and salvation in one, and is therefore just as compelling. Even if it's invented, it is still powerful. The effort we expend on these projects often rivals and sometimes surpasses devotion to god, for better and for worse.

Show Me the Money

I found something else in Murray's book; I found the kind of people I had been looking for. "My point," wrote Murray, "is that a person with a strong sense of *this is what I have been put on earth to do* is more likely to accomplish great things than someone who doesn't."[6] In addition, Murray wrote, "a common theme in the biographies of the giants (and in the analyses of creative people in general) is that their work expresses the purpose they saw in their lives, a purpose they usually had felt before they had achieved anything."[7]

Here we have no drifting entities from the Bronson book, complaining that they can't find their place in life. Shakespeare, Newton, Aristotle, Einstein, Darwin, Michelangelo, and Beethoven never doubted their life's purpose. Murray is quick to point out that these people weren't saints. Money, power, and fame were part of their motivation. "Some were vain about their celebrity or bitter about their obscurity."[8] But they knew what they were meant to do, and that overwhelming drive gave focus, direction, substance, joy, and even transcendence to their lives.

"So, show me the money!"

"What?" I looked up from the book.

An aging man with a paunch and a baseball cap was talking to me. "You winning anything?"

I had been absorbed in the book, writing notes in the margins, and underlining passages. He thought it was a book on gambling and that I was figuring out the odds.

"No," I said, a bit startled, "It's not a book on gambling."

"So you're not winning?" he said, not seeming to hear me.

I nodded. He shrugged and walked off. And I wondered if my absorption in the book was itself a form of flow.

23

waiting for the secular messiah

I can understand Fred's drive to write a book and admire him for it. Fred, probably like most of us who don't believe in eternal life of the soul, would like to leave some trace of himself that would live longer than he. "Paper tombstones," after all, can be more enduring than those of granite. . . . Considering the divergence of your backgrounds, I think your and Fred's marriage has done very well.
—Dr. Frank Leitnaker, Becky's dad

The only moment of unalloyed happiness I ever had was when I received a wire from Harper telling me that they would publish *The True Believer.* I felt like a darling of fate, an immortal raised above the common run of humanity. There were no doubts about my worthiness and no fear about the future.[1]
—Eric Hoffer, *Truth Imagined*

It's easy enough to find people who love their creative and productive immortality projects. But how can any of us know if our pursuits are good or bad, productive or destructive? As we have already seen, we are all quite adept at fooling ourselves. In our own minds, our goals are always genuine, altruistic, noble, useful, important, meaningful, and so on. How do we distinguish between good and bad methods of justifying our lives?

For the most part, good immortality projects derive from genuine interests and talents, are generally not harmful to others and one's self, and have a positive outcome. Bad projects are fabricated and . . .

It's Just Your Opinion

"That's okay as far as it goes," Becky interrupted, "but you're basically just giving *your* opinion, and that's not good enough. You need an objective set of standards."

"Well, it's not rocket science. If you blow people up in a crowded market place, it's bad, and if you discover a cure for polio after years of effort, it's good."

"But it's not that simple," she said, pleasantly but firmly.

"I didn't say it was simple, but some things are obvious."

"And some things are not so obvious."

"Like what?"

"Like being unwilling to lay one's ambition down," she said, harkening back to a night in Germany so many years ago, when she and I and C.S. Lewis listened to Johnny Mathis.

"Like I didn't," I said.

She nodded "Like you didn't."

We had been reading *Tuesday's With Morrie* together at night as an activity we could do together. It was Becky's idea. It would bring us closer. I was too absorbed in my books. I was always too absorbed in my books. On the surface, my reading and writing was a positive and productive immortality project that didn't hurt others, but as Becky has often pointed out, if you are not willing to lay it down, someone, somewhere, somehow will invariably be hurt.

I wasn't laying it down.

As a result, there were periodic scenes. She wanted my attention, and I wanted significance. So after one of those scenes, where I was forced to feel miserable and helpless, we decided to read together at night. *Tuesdays With Morrie* seemed like a good place to start.

Thus, while there is often an element of joy in one's pursuit of a meaningful life, there is often an element of pain. It is not as simple as good or bad. Even when one's immortality project is genuine, it can also have negative consequences. So, in this regard, our marriage was spiritually dysfunctional, not only because of the religious disparity but also because I worshipped my god a little too much. So before we go any further in trying to distinguish between good and bad pursuits, we'll take a look at an immortality project that has elements of both—my own.

A Short History of Four Decades

Some time around 1980, I came to the conclusion that I was more religious than Becky. We both independently determined that life was too short to waste time on say, reading novels, when there was so much to learn. We both became more focused than ever on our immortality projects. She on the church, me on my books. She had her Messiah, and I had mine. But was I waiting for a messiah or waiting for Godot?

From my early twenties to the Big Six O, I lived parallel lives. Standard job and standard family on the one hand, but driven to write by the triple furies of genuine interest, questing for significance, and existential dread. At any given time over those decades, I had manuscripts circulating. Or letters to agents. Or stories to magazines. Or book proposals to publishers. Or queries to syndicates. Every day I approached the mailbox with a hopeful expectation, sort of the way the Jews approach the Sabbath. As the Friday Sabbath nears, there is an upsurge of hope among the righteous that perhaps *finally* on this Sabbath the Messiah will appear. And in a very real sense, I was looking for my own messiah in the daily mail. Maybe this will be the day the acceptance arrives that will not only change my life, but justify it. And since my mind automatically puts everything into prose, as I approached the mailbox, day after day, decade after decade, I wrote the scene in my head.

I was sitting at my desk grading papers in our Bronx apartment soon after I graduated from college, when Dad came in with the day's mail. "You've got a letter here from Random House," he said with a hint of curiosity.

It had been a particularly bad day. My second hour class was as insane as ever, and the snow was piling up in Stuttgart, Germany. I made a quick stop at my mailbox in the teacher's lounge, where all the talk was about Nixon's election, and there among the usual blizzard of notes was an envelope . . .

Four days after Ashlie was born, I was back at school, trying to concentrate, and counting the moments until I could get home and hold her in my arms. I made my way to the mailbox in the office, talking first with the counselor, then to a colleague. I grabbed the mail, and found a large clasp envelope which . . .

I had a million errands to run after school: bank, commissary, dry cleaning, check the mail, and pick up Melanie at the elementary school play rehearsal. Another torrential tropical rain was falling on Okinawa. I closed the huge Wilson golf umbrella and watched the rivulets of rain pool on the floor. I dialed the combination and found a letter from my mother, assorted junk, and a letter from that New York agent saying . . .

We came home from a long day of Christmas shopping at the Greeley, Colorado mall. I was anxious to get back to the computer, but impatiently checked the four voice mails. The last one was from a publisher who raved about . . .

After dinner, we talked to Mandy about how her the baby was doing, watched the news from Iraq, and then I headed down to the den to work on the chapter about immortality projects. I checked the e-mail and to my great surprise was a note from . . .

The Greyhound and the Englishman

During those years of fantasizing around mailboxes, I rendered unto Caesar the things that are Caesar's, and unto my god the things that were god's. Jesus's warning to Christians two thousand years ago was to give God his due, but not to forget that one had to also function in the secular world and obey its laws. My rendering unto Caesar was to have a job and go about the usual business of living. My rendering unto god was the pursuit of my immortality project. Shortly after my thirtieth birthday, I took a sabbatical and spent a year in Spain rendering unto Caesar not at all.

In January 1974, I strapped a tent to the luggage rack of my car and headed for Gibraltar. I had already been in Spain four months. I was tired of speaking German to the Germans I had met and tired of struggling to understand Spanish. I wanted English. I had taken a year off from teaching to live in Spain and write the Great American Novel. After meandering through Switzerland, France, and Spain, I had ended up in a small stucco bungalow overlooking the beach on the *Costa del Sol,* reputed to have "the best weather in continental Europe." But it was time to move on. Gibraltar seemed like a good change of pace.

Unfortunately, the road to Gibraltar was closed. I sat on the hood of my car at the end of a deserted highway, squinting alternately at my maps and the barrier in the middle of the road. A large sign announced that a territorial spat between Spain and Great Britain had closed the only road to Gibraltar. I could hear English radio stations, but unless I wanted to ferry back to Morocco and then to Gibraltar, I would have to forego it.

I ended up down the coast from Malaga and for the princely sum of one hundred dollars per month, rented another bungalow where I continued pounding out the novel on a manual typewriter.

Every morning I walked along the empty beach, enjoying the wonderful salty odor and sounds of the ocean, clearing my head, going over dialogue, and disappearing into the inner world of the novel.

One morning, around eight a.m., I came across a lone man on the beach, sitting on a blanket.

"Nice day," he said, probing to see if I spoke English. Yes, I said, it is. And being the only two people on the beach, we got to talking. He had dark hair, pale skin, and was edging towards paunch. Yes, I'm an American, I told him. Yes, I took a year off to write a great novel. Yes, I've been rejected dozens of times.

And then he gave me a bit of advice. You have to assume, he told me, that all those editors are crazy. You can't get discouraged. They don't know what they're talking about. Good stuff often gets rejected. You know you are writing well. Rejections show you are keeping at it. The editors are making a mistake.

It was as if he had been there, as if he had been a writer. He just knew what I was going though.

We said our good-byes, and I continued along the beach, trying to jump back into the book where I would be living the scene; but something nagged at me. It was nice enough to get such encouragement from a total stranger, and no, there was nothing mystical about it. But there is a point to this story and in order to get to it, we need to jump back two months to when I was living in that first bungalow along the coast near Fuengirola.

My neighbor in that complex was a retired German waiter named Wolfgang. He gave credence to the idea that people bought dogs that were similar to themselves. Wolfgang looked like his greyhound, Fella. Both were sleek, lithe, and gray. Wolfgang had a gray spade beard and a gray combover. Many a night we walked over the hills to a little restaurant where we devoured fresh grilled squid. Wolfgang's wife had died the year before, and with nothing to do, he spent the winter in Spain, perfecting his Spanish. He was something of a linguist. His English was excellent, and he taught me lots of colloquial German expressions.

The problem was that he kept Fella on a leash. Although he walked the dog in the hills behind the bungalows, the dog never got to run. Most of the time he was tethered to a leash out back.

Spain had packs of wild, abandoned dogs. They weren't wolves, just an assortment of cute little dogs scavenging for food. Of course, when they trotted by, Fella would go crazy, not only because of his territorial urges, but also because he never got to run. He was never free. Here was a greyhound, born to run, tied forever to his leash.

One night, around nine, Wolfgang banged on my door. Fella had escaped. Would I help? We drove around the complex and into the hills, got out and shouted for the dog, then walked to the beach. The moon was bright, the surf was gentle and foaming. And there he was! "*Com, Fella, com, comst du hier.*" But the dog would have none of it. He was racing along the edge of the surf having the time of his life. He didn't care about Wolfgang.

I kneeled down at the water's edge, sneakers soaked, the waves gently lapping. Kneeling is somehow less threatening to a dog. Fella crept close to me, but when I reached out he darted away, as if he were playing a game.

Eventually, Wolfgang got the leash around him and returned the dog to his tether in the yard.

And I was thinking about all this after those encouraging words from the Englishman. It took a while for those incidents to coalesce. There is a point here . . .

About a decade later it came to me. *The Englishman's advice was worthless.* Something Fella would have understood.

Fella was a greyhound. He was born to run. His genetic imperative insisted he run. He hungered to get out there and race around the hills. Yet he was denied this by Wolfgang. No one had to whisper to him, "Now Fella, when I let you go, I want you to run. Don't be afraid, there, boy, and I'll give you a dog biscuit if you race across the beach." Similarly, no one had to tell me to ignore the rejections, to keep at it, to keep writing, that the editors were mistaken, and so on. Unlike the unfocused people Po Bronson commiserated with, I knew my calling. The dog and I both knew what we were meant to do.

What Should the Teacher Do?

The lengthy novel I had written in Spain has been gathering dust in my basement for over thirty years. It became increasingly evident that if writing was an immortality project, I was going to have to become immortal to see it come to pass.

By the end of 1996, I had been rendering unto Caesar for almost three decades, and it was getting old. Sometimes I went through the day in a cynical funk.

Here's Mr. Singer walking the dog in the morning.

Here's Mr. Singer pulling into the middle school parking lot.

Here's Mr. Singer putting the key in the door of his classroom.

Here's Mr. Singer putting the aim of the lesson on the board.

What lesson are we doing today?

Was the New Deal successful?

How did Athens become the most important city-state?

Why did the Boston Tea Party lead directly to the American Revolution?

How did Napoleon gain power in France?

What caused the Protestant Reformation?

Why has the Constitution been successful?

Why did Rome change from a Republic to an Empire?

Why was the United States unable to remain neutral during World War I?

How did the feudal system operate?

Why did the Renaissance begin in Italy?

Why am I still here?

Why am I still here?

TODAY'S LESSON:

"WHAT SHOULD THE TEACHER DO WITH THE REST OF HIS LIFE?"

"OK, class, what do you think? Is it time for Mr. Singer to admit it's never going to happen? Is it time for him to quit?"

Several hands go up.

The teacher calls on Lakisha.

"Oh, I don't think he is capable of quitting."

"What do you mean by that, Lakisha?"

"Well, he's been doing it for decades. He can't just stop."

"Besides," says Chris, "he still believes he has something to say. Still believes with a break here or there he can get published."

"But isn't he being unrealistic?" asks the teacher. "I mean, after almost thirty years, isn't it time he accepted reality? We have to give him credit for tenacity, but at this point, it should be obvious it's never going to happen."

Several more hands go up. The teacher calls on Debbie.

Debbie says, "I agree. The fact is that there are plenty of talented people out there, but only room for a few, so even if he's good, even if he's great, it doesn't matter."

"OK," says the teacher. "Let's look at this way. What are his alternatives at this point? We'll list them on the board."

Paul raises his hand in the back of the room. "I think he should just sit back and enjoy his life. Enjoy his kids, retire to Colorado, read, watch movies . . ."

"That's ridiculous," Naomi interjects. "He'd go crazy. He's said it himself a million times that the only way to live is to be embroiled in a project, to be so energized that you can't wait to jump out of bed and get back to it. He needs to retire and work full time on his books."

"That would take years of work," says the teacher, playing devil's advocate. "Should he make such a commitment?"

"What would he do instead," said Chris. "Watch soap operas?"

"And there is something else to consider," Anita adds. "The guy is fifty-two. He is well aware of his mortality and that we have to prove our worth before death catches up to us. He knows he's in a race and he knows he's losing that race."

Juan was frantically waving his arm in the air. "Like don't forget his father's last words: Time is precious."

"But what exactly did that mean? That he should mellow out and enjoy life instead of obsessing over impossible goals. That he should enjoy his time?"

Juan was shaking his head. "No, man, it meant that he is running *out* of time, that he should retire and write that book."

The bell rang, the class filed out, the teacher packed his papers, turned off the computers, switched off the lights, closed the door, locked the door, retired, returned to the States, started teaching at a university, and wrote a five-hundred-page book called *The Quest for Significance,* followed by another huge tome, *The Crisis of 2020,* explaining how home-grown zealots on holy missions are leading the country into social upheaval.

Each was rejected hundreds of times

Then Uncle Sonny came to Colorado . . .

Sounds Like You're on an Ego Trip

"I think you should leave this whole chapter out," Becky said. "It sounds like you're on an ego trip."

She read this chapter at the end of August, ten years after we had returned to the States. We were both embroiled in our various projects. I was finishing up a course on the Renaissance and the Reformation at the university. She was gearing up for another year of writing complex theological papers for her master's in theology. Uncle Sonny continued his weekly eruptions about going back to the Bronx.

I agreed with her. "I know, I had mixed feelings about it. It was fun to write but on the other hand I sometimes cringe writing about myself."

"So why do it?"

"Because, we are both examples of religious intensity. We are characters in our own book, and there is a certain literary responsibility to carry it though. I really do want those *paper tombstones*. It's the only road I have to salvation."

"There's another road to salvation," she said.

I looked at her with a mock cynical expression.

"Well, it's true."

"You have your gods," I said with a good-natured prod. "And I have mine."

"But you can have both! You don't have to give up your writing. God wants you to be who you are."

"This is exactly what I've always said. I am who I am. I can't believe what I don't believe."

"I know you feel that way. I know you think that your non-believing is an impenetrable wall, that nothing can break its way in. You can't imagine how it could happen."

"That's right, I can't. I've said it enough times. How can you change a lifetime mindset? People who suddenly convert have really been looking for answers. You know, 'seek and ye shall find.'"

"But that's not true, you *are* seeking, you're just not convinced it's God you're looking for. You have a prejudice against God being the answer."

"No, I'm just rejecting the answer. Look, I've given it decades of thought, and I've come to a rational conclusion about what I believe and what I don't believe. If it's a prejudice, it's based on facts and reasoning."

"But it's still a prejudice. You have said many times that God can't be the answer because He's supernatural, and the supernatural doesn't exist–and that's a prejudice."

I shook my head. "But I'm not against religion; I'm for it. It brings people comfort. It promises them eternal life. Don't you think I want eternal life? Of course I do. I'm almost sixty. I'm running out of time."

"I know," she said softly. "But there's still time. I haven't given up on you, and neither has God."

24

thomas aquinas weighs-in on immortality projects

Since . . . Happiness is to be gained by . . . certain acts, we must in due sequence consider human acts, in order to know by what acts we may obtain Happiness, and by what acts we are prevented from obtaining it.

—Saint Thomas Aquinas, *Summa Theologica*

Now we need to get back to the question Becky raised. How do we determine if our own immortality project is good or bad? How can we know if our attempts at justifying our lives are worthwhile or worthless, or even worse, harmful to ourselves or others? My trip to Spain to write a book seems to be in the realm of *good;* the interest was genuine, and it hurt no one. But retreating to my den night after night, leaving Becky alone with the kids, was admittedly a negative. Becky is right—we need an objective paradigm, and she found one with Saint Thomas Aquinas.

The Good Act According to Thomas Aquinas

"I think there could be a parallel between how St. Thomas evaluates a 'good act' and how you could evaluate a good immortality project," Becky said. "When Thomas looks at a good or moral act he sees . . .

"Wait a minute," I interrupted. "You called him *Thomas*. Are you on a first name basis with a Saint of the Catholic Church? I mean, don't you think you should call him *Saint* Thomas. Or at the very least, show some deference and call him *Mister* Aquinas.

"*Fred!*"

"Really, Becky. Think about it. Would you refer to Pope John Paul II as 'John,' as if he were someone in your bowling league?"

Becky was shaking her head and laughing. "I'm not in a bowling league."

"Well, if you were?"

"Do you want this information or not?"

"Go ahead . . . but keep it respectful."

"The three elements that Thomas sees as necessary for a good act are the action, the intention, and the circumstances. First, there is the action, the who-did-what-to-whom. For example, let's say that you, my husband, gave me a kiss on the lips."

"Hmm, that sounds very interesting. Perhaps we should try it right now?"

Becky wasn't amused. "Do you want to talk about this or what?"

"I'd prefer the *what,* but go ahead."

"So, first you look at the three parts of the action. Husband giving a kiss on the lips to his wife is a good or at least a neutral act. But suppose that instead of you giving me the kiss, it was some stranger who grabs me in the mall. That changes the 'goodness' of the act. Or if it was not me you kissed, but someone else—again that changes the nature of the act."

"Especially if I'm kissing my brother-in-law, Big Dave," I interrupted.

She ignored me. "So the first thing to consider in evaluating an act is *who-did-what-to-whom.*

"Second, St. Thomas looks at the *intention* of the act. For example, let's say that your kiss is not one of affection. We have been fighting all week, but you don't want our dinner company to know, so you kiss me. Because there is an element of dishonesty, you don't have a good intention. The act that started out good has been spoiled by a dishonest intention."

"I think I'm getting a bad deal here," I said. "What if I am genuinely sorry and I want to make up and I am overwhelmed with your sweetness and charm, now that's not a bad intention is it?"

"That's a different intention. Making up could be an acceptable intention, but that brings us to St. Thomas's third element: *circumstance.* Circumstances usually have to do with *where, when,* and sometimes *how.* For example, the when and where of your apology, in front of dinner company, is not very appropriate. You should probably apologize in private where you could give a heartfelt apology, and I could respond in kind."

"I could apologize in private right now for all my many sins. What do you think?"

"I think you're being sarcastic as usual, but speaking of your many sins, we could return to your intentions on that first date of ours when I wouldn't go back to your apartment."

"That," I said suddenly animated, "is a perfect example of *good* intentions. There wasn't an ounce of deviousness. I just wanted to spend more time with you. That was all I had in mind. It was quite obvious nothing was going to happen. And since it was a 'good act,' why did you turn it down?"

Becky shook her head and smiled that knowing smile. "Because I couldn't be sure of your intentions."

Now it was my turn to shake my head. "It's not that you weren't sure; it's that you thought you *were sure.* You assumed the worst–that I was going to assault you or some such thing. But the truth is that I had no desire to put you in an uncomfortable situation. Therefore, my intentions were good, but your misinterpretation turned a good act into a questionable one."

"You're wrong, Fred. My 'misinterpretation' didn't change a good act into a questionable one. In fact, that brings us to another important point in Thomas's paradigm. What you just said is an example of a misunderstanding that people often have about acts and consequences. They think that consequences change an act; if an act has a bad outcome, then they think it wasn't a good act. But that is not necessarily true. So my negative reaction didn't change the fact that your invitation was 'good.' All of us can think of good *actions* that we have done, with the best of *intentions,* in appropriate *circumstances* that have had unforeseen negative consequences. That doesn't change the fact that it was a morally good act. We cannot always foresee how people will react or how events will unfold.

Dr. Mengele and Thomas Aquinas

"An even more common misunderstanding about consequences is that an evil act can be 'redeemed' by positive outcomes." Becky was in her element now–teaching. "Take someone like the Nazi doctor, Mengele, who performed horrific experiments on human beings in the concentration camps. Mengele argued that he was trying to make discoveries for the good of mankind, so not only were his intentions good, but also the consequences were potentially good. However, the Church would rightly say that an evil act is an evil act, regardless of the outcome. There is *nothing* that could have justified the terror, horror, and pain that so many innocent people suffered at the hands of the Nazi doctors. The act itself is evil. Period. You cannot do an evil act, even if it has a good intention or a good outcome."

"Mengele is an easy one," I said, "but how about something morally ambiguous, like embryonic stem cell research?"

"There is nothing morally ambiguous about it," Becky replied quickly. "Embryonic stem cell research removes a layer of cells and kills this small human person."

"But that's just your opinion. You think it's wrong because the Church frowns on anything resembling an abortion, but to me what is wrong is standing in the way of research that might end all sorts of diseases."

"I wasn't giving an opinion; I was simply stating a fact. Removing the cells kills a living being. And what kind of living being are we talking about? It is not a fish or a parakeet. It is a human person, a young person who is not fully herself or himself yet, but nevertheless already a unique person complete with a full genetic code."

"I'll tell you what a bad act is," I said, getting a bit worked up. "Sacrificing the health of millions of people because of the Church's interpretation of morality. Look, suppose you were faced with a choice—if aborting a fetus would ultimately have saved Johnnie's life, how could you possibly choose unborn cells over a living being? That," I said with finality, "would be the real immoral act."

She shook her head. "You are using Mengele's arguments again. You can't justify an evil act because it is for some greater good. The Church is trying to protect the human person; the human person must be protected from birth to death, or we begin down a slippery slope. Killing the embryo because some good might come from it is wrong."

Thinking Through Our Own Immortality Projects

It was obvious we weren't going to be agreeing on much, so let's get back to the purpose of this discussion: what makes an immortality project good? How can we know that the things we do are essentially good, not harmful and not self-delusional?

Here is Becky's version of St.Thomas's template that might be useful for those who are willing to look at their own immortality projects.

The Project Itself: Who-Does-What-to-Whom?

The who in immortality projects is, of course, always ourselves; I will refer to the creator of an immortality project as the *Designer*. It is important, however, always to ask: How will this project affect those with whom I have my closest relationships? The Designer needs to be sure that if the project affects the time or money of significant others, that he involves them in the decision making or planning.

Does what? There are obviously endless possibilities. The only limits would be that the action does not harm the health or welfare of others. It will likely produce something positive, creative, or innovative.

To whom: The Designer originally creates the project for his own personal satisfaction, so in this regard he is also the recipient. This is the feasting on ambrosia. In other cases the recipient is the family, the community, or even civilization as in the case of the invention of the car, the light bulb, or medical breakthroughs.

THE INTENTION

The greatest danger in the intention is self-deception. Our deepest motivations are often self-serving. We hope for recognition, fame, power, or some kind of ego-gratification; but because we can't admit that to ourselves, we unconsciously put on a mask of altruism, heroism, sacrifice, struggle, or nobility. Since we are not able to admit these motivations to ourselves, they stay beneath the surface and often drive us more powerfully than if they were openly acknowledged. These are the kinds of situations that usually lead someone else to pay the price for one's attempt at achieving a meaningful life.

A good intention focuses on the project itself, its validity, and the potential it holds to bring joy or health or well-being, etc. The sense of meaning exists in the project, and the Designer is pleased that it is successful. His own recognition is secondary. On the other hand, when recognition or fame are the driving force, then the project is *just a thing to be used* for oneself.

When is probably the most important circumstance in evaluation of a proposed project. For example, many parents delay the pursuit of degrees or prestigious jobs because their children might suffer as a result.

Immortality projects may or may not reap great rewards personally or financially. So the Designer should not be discouraged by the outcomes or consequences.

They Worship Their False Gods

The problem with this template, if I may interrupt Becky for a moment, is that while it makes sense, and some may use it to analyze or alter their behavior, those on holy missions *do not have the slightest inclination* to understand their actions. They have, after all, connected with destiny. They know with absolute certainty why they exist. Why should they question it? They love their holy missions, they worship their false gods, their eternal salvation is on the line, and woe be unto the person who tries to burst their existential bubbles.

Imagine trying to talk Susan Stern out of her "world-wide liberation"; imagine trying to convince suicide bombers that they are evil instead of holy; imagine attempting to reason with Samuel Adams as he rounded up thugs to throw the tea overboard . . .

"And imagine," said Becky, "trying to talk *you* into giving up your writing."

"That's completely unfair. My immortality project doesn't hurt anyone."

"Hmmm."

"Okay, it's true, I admit it. But the point is . . ."

And so, as the sun sets over the distant hills in streaks of orange and blue, we leave the happy couple once again agreeing on almost nothing. Tune in again to the next chapter where we hear Fred saying to Becky, "Then what about Butterfly the Tree Hugger?"

25

the joy of martyrdom versus veal piccata sauteéd lightly in a lemon sauce

If there is a meaning in life at all, then there must be a meaning in suffering. Suffering is an ineradicable part of life, even as fate and death. Without suffering and death human life cannot be complete.[1]

—Viktor Frankl, *Man's Search for Meaning*

The point I was trying to make at the end of the last chapter is that the Aquinas system is only useful for those who are willing and able to analyze their behavior. It can only work for people who recognize the value of self-examination and who have a certain integrity about their lives. Unfortunately, since most of us are convinced that our intentions are honest, genuine, and benign, we feel no need to analyze. As a result, many of our immortality projects go awry.

Consider the case of Julia "Butterfly" Hill, who lived eighteen stories high in a California redwood for two years to protest the logging efforts of the Pacific Lumber Company. She lifted food and supplies by a rope, bathed in a bucket, and slept on an eight-by-eight-foot plywood platform, covered by a tarp. She stayed there through howling winds and rainy winters. When she finally came down after reaching a compromise with loggers, she walked barefoot two miles to a press conference. She named the tree "Luna," and referred to the other trees as "ancient beings."[2]

Her actions had spirituality written all over them. Compare her experience to that of Simeon Stilites, a fifth-century Christian monk who lived atop a sixty-foot pillar for thirty years. He endured heat, cold, and rain. The circumference of his home was around three feet. A railing kept him from falling while sleeping. Disciples climbed a ladder to bring him food and water. He bound himself to the pillar with a rope that became embedded in his flesh, rotted, and became infested with worms. When worms fell from his flesh, he would pick them up and replace them, saying, "Eat what God has given you."

Good Butterfly or Bad Butterfly?

Was Butterfly's two-year stint on the tree altruistic or self-serving? Fabricated or genuine? Heroism or false heroism? In short, was her immortality project good or bad? Let's assume she's not married so she is not inconveniencing her husband or children. Let's also assume that the loggers were inconvenienced, but not overly so, since they could chop down other trees.

On the surface then, because the intention, the circumstances, and even the consequences were benign, her actions could be deemed acceptable. But it always comes back to the intent of the act, which is why subjectivity creeps into the picture. In her mind, her intent was noble and heroic; in my mind, she is doing it more for her own satisfaction than for her supposed cause. She puts on a public face of altruism, but she really does it for the good feeling of defiant heroism, or fighting the good fight. She wanted to struggle because when one puts out effort, when one suffers and sacrifices to pursue a righteous cause, then it is all the more satisfying. Both she and Stilites seemed to be saying, "If I endure pain, I am worthy; I have done something significant." Both were on holy missions. They wanted to be martyrs.

"But how can you know that?" Becky interjected once again.

"Maybe I can't know it in some absolute sense, but her motivation seems obvious to me. And in the end, in spite of the Aquinas paradigm, identifying spiritually dysfunctional holy missions will have an element of subjectivity in it. Remember, that no one on a holy mission could possibly think they have anything but the most selfless of motives, but it is often an existential delusion. They are motivated by a hidden psychological agenda. Those who choose martyrdom are, in my opinion, clearly on an artificial, spiritually dysfunctional quest.

"In addition, Hill had another motive. Nestled on her perch, high in the California redwood, she rewrote her life script."

The Nuclear Nuns

While I was mixing the morning coffee in mid-July 2003, and preparing to head over to Garden Square to take Uncle Sonny food shopping, Becky became engrossed in a front page article titled, *God's work facing man's judgment: as sentencing looms for missile protest, sisters don't regret their "joyful" disobedience.*[3]

I suppose any article about "God's work" would attract her attention.

"What do you think about those nuns?" I asked her, already halfway though the oatmeal.

She shrugged. "They're ridiculous. War is terrible, but if we don't fight back, if we don't have an army, then we become victims of the Stalins and Hitlers."

The Nuclear Nuns

The year before, three nuns in their fifties and sixties had broken into a missile silo about an hour from where we live. They hammered the silos' 110-ton concrete lid and painted crosses in their own blood. They were found guilty and their sentencing was due in less than a week.

Two years before, in a similar incident, they had spilled blood and pounded hammers on a jet fighter in Colorado Springs.

Why did they do it? "Our motivation was symbolic disarmament," said one. "Our intention was to stop these weapons."

"I believe I had to go there to stop a crime against humanity," said another. The existence of such weapons, she said "is a crime of genocide."[4]

To many they are heroes. Elizabeth McAllister, the widow of radical 1960s' priest Philip Berrigan, called them "extraordinary women." A local pundit wrote, "They are sort of like angels."[5] *The Denver Post* suggested that, "To supporters they are courageous, dedicated, faithful, wise—even martyrs."

Their real motivation, they tell us, is to serve God. "Whatever God asks of us, whatever we have to sacrifice, we will do it, and we will do it with joy," said Ardeth Platte.

They derive "joy" from the "sacrifice." But why joy? Because these actions give their lives meaning. To defy the American government, to be for peace, to struggle, to suffer, even to go to jail, is, for them, the defiant road to salvation, nothing less.

Consider what they have achieved by their civil disobedience. The world has taken notice. Thousands if not millions of people admire them, know they are heroic, and know they stand for goodness. *The more they suffer, the better they feel.* They want to go to jail, and every day in that prison will be an existential pleasure.

There are those who would say the nuns were sincere, but their actions were so outrageous and pointless that we can only conclude they were the opposite of sincere: they were on an artificial holy mission that had it all—defiance, heroism, and self-importance. In addition, they got to suffer for their cause. Suffering, they say, is good for the soul, but even more to the point, it is good for the immortal soul. For those who crave it, martyrdom is the ultimate high because it is the ultimate heroism. *To suffer for the cause is heroic; to fight for it is defiant; to die for it is cosmic.*

Coraggio's Italian Deli

The day the nuns were sentenced, I was reading about them in the local paper and munching on two slices of genuine New York pizza at Coraggio's, a small deli run by a New Jersey transplant, Tom Coraggio. Tom worked his buns off. He lived in that deli. He worked extraordinarily long hours, and I admired him for it.

Coraggio's was located across the street from the university. He had expected the student crowd to bring in business for his giant submarine sandwiches, but it didn't work out that way. Lunch crowds were big enough, but the rest of the time it was relatively empty.

I was at Coraggio's to order food for my oldest daughter's wedding reception. She had been married the previous March in Seattle, and now we were having a lawn party for the Colorado crowd. It was 4:45, Friday afternoon. Tom and his crew of five had been working since four in the morning preparing for his Friday night buffet. All you can eat for $12.95. And what a spread it was. Huge fresh shrimp, steamed mussels in the shell over linguini, veal piccata sautéed lightly in a lemon sauce, Chicken Sorrento—lightly breaded and fried with prosciutto, eggplant, and melted mozzarella in a tomato wine sauce. Fresh baked delicate pastries and breads. It was enough to make a grown man cry.

Tom showed me the mussels in linguini. "How does that look?" he said proudly.

It looked good enough to eat.

We ordered platters of baked ziti with meat, veal marsala, chicken breast with wine mushrooms, veal and peppers, filet of sole almondine, and so on.

Tom was in his late-forties, slim (in spite of all those culinary delights), a fringe of brown, graying hair. He was calm, almost placid. He worked steadily, consistently, rarely complaining, just dealing with life, taking pride in his efforts, making ends meet.

Kierkegaard would say he was tranquilizing on the trivial, that he was gaining his reason-to-be through work, as most of us do. But I wondered as I watched him bring out the platters, if there was not a hint of feasting on ambrosia (or in this case feasting on Scungilli and Calamari Marinara). Yes he worked hard, yes he struggled, but his dishes were works of art. He gained a sense of satisfaction in creating these foods. I don't know if Abraham Maslow would consider him self-actualized, but I think he was.

(In October 2005, Tom's dream came true when he opened a family-style Italian restaurant in Greeley, complete with an Italian lounge singer and beautiful frescoes of his ancestral home in Italy decorating the walls.)

The Fear That Fills Me Is Not Having Lived Hard Enough

Saturday's papers announced that the nuns were sentenced to up to three and a half years in prison. They were predictably defiant, energized, and happy. Just prior to the sentencing, Ardeth Platte said, "Whatever sentence I receive today will be *joyfully* [emphasis mine] accepted as an offering for peace. With God's help it will not alter my spirits." Carol Gilbert announced with bravado that "what the government fails to recognize is that long prison sentences will only energize the movement." [6] In other words, the more we suffer, the greater will be our martyrdom and the more effective will be our holy mission. And then Gilbert made a statement indicating her real motivation. "I don't fear going to prison. I don't fear loss of freedom to move about. I don't even fear death. The fear that fills me is not having lived hard enough, deep enough and sweet enough with whatever gifts God has given me."

The fear that fills her is that she has not struggled and suffered enough to feel worthy of eternity.

Defiant heroism is particularly gratifying when it takes struggle, sacrifice, and pain. People on holy missions are generally out of control and beyond reason. Once they have linked to their eternal reason-to-be, nothing can shake them from their cause which they see as the only way to invest their lives with meaning. The surface manifestation is almost always altruistic, i.e., "I'm doing this to help people," or, "I'm sacrificing for the betterment of mankind." But they are really motivated by the betterment of themselves.

A Relentless Quest for Martyrdom

Perhaps the best example of gaining immortality through suffering is the early Quakers, who, according to the eminent historian, Daniel J. Boorstin, "engaged in a relentless quest for martyrdom."[7] English Quaker, William Dewsbury, said he "as joyfully entered prisons as palaces, and in the prison-house, I sang praises to my God and esteemed the bolts and locks upon me as jewels."

"One after another of them," wrote Boorstin, "seemed to lust after hardships, trudging thousands of wilderness miles, risking Indians and wild animals, to find the crown of martyrdom. Never before perhaps have people gone to such trouble or traveled so far for the joys of suffering for their Lord."

In 1659, Quaker Mary Dyer was banished from Boston on pain of death for preaching to the Puritans. Undaunted, she soon returned to her preaching, and along with some others, was sentenced to death. Her response? "Yea, joyfully shall I go."

As she was marched to the scaffold she announced, "It is an Hour of the greatest Joy I can enjoy in this World. No Eye can see, No ear can hear, No Tongue can speak, No Heart can understand the sweet incomings and refreshings of the Spirit of the Lord which I now enjoy."

The two other Quakers were executed, but the Puritans did not have the stomach to hang a woman, and let her go, warning her not to return. However, Mary Dyer would not be denied a martyr's fate, and in less than a year she returned, and was again condemned to death. Standing on the gallows ladder, the Puritans again offered to spare her life if she promised to leave the colony. She refused and they hung her.

The key operating word is *joy*. While to others, martyrs are suffering, the martyrs themselves are in ecstasy because dying for the cause justifies their lives and earns them eternal salvation. Like the nuns in Colorado, their immortality projects are transcendent. Death and suffering are inconsequential; their martyrdom, joy, and salvation assured.

The *joy* in martyrdom underlines the fact that they do it for themselves, not because of their altruistic pretensions. They do it for the internal happiness and existential satisfaction that accompanies suffering for a holy cause.

If anyone doubts the joy of martyrdom and its link to god, they need only listen to the widow of Raed Abdel-Hamed Mesk, who blew himself up on an Israeli bus on August 20, 2003. "God gave Raed something he always dreamed of. All his life he dreamed of being a martyr."[8]

Struggle, Danger, and Death

In 1940, George Orwell wrote the following in an attempt to understand the Nazi phenomenon:

> Hitler knows that human beings don't only want comfort, safety, short working hours, hygiene, birth control, and, in general, common sense; they also, at least intermittently, want struggle and self-sacrifice, not to mention drums, flags, and loyalty parades. Where capitalism and even socialism, have said to people, "I offer you a good time," Hitler has said to them, "I offer you struggle, danger and death," and as a result a whole nation flings itself at his feet.

In the right circumstances, "struggle, danger and death" have a greater appeal than the dull monotony of security. We want problems to solve, an enemy to defeat, a devil to destroy. H.L. Menken may have been right when he said that human beings can only stand peace for so long before we begin to "fume and lather." Then we turn to wars and revolutions to feed our souls.

Hitler instinctively knew what motivated people, and he used those needs to manipulate an entire nation. He understood that suffering and sacrifice were actually desirable if it gave people meaning. All men, said Hitler, had an inner sense of unfulfillment:

> Slumbering somewhere is the readiness to risk some final sacrifice, some adventure, in order to give new shape to their lives.

They will spend their last money on a lottery ticket . . . The humbler people are, the greater the craving to identify themselves with a cause bigger than themselves, and if I can persuade them that the fate of the German nation is at stake, then they will become part of an irresistible movement embracing all classes.[9]

In other words, give people a sense of noble purpose, and they will follow you anywhere. When one suffers and even dies for a great cause, he endures the suffering happily, because he has gained the existential trophies he so craves. One would guess that reasonably rational creatures would prefer comfort to pain, yet time and again we choose to sacrifice, to suffer, and to die because struggle defines us and provides a sense of having earned personal significance which is a ticket to immortality.

More Respect

Tom Coraggio does not make headlines, but I have more respect for the way he pursues significance, than I do for tree-hugging martyrs and those headline-grabbing, self-serving, martyrdom-seeking nuclear nuns who say they are doing god's work, but are really just tending to their own immortal souls.

26

mandy in the middle

> The only way to be saved is to spend your lifetime on a pilgrimage
> . . . it is the journey itself that is his salvation.[1]
> —Psychotherapist, Sheldon Kopp, *If You Meet Buddha on the Road, Kill Him*

What about the rest of humanity?

We have talked quite a bit about holy missions and the spiritually dysfunctional fanatics who pursue them. But most people do not inhabit the religiously scorching edge on the one hand, or the cold blue extreme of atheism on the other. The majority of people do not exhaust their energies on false and destructive holy missions. Most inhabit the tepid middle. And for that point of view, we turn to my eldest daughter who inhabits the spiritual center of my religiously diverse family.

Mandy has always been running, but she is not sure where she is running to.

RUNNING: A PLAY IN THREE ACTS

Act I: A German Forest

I'm running with Mandy and Ashlie across a field toward a German forest.

It's 1988. Mandy is ten. Ashlie is eight. They can't keep up. Mandy is breathing heavily; Ashlie is almost gasping.

"Stop and rest," I tell them as I keep running back and forth to maintain my pace. It's all right, don't worry about keeping up. Just walk until you get your breath back." I run some circles around them. I don't want them to hyperventilate or god-knows-what. When they have sufficiently recovered, we plunge into the forest. It is dark and damp. Huge trees tower over us. We pass a giant ant hill. Mushrooms sprout erratically along the trail. Dead trunks lie on the ground. It's Saturday morning and the sun breaks through the trees, momentarily brightening the upper branches and splattering patterns on the ground.

"Let's walk for a minute." They are out of breath again. I know that someday they will outrun me. I'm getting older, and they're getting stronger. But that day seems years away. I can't imagine them as teenagers; it has no reality. We go deeper into the forest. There is no danger, nothing to worry about. It's not New York's Central Park. The German forest is free of thugs. Nevertheless, one feels somewhat edgy. The forest is quiet. Foreboding. The girls stay close to me. This afternoon, we'll go to the kiddie matinee to see *Pippy Longstocking, The Strongest Girl in the World.*

Act II: Japanese Streets

Mandy and I are jogging through the streets of Koza, Okinawa. We have been on the island for three months. We are heading towards Kadena Air Base. It's December 1990, but feels like May. She just turned thirteen. Her hair is pulled back in a ponytail that bobs all over the place. She is running ahead of me. I'm having a little trouble keeping up. I pick up the pace. She turns, sees me gaining, and starts to sprint. I can see her smiling. I am not smiling.

Every so often she turns to make sure I'm not catching up. After she turns again and races forward, I suddenly pick up the pace. This time I'll catch her before she realizes how close I've come. "Hurry up, Mandy," I'll say as I glide by. "Try to keep up, willya." I'm running quietly. I don't want her to hear me approaching, but she senses my presence, turns, and takes off.

I can't catch her.

By the time I reach home she has already raced up the stairs and is sitting on the couch. Our apartment is typically Japanese—sliding paper walls and tatami mat bedrooms. Becky and I worry that the girls will punch holes in the paper walls. I am out of breath. She looks very, very pleased with herself. Smug and amused, actually. "What took you so long, Dad?" she says.

"I knew you were going to say that," I say in between breaths.

It's the end of an era.

Act III: Running with Baby in Washington State

Mandy straps her nine-month-old son, Sam, into a three-wheel stroller used for joggers. It's a yuppie thing. They don't use these things in the inner cities of Los Angeles or Chicago, but here in Washington, there are plenty of *Young Upwardly Mobile Professionals,* of which she is one. It's June 2006. She is twenty-eight and training for a triathlon.

"How about if we jog together, like in the old days," I suggest.

"I'd rather just walk," she says, "then we can stop at Starbucks to talk."

We have a lot to talk about . . .

We wheel Sammy into Starbucks. He is not impressed, preferring a bottle to a cup of coffee. Mandy sips a caramel macchiato. Sammy sits on my lap and reaches for my frappuccino. I give him a taste of the whipped cream. He seems to like it and reaches for more. I give Sammy another spoonful. I'm thinking it tastes so good after that long, hot walk, that I really don't want to give him any more. "Mandy, why don't you give him some of yours?" I say.

She gives me an amused look and offers the baby a spoonful.

Now we are ready to talk about her place on the spirituality spectrum.

I ask if she has any Jewish identity at all. Without hesitating, she answers, "Oh, yes, my nose."

The Funny One

Mandy is the funny one, her satirical streak isn't far from the surface, as her many childhood video productions attest. With her sisters and cousins as extras in her productions, pre-pubescent Director Mandy was in her element.

Click: Slapping her thigh. "Lost me leg in the war, nine-teeeen-fourteeen."

Click: Plaintively. "Excuse me, suh, I'm a little Czechoslovakian girl, suh, and I don't even know where Czechoslovakia is . . . or what it is, or even how to spell it . . .and does it taste good with peanut butter . . ."

But that was then and this is now. She went on to acquire a master's degree in occupational therapy, a husband, a house, a mortgage, and a baby, so she was clearly on the American Mainstream path.

Spiritually, though, she is neither here nor there.

Sometimes I Feel Restless

"I'm not very religious at this point in my life," Mandy says. "There have been times when I was more religious. I'm not feeling the connection that I once felt. Sometimes it seems like I have too many distractions in my life to focus on religion.

"I slowly disengaged from religion in college and after being away from the routine with Mom."

Distractions will do it. Call them short-term goals. Life's bumps to get over. College, studying in Mexico, boyfriend, marriage, graduate school, backpacking with Brandon in Central America, new job, problems on the job, pregnancy, baby, baby crying, baby not feeding well, and so on. Achieving the immediate goals of life required far more attention than church. And in many ways, achieving those goals was far more tangible for Mandy than the vague presence of God.

But now, in-between working, caring for Sammy, and training for the triathlon, there are moments when she has her doubts about the muted presence of God in her life. Mandy admits she would like to be more religious because "I don't always feel fulfilled. I've been really asking myself lately, what is it that makes me happy? I have a baby and this wonderful house and a wonderful husband, but sometimes I feel restless, and I just don't feel happy, and sometimes I think maybe I need to pursue getting back to God and faith; maybe that would fill what was missing. I know that sounds like a cliché, but that's how I feel."

"Could it be," I say, raising a key point of this book, "that you don't feel you have enough challenge or that you need a greater sense of purpose? You have everything you need, and yet somehow you need more struggle in your life."

Sammy starts to fuss. His big, dark eyes are wet. Mandy pats his back, stalling a bit so she can say what is on her mind. "It's not struggle I need, but maybe more passion. There's nothing I really feel passionate about. Brandon has a lot of passions, scuba diving, mush-rooms, space, and even seaweed." She pauses for a minute, trying to settle-down Sammy. And with a questioning look, she adds, "But is it really that I need more *hobbies,* or is what I'm missing the need to pursue my faith again?"

"I have a feeling," I say, "that as long as you have enough distrac-tions, you will be okay. As long as you have short-term meaningful goals, you won't have time to feel like you are missing out."

I was thinking about Eric Hoffer's statement that the next best thing to a meaningful life is a busy life. As long as we are busy, as long as we are achieving those short-term goals, as long as we are preoccu-pied with making our way through life, we can be reasonably satisfied. It's not that our day-to-day affairs are meaningless; they are obviously very important. But they lack drama, they lack importance in the greater scheme of things. And when our prosaic goals are not enough, we start creating new goals. Ernest Becker alluded to all this, and most notably, the need for "passion" as Mandy put it, when he wrote that we human beings do not want to admit that:

> We do not stand alone, that we always rely on something that transcends us, some system of ideas and powers in which we are embedded and which support us. This power is not always obvi-ous. It need not be overtly a god or openly a stronger person, but it can be the power of an all-absorbing activity, a passion, a dedi-cation to a game, a way of life, that like a comfortable web, keeps a person buoyed-up.[2]

"But don't you think," I say to Mandy, "that a truly religious per-son wouldn't be distracted by secular pursuits? That no matter what was going on, Jesus would be the most important thing in her life."

"That may be," she says, "but although I'm not feeling the fervor at this point right now, I still see myself as religious. I still believe in God."

"Mandy," I say, "ninety-five percent of Americans claim to believe in God, but they sure don't act like it. It's easy enough to talk the talk, but a truly religious person also walks the walk. It sounds to me like you are closer to me than to Mom in your religious feelings."

"I don't think so, Dad. I really do believe in God and feel the presence of God at different times of my life. *Even now.* But I'm not feeling very Catholic, very religious. It's just not on my mind on a daily basis."

"Do you go to church?"

"I sometimes feel a compulsion to go to church, so I go now and then, but I don't feel inspired in church. I'm not feeling anything anymore, so I tend to not go.

"What do you want to feel?"

"A connection to God again."

"What about praying?" I ask. "Do you pray?"

Sammy reaches out for the toy Mandy had placed on the table. "Yeah, I do. Maybe not every day, but definitely a few times a week. Kind of short, intense prayers like to help someone in strife, or I pray for help, guidance, or peace. Sometimes I pray to keep my family safe and healthy."

"Does it work?"

"In that moment, I feel a connection. It's what everyone wants—a feeling that there is something greater than you that loves you, that takes care of you, that looks out for you."

"From my point of view, it sounds like you want a surrogate parent. I've always thought that god is a substitute for parents who loom as gods in the eyes of infants. Look at Sammy, here," I say. "When he starts perceiving us more clearly in a few years, the only conclusion he can come to is that he is small, the world around him is incomprehensible, and that you and Brandon are huge, powerful, all-knowing and all-loving beings. From his little vantage point, you and Brandon have always existed, just like god. He is utterly dependent on you; you provide life and food and warmth and the hugs he craves. He doesn't understand why he is so small and helpless and you are so big and powerful. He only knows one thing—that big people are inscrutable beings, and that you and Brandon are the most important Loving Beings in Creation. As adults, that's what we subliminally crave—a continuation of the love and security of our god-like parents, and, as a result, we create god."

Not on a Quest for Significance

Someone like Mandy, who has a fuzzy sense of lacking purpose and meaning but who is otherwise successful and happy, represents people who are not on a quest for significance because *they have already arrived*. Everything is going well: husband, child, education, job, family, and friends. No struggles, no ego deficiencies, no overarching problems. For Mandy, as for most of us, there are no holy missions, no fabricated heroism, no transcendent causes, no destructive jihads, no martyrdom, just short-term goals of husband, job, and children. Consequently, a vague sense of the need for struggle and sacrifice is perhaps creeping in, in order to beef up her immortality project. If Mandy was intensely religious, she might not need more meaning. Perhaps that is why she is training for a triathlon—it's a short-term goal requiring effort, energy, and planning that will result in a feeling of accomplishment.

Raising a family and running a triathlon isn't tree hugging, but it certainly is real.

27

ernest becker and temple grandin: a slam dunk confirmation of spiritual hunger

The real world is simply too terrible to admit; it tells man that he is a small, trembling animal who will decay and die. Illusion changes all this, makes man seem important, vital to the universe, immortal in some way.[1]

—Ernest Becker, *The Denial of Death*

Of all the people who clearly understand our need for making a dent in the cosmos, Ernest Becker is the most articulate. In his 1974 Pulitzer Prize-winning book, *The Denial of Death*, Becker described in stunning detail and absolute clarity, the dilemma of being a smart creature—one that is simultaneously aware of its own existence and its impending death. Writing with energy and conviction, Becker discussed our immortality projects, (although he didn't use that term), our hunger for defiant heroism, the wars and revolutions we create for spiritual purpose, and the pressure that fear of death brings to bear on our quests for cosmic significance and salvation. Children, Becker wrote, "openly express man's tragic destiny. He must desperately justify himself as an object of primary value in the universe. He must stand out, be a hero, make the biggest possible contribution to world life, show that he counts more than anything or anyone else."[2]

In other words, we are all on a lifelong quest for significance. Our lives are immortality projects. We tell ourselves that we are the most important part of creation to compensate for the nagging suspicion that we are nothing.

Becker understood all this as clearly as anyone has; after all, he wrote the book.

Then he got cancer. And died.

The year he won the Pulitzer for *The Denial of Death*, cancer struck him down. And on his deathbed, he made a startling admission.

A Breathtaking Deathbed Interview

Throughout his book, Becker implied that we created God, and we create immortality projects to give our lives meaning in the cosmos. But now that he was faced with a premature death at the age of fifty, what would he have to say? Did he still believe that God is a fabrication to infuse our lives with significance? It may be true that there are no atheists in foxholes, but Becker was no ordinary atheist. In a breathtaking deathbed interview with *Psychology Today*, Becker said the following: "I am lying in a hospital bed dying, and I am putting everything I have got into this interview, as though it were really important, right? And I consider myself to be a self-realized person in the sense of having . . . broken my character armor. But if I'm going to live as a creature, I have to focus my energies in a driven way."[3]

In other words, the only way to live as a functioning entity—in spite of one's insight into the reality of his mortal animal nature and cosmic insignificance—is to believe that what we do is important. Even as he lies dying, and he knows that we are all dust, he can focus his energies on the interview, knowing on the one hand that it is meaningless, yet feeling on the other that it is genuinely important. We ignore eternity; what we do now is important. Recognizing the truth—as Becker does—does not necessarily prevent someone from living vitally.

This is exactly what one would expect from Becker.

Then he dropped a bombshell.

But before I reveal his bombshell, I need to give Becker his due.

Ernest Becker's *The Denial of Death*, put everything together for me. Every page seemed to shout the truth; it was pure excitement. Until I read the book, my own work was a jumble without form. *The Denial of Death* was the glue that held it all together; it was the missing link that filled in the blanks. The book was a joy and a revelation and a relief. It was a relief because I wanted to make sense of things, because I had read many books and felt there was some kind of elusive truth out there, drifting on the wind. I wasn't exactly "dazzled by a thousand sparkling lights" like Rousseau, and the scales didn't fall from my eyes like Paul. I had no religious conversion, but it gave focus to what I was already trying to do. And it was therefore a relief to feel that I had been on the right track, and with Becker's help, I was starting to understand.

Then, on his death bed, Becker became a heretic to his own existential creed.

Said Becker, ". . . I believe in God."

He believes in God?

Becker, who so beautifully articulates our fabricated heroism and artificial transcendence; Becker who tells us we deny our animal natures because it reminds us we are mortal, transient and insignificant; Becker who says that god is a surrogate parent; Becker who says the human race is "a trembling (biological) accident germinated on a hot house planet;" Becker who says that human evil derives from our existential dread; Becker who knows our cultural facades are "vital lies" to hide our minuteness and utter insignificance to creation—now says he believes in God!

Hanging over the eternal abyss, he gives in to the vital lie.

Listen to Becker as he speaks from his hospital bed in 1974:

> What makes dying easier is to be able to transcend the world into some kind of religious dimension. I would say that the most important thing is to know that beyond the human viewpoint, beyond what is happening to us, there is the fact of the tremendous creative energies of the cosmos that are using us for some purpose we don't know. To be used for divine purposes, however we may be misused, this is the thing that consoles me.

Frankl said something similar in the concentration camps—maybe there is another dimension we are unaware of. Well, maybe there are beautiful ten foot women on the planet Mongo. I expect others to give in to wishful thinking, not Becker. But looking into the jaws of eternity, Becker talks about "divine purpose." It's what we all so fervently and poignantly ache to believe, so why not believe it. If Becker gave in, then the rest of us—given the opportunity as we face death—are also vulnerable.

On his deathbed, Voltaire who had little use for the Catholic

Church, remained consistent. He was being prodded to accept Jesus, but maintaining his satirical wit to the end, reportedly said, "Don't talk to me about that man!"

And finally, Uncle Sonny, who is in good company with Becker, Frankl, and Voltaire to be sure, said essentially the same thing. He was in particularly good spirits after watching the first Broncos pre-season game at our house, and we sat for a while out front on the rockers. He opined how he loved the sunsets. "Each one is different and beautiful," he said. "And all those stars are so amazing. The universe is so incomprehensible." His cigarette smoke wafted in my face as the idea of sunsets and stars led him back to the "Alpha-Centauri Conversation" and the rare possibility of alien life. "We are all so small," he said. "And why are we here?"

"The eternal questions," I offered.

"Right, why are we here and where are we going?" And then he got to it—what we all want to believe. "I think we all become part of the universe in some way."

"Well, our essence goes back into the soil and helps the plants grow."

"Or maybe other ways, we don't know about."

It so often comes back to that. We hope there are other dimensions. We speculate, we write thousands of years of theology, we sit in our rockers on warm August nights and hope . . .

Decoding Human Behavior

Temple Grandin gives us another unique and extraordinary example of why the quest for immortality through spiritual purpose is so ubiquitous and powerful. Grandin is an autistic woman with a PhD.[4] Those with autism live within their minds, seeming to exist in another dimension or a separate psychological plane. We associate autism with children who are completely out of touch with reality, "profoundly disabled . . . perhaps head banging; rudimentary language; almost inaccessible . . ."

But Temple was different. She was able to bridge the gap between her inner world and ours, but was never quite in tune with us. She took things literally, missed sarcasm completely, along with metaphor and symbolism. She can "decode" human behavior, understand it perhaps, but does not feel it herself. She compares herself to Data, the android on Star Trek. Data looks human and can objectively understand human emotions. He can conceptualize humor, comprehend hate, and abstractly understand love, but can never internalize them. And so it is with Temple Grandin.

As a result, she never dated, had sex, or fell in love. The whole thing mystifies her. "She found such interactions completely baffling and too complex to deal with; she was never sure what was being said, or implied, or asked, or expected. She did not know at such times, where people were coming from, or their assumptions or presuppositions, or intentions."

Her story was recounted in a book of her reminiscences, *Thinking in Pictures*, and in *An Anthropologist From Mars*, by Oliver Sacks, a professor of clinical neurology. When Sacks asked her if she had ever cared for another person, she hesitated and answered, "I think lots of times there are things that are missing from my life."

"Is this painful," he asked.

"Yeah, I guess."

Just before they parted company at the airport, Grandin spoke with some urgency. She wanted to talk about God:

> "I believe," she said, "there is some ultimate ordering force for good in the universe—not a personal thing, not Buddha or Jesus, maybe something like order out of disorder. I like to hope that even if there's no personal afterlife, some energy impression is left in the universe . . . Most people can pass on genes—I can pass on thoughts or what I write.
>
> This is what I get very upset at," said Temple, crying. "I've read that libraries are where immortality lies . . . I don't want my thoughts to die with me . . . I want to have done something . . . I'm not interested in power, or piles of money. I want to leave something behind. I want to make a positive contribution—know that my life has meaning. Right now, I'm talking about things at the very core of my existence."

This statement by Temple Grandin is as dramatic and stunning as Becker's death bed retreat. Here is a woman who has to "decode" human behavior, who is incapable of feeling love or of understanding sarcasm, who is baffled by common human assumptions. Yet the one thing she shares with us, the one thing she understands, the one thing that shakes her to the existential core is the need for her life to have meaning. She doesn't understand human emotion, yet she weeps—aches—for immortality, for her life to be worthy of eternity.

Temple wants what we all want—call them "paper tombstones," as my father-in-law put it—call them leaving footprints in the sands of time. It's why we carve our initials in a tree, because we know the tree will outlast us and our initials will tell the world we were here.

So What Does It All Mean?

The purpose of Part 2 was to discuss the question: What do people want? The answer in a nutshell is that we want to be better than who we are. We want to make our lives worthy so that we have added something to eternity. We do this through a multiplicity of immortality projects, running the range from the prosaic (changing our name to Santa Claus), to the fantastic (fighting a war), to the artificial (fabricating revolutions), and to the horrific (killing millions in the name of our chosen god).

And one of the most dramatic examples of this is September 11th.

PART 3

FROM THE BRONX TO THE ALAMO

Glory is largely a theatrical concept. There is no striving for glory without a vivid awareness of an audience—the knowledge that our mighty deeds will come to the ears of our contemporaries or "of those who are to be." We are ready to sacrifice our true, transitory selves for the imaginary external self we are building up by our heroic deeds . . .

—Eric Hoffer, *The True Believer*

28

september 11th

Democratic Civilization is the first in history to blame itself because
another power is trying to destroy it.

—Jean-Francois Revel, 1970

On September 11th, 2001, I was in New York City helping my uncle
move his assets around and move my aunt into a nursing home. Every
day I drove to the Bronx from my sister's house in the suburbs to
spend eight to ten hours taking care of business—lawyers, bankers, social workers, doctors. It was a painfully slow process. Uncle Sonny
moved cautiously and suspiciously. On September 11th, we had an
appointment at a bank in lower Manhattan, not far from the World
Trade Center. We never made it.

I listened to the unfolding horror driving to the Bronx. A fire was
burning at the Pentagon. A plane had crashed in Pennsylvania. Crossing the Hudson River on the Tappan Zee Bridge on that warm, clear
morning, I could see both towers smoking far in the distance. By the
time I got to the toll booth, Peter Jennings was saying something like
"Oh, my God, the tower is falling."

Afraid of Eternity

When terrorists set off bombs in crowded market places or crash planes

225

into buildings, most of us have trouble understanding how any cause could justify such atrocities. But if we take a close look at the people who commit these crimes, we begin to understand that they are not motivated by injustice, or tyranny, or oppression, or any of the other standard laments. They are motivated by *existential dread*. They are afraid of eternity and are desperately trying to make their lives worthy. In addition, they are motivated by their anger at a world that has not given them the recognition and respect they feel they deserve. They are trying to have an effect on events. They want to make a dent in life, and they want the rest of the world to notice them. They are attempting to justify their lives by rewriting their life scripts into scenarios of defiance, heroism, and transcendence. They are on a cosmic power trip. Because they have connected with their immortality projects, the deaths of others—even the deaths of millions of others—are inconsequential. Others may die, but they will live on forever.

During the spring of 2003, when suicide bombers in the Middle East were out in full force, President Bush stated the obvious when he said, "It is clear there are people in the Middle East who hate peace." But why? Doesn't everyone want peace? The answer is decidedly not. Peace eliminates the heroic identity of the freedom fighter. Engaging a demonized enemy—and the sense of purpose, direction, and camaraderie it provides—is so psychologically satisfying, that they want that feeling to go on forever. They cannot be talked out of their hatred because fighting against Israel and the West is their true religion. Peace would negate their reason-to-be, so peace is opposed with fanatical zeal. For them it's not that the ends justify the means, but the means are a spiritual end unto themselves. Winning is not their motive. The *process* of fighting for the cause is their salvation. They don't want to win. They want either perpetual struggle or a martyr's death. The reason that militant Islam is particularly powerful is that it combines a mainstream religion with the secular religion of pursuing a noble and heroic cause.

His Face Turned as White as His T-Shirt

Aunt Millie, Uncle Sonny, their neighbor Steve, and their home-health aid, Norma, were sitting around the kitchen table when I arrived at the apartment on September 11th. Two glasses of wine sat on the table. Sunlight poured into the room, doing little to brighten the dismal, edgy mood. As usual the air was rancid with smoke, and I immediately opened the balcony door. My uncle wore a white T-shirt with his usual impassive, stony expression. Thick cigarette smoke curled out of his mouth. Everything in the apartment reeked of smoke–the furniture, the walls, their clothing, papers in the draws, towels, everything. The small black-and-white set on the kitchen table replayed images of the twin towers smoking and falling.

We talked a bit about the attacks and then got down to business. My time was limited. I made a few calls, gave him some papers to sign; and in the midst of all this, with the 9/11 chatter on the little set, Uncle Sonny's face turned as white as his T-shirt, and a fierce, visceral rage crossed his face. He looked at me as if I had just murdered his wife. He rose up from the chair on shaky legs and came at me. "You f------ son-of-a-b-----. You f------ c--- sucker."

His fists were clenched, jaw tight, eyes flaming with hatred. I was cornered in the back of the dining room, and as I tried to slip past he lunged at me with his fist, his face contorted and twisted. Uncle Sonny was still strong–all muscle and grizzle. As a kid I had marveled at his vice-like grip that could have crushed every bone in my hand. I managed to duck out of the way, grabbed my files, and fled the apartment.

THE KING OF HIS BRONX DOMAIN; NY YANKEES CAP CLOSE AT HAND.

Perhaps it was the alcohol, or the fact that his wife of over fifty years was dying, or the pressure of my visits and the business we transacted, or his dementia, or the painful years helplessly watching Johnnie deteriorate and die, or September 11th—or all these things.

I made my way to Applebee's across the street for lunch. It was surprisingly deserted. The waiters and waitresses hovered around. I had no appetite but just needed to sit quietly. The multiple televisions at Applebee's, which generally show sporting events, were showing scenes from lower Manhattan—the Twin Towers burning and then falling, huge billows of white smoke, people running for their lives. The talking heads made reference to Muslim terrorists and an organization called "al-Qaida." Already there was talk about what the United States had done to cause such an attack.

The waiter was standing by, but I was shaking my head. *Don't they understand?* It has nothing to do with our policies, or logic, or reason. They are Muslims on a holy mission killing for god, killing to gain entrance into eternity. They are Samuel Adams and Thomas Paine. They are Hitler and Rousseau falling to their knees in rapturous enthusiasm. It's a combustible manifestation of the *spiritual perfect storm*, igniting nationalism, ethnicity, and religion into a destructive force. And they want to know what *we* did to provoke these attacks.

"Excuse me?" said the waiter.

"What?"

"Did you say something?"

I ordered a chicken salad and called Becky on the cell phone. There would be roaming charges but I didn't care. I had to talk to the one sane person in the universe (well, besides me). "The world is such a dangerous place because of spiritual hungers. You can't reason with people on deadly holy missions."

As I sat there picking at my food and sipping the Coke, it seemed as if the world had once again gone mad. Voltaire was right; we are just atoms on a ball of mud killing each other. But we want to be the opposite of atoms. We want to transform ourselves from the ciphers of the universe into the focal point of existence. Some turn to god as the source of their spirituality; others fly planes into buildings. Still others attack their nephews to strike back at a universe and a god that doesn't seem to care.

29

the quest for significance in the bronx

Don't laugh at a youth for his affectations; he's only trying on one face after another till he finds his own.

—Logan Pearsall Smith, *Afterthoughts*

On September 12th, I was back in the Bronx transferring my aunt to a nursing home. Uncle Sonny had calmed down. "Look upon this as your finest hour," Becky said to me as I drove across the Hudson River.

I wasn't encouraged. "I just want to be finished with this and get out of here." But it was nice to talk to her as I drove to the Bronx. I was longing to get back to Colorado.

My aunt had Alzheimer's and–as we later learned–cancer. Her stomach was bloated. Her chattiness had morphed into a befuddled quietness. "I feel very strange," she said over and over, lying in the nursing-home bed. "I don't know what's going on. Why am I here? What is this place? I feel very strange." Another time she said, "My life is over. The children died. It was terrible. I don't understand. I feel very strange. Why am I here?"

This is the woman who lost her loving brother Eddie to muscular dystrophy when she was twenty, who at twenty-two was flirting with the communist party, who at forty was writing frantic letters to Jerry Lewis and John F. Kennedy, and who at eighty was falling victim to Alzheimer's and wine.

Back to the Old Neighborhood

Tired from making my way through the bureaucracy of nursing homes, social workers, and health-insurance hassles, I drove to my old neighborhood in the Bronx. The Loews Paradise Theater on the Grand Concourse was shuttered. The faded outline of the name announced it had long since closed down. In its time, it was the quintessential ornate theater with marble statues, Roman decor, a huge foyer with a giant marble pool full of fat goldfish, and a sky filled with stars and moving clouds. A National Geographic coffee table book on Americana gave it a two-page spread. I went on my first date there in the sixth grade, graduated from high school there, and according to Uncle Sonny, my mother placed second in a beauty contest on the Paradise's stage.

The Paradise had a "children's section," where a thin, tight-lipped woman in a white coat rounded us up like sheep and prowled the area like a Gestapo chief. She wielded a flashlight like a laser weapon, pointing it at us if we made too much noise. After we turned twelve and paid adult prices, they still forced us into the children's section, which seemed to me to be a great injustice. Consequently, on some Saturday afternoons, we would sneak away from our assigned seating to sit among the adults, probably annoying them with junior high antics.

Now it was dead, boarded-up.

My old neighborhood was the same yet different. Every single building that had stood in that concrete canyon in the 1950s remained intact in 2001, but while the neighborhood had been primarily Jewish, it was now completely Hispanic. Becky often marveled at the hundreds of six-story apartment buildings that seemed to stretch in every direction. There were endless neighborhoods and buildings, but this two-block stretch from 181st Street to 183rd and from the Grand Concourse to Jerome Avenue was the only one that mattered. Like the Paradise Theater, the buildings with their large lobbies and doormen had seen better days.

I parked across the street from the school yard of PS 79 and walked rapidly around the streets, marveling again at the familiarity of the buildings. The day was broiling, and I bought some cherry ices from a voodoo-looking, dark black Haitian woman. They were cold and full of flavor, and I savored every icy mouthful.

The building directly across the street from mine had a long concrete facade about three feet high, which was perfect for ten-year-olds playing "off the point." If a guy hit the point just right, the spaldeen (a pink little rubber ball manufactured by Spalding) would fly all the way across the street for a home run. The trouble was that sometimes the ball would end up on a fire escape, or even worse, in the mean old lady's house.

The old lady spent most of her time sitting at the window watching the world go by. I had a sense that she was sad, that she had no life. She was, after all, old with short straight gray hair; she existed in another dimension from ten-year-old boys. I never thought of her as ever being young, or having a job, or being married. But mainly we hated it when she chased us away. She was nothing but mean.

One fine day in May, we were playing off the point with *my* brand new spaldeen and sure enough, someone hit a home run right into the old lady's window. It was one of those rare times she wasn't actually sitting there. And I wanted the ball back. After all, it was brand new—fresh and pink and full of bounce. I had spent a full twenty-five cents for it! But what could I do? Ring her bell? People said she was a witch. She was always yelling that the ball would hurt her and that she would tell our parents.

But I wanted my brand new spaldeen back.

I went up to her door and rang the bell hoping she wouldn't answer, but knowing that she would because she never left. I was ready to run full speed back to our apartment, which happened to be on the same floor. I gauged the distance, estimating that I could be home in maybe three seconds. Why am I doing this? It's only a stupid ball. I braced myself to run. She opened the door and looked down at me. "Yes?"

I didn't want to actually look at her face, so I announced to the wall that my ball had gone through her window.

"Well, come in," she said.

I was surprised she had a normal speaking voice. I quickly glanced up at her. Was this going to be a Hansel and Gretel thing? I didn't want to end up in an oven. She wasn't angry at all. "Come in," she said again.

The apartment was neat as a pin and spartan in appearance—hardwood floors, a few throw rugs, a piano. "Well, let's look around for it," she said. I was relieved but still on my guard. Why was she being so friendly? "There it is," she said, "behind the chair."

I didn't know what to do. "Well, go on, dear, get your ball."

Dear? The old lady called me dear, like she was my grandma or something. I carefully went behind the chair, retrieved the ball, and headed for the door. She just stood there looking at me.

"Thanks," I said at her front door. She didn't say a thing. She continued to stare silently at me. I looked passed her to the big window and then to the piano. I squeezed the spaldeen. Still she said nothing.

"Well," I stammered, "thanks, really thanks." And as an afterthought, I added, "I'm sorry."

By the time I got back to the street, she was sitting in her usual place, staring out at nothing.

Now, almost fifty years later, I wonder why I was sorry. Because the ball had gone in her window, or that I was sorry to bother her, or was it because she seemed to be so spiritually void?

Hierarchy of Smart Jewish Kids

Many of my parents' lifelong friends came from this neighborhood. But mostly I remember their kids and how smart they were. In that building was Lennie, who had a 98 percent high school average, and Matthew, who had a photographic memory and was "brilliant." In that same building was Roy, who would eventually become a millionaire businessman and live for a time next door to O.J. Simpson in California. Across the street lived Jeffrey, who became a Hollywood agent and married a famous singer. Also in that building was my best friend Jay, who, with his 92 percent average, was just mediocre by smart-Jewish-kid standards. And me? I eked out an 83.8 percent high school average; better than most kids, but a million miles away from the Holy Grail of high school, the 85 percent needed to get into the city colleges. And I wondered if my drive to write—one of the few avenues I had to gain real significance—was due in part to my lowly status on the hierarchical totem poll of smart Jewish kids from the Bronx.

Emerging from the Garden of Eden

I walked back to PS 79 to use the rest room. It was my only option in the neighborhood and finding relief took precedence over old memories. The four-story red brick building with its wrought iron fence was exactly the same on the outside, but inside it was different. A Hispanic man sat at a table and asked me if he could help. "I'd like to use the rest room."

"Sorry," he shrugged, looking over my shoulder at nothing in particular. "It's not allowed."

Look, I wanted to say to him. *I'm not a child molester. I went to this school from kindergarten through eighth grade. And I desperately need to use the rest room.*

I somehow talked him into it and took a quick look around the school. Nothing looked familiar. But if I didn't remember the building, I certainly remembered the transition from elementary school to junior high. Graduation was simply a matter of going from the second floor to the third, but in that moment the world changed. The girls went to an all-girls junior high, and we went up to the top two floors otherwise known as Creston Junior High.

Sixth grade had been idyllic; seventh grade was a shock. In sixth grade, life flowed from day to day with nary an insecure thought. Looming above us was a network of parents, teachers, the principal, the police, the local barber Archie, Mr. Zimmerman who ran a small local grocery store, and somewhere far off was President Eisenhower. Life was fair, orderly, and secure. Friends were always there; acceptance and belonging were as natural a part of existence as the buildings that towered over us.

Back then the vast majority of people in the world were Jewish. At Jewish holiday time, Mr. Weinstein, our sixth-grade teacher would ask for a show of hands as to who would be out of school. Eighty percent of us raised our hands, and we exchanged knowing glances. The "Catholic" kids may have gotten out of school early twice a week for some mysterious rite called "catechism," but we got to take entire days off to put on a tie and hang around and not play off the point. But it was okay because anything was better than being in school. Then the teacher would ask which boys and girls would be in school on the Holy days, and the four or five "Catholic" kids would raise their hands. We would look around through hooded eyes at the Irish boys with sandy hair and freckles and the girls with Italian names and thick black hair, confirming once again who was in and who was out in Mr. Weinstein's sixth-grade class.

Mr. Weinstein must have been in pedagogical heaven. He had the "smart" class. We all did our work. Our parents were involved in school. We were so enthusiastic about social studies reports that we met on weekends and after school at someone's house to prepare our presentations.

And then we went upstairs to the junior high, where the real world began to show itself. In seventh grade, we came to the uncomfortable realization that the majority of people in the world were not actually Jewish. There were many more "Catholic" kids in our classes, and the world somehow felt different.

Sitting in front of me in homeroom class was a short kid named Thomas who had a pinched face and the nervous mannerisms of a mouse. Instead of contemplating the wonders of Marilyn Finklestein's ponytail, as I had in the sixth grade, I spent the year looking at the spectacularly uninspiring view of Thomas's dirty brown hair.

In my homeroom class were four juvenile delinquents. They were fifteen or sixteen years old; we were twelve. Some were over six feet tall; we were closer to five feet. They had been kept back three or four times. The rest of us kept our distance from them. They inhabited a different dimension. Blaylock was just plain mean. He squinted all the time. His hair was greasy and blond. He wore a T-shirt with a black leather motorcycle jacket, the collar turned up menacingly. Carson had a big black pompadour and seemed a bit dreamy. Sullivan, a big, friendly kid, came to class every so often with cuts and bruises on his face because his father regularly beat him. Around the middle of the year, I walked into class and Nathan motioned with his head, "We've got another one." Sure enough, a handsome Italian kid who could have been Sylvester Stallone had transferred in. He wore a cross over his T-shirt. Now we had five.

My friend Stevie and I concluded that these guys were "phonies." The upturned collars on the black leather jackets, the greased hair, the taps on the shoes, which they scraped when they walked, and the cigarette tucked behind the ear all smacked of affectation. They were not happy with who they were, so they reinvented themselves with a sub-cultural pose designed to improve their images.

Speaking of images, when the weather turned colder, Stevie asked me if I was going to wear the usual hat with the aviator earflaps that tied beneath our chin. I had been thinking the very same thing.

"They look faggy," Stevie opined.

"They're not sporty," I added.

"What would the girls think if they saw us with those stupid ear-muffs?" Stevie said, more of a statement than a question.

And what would those greasy JDs think?

We had become self-aware. Moving from sixth to seventh grade was akin to expulsion from the Garden of Eden. *We knew we were naked;* we knew we were vulnerable. Uncertainty crept in like the mists of death on Passover night. Do I look right? Do I act right? What do other people think of me? What do I think of myself? Do I measure up? And if I don't, what can I do to spruce-up my image?

Puberty changed everything. Masks became a way of life, and there was no going back to the Garden of Eden of our childhoods.

Meanwhile, the really smart kids were winning academic awards and I wasn't. More uncertainty. Not everyone was Jewish. More un-certainty. We wanted to look cool. I wouldn't be caught dead in a hat with earmuffs. The world grew more ominous. The girls filled out, and it wasn't just bobbing ponytails that held my attention.

Is that where the quest for significance starts? At puberty? With self-awareness and self-doubt? Is that where we start those affectations

CLIMBING THE SCHOOL-YARD FENCE. WE KNEW WE WERE NAKED.

to boost our images? Or is Adler right that because we start out as powerless children, we spend the rest of our lives striving for power?

I crossed the street to my rented car and looked back at the chain-link fence surrounding the school yard. The late afternoon sun was just about to dip behind a building, which would bathe the neighborhood in shadow. On the passenger seat were files and pages of scribbled notes. I'd be back with Uncle Sonny tomorrow.

30

strangers in a strange land

It's what you expect here in the bible belt. Look, I walk down the hall and don't see any New York names: no Italian, no Jewish, no Polish names.

—Uncle Sonny

Throughout the beautiful, dry, and sunny Colorado summer, Uncle Sonny remained as inscrutable as ever. He spoke carefully and precisely, enunciating each word. He spoke like he had lived, unhurried. His handwriting was similarly precise. Each letter was carefully formed and rounded. Every letter of every word was in place. He wrote as he spoke, slowly and accurately.

During the first three months, he never used a four-letter word. He never swore in frustration, as in, "S---, I can't tie my shoe lace." The closest thing he came to swearing was to mutter in his clear baritone rumble, "I needa take a leak."

My uncle probably had an addictive personality–cigarettes and booze–and since he was denied alcohol, he fixated on his new addiction: Starbucks. He was ready to go every day. Starbucks was the drug of choice.

When I thought about him coming to Colorado, I imagined the icon of the experience would be me pushing him in a wheelchair around the lake across the street. But that wasn't it at all. The icon was this little old man, shriveled down to 125 pounds, wearing a New York

Yankees baseball cap, resting on his walker, his lined face a mask, sitting among the yuppies and college students with their books and cell phones, sucking mocha frappuccinos through a straw.

His drunken, paranoid rages seemed to be a thing of the past. Without alcohol and endless hours isolated in his apartment to ruminate upon all the people who were trying to cheat him, and with normal interaction with normal people on a daily basis, he was, at times, downright pleasant. As we would get in and out of the van, and I folded his walker, he would mutter in his deep voice, "Thanks, Fred." He was soooo polite.

A "Screw You" Kind of Guy

But just when things seemed to be going well, his anger and profanity would surface, sometimes with volcanic fury. His mind was compartmentalized. We would be sitting around Starbucks and he would suddenly be talking again about his father, or the distance to Alpha Centauri, or his army days in Manchester, England, or "my aunt Dora."

But then the negative files would pop out.

"My neighbor Steve told people that I used the N-word. That's why I punched his other eye out."

"Those f------ Italians are trying to keep me from getting the insurance money." "I don't want any more f------ Jewish lawyers."

Although we saw him every day, and he did indeed have normal people around, he tended to keep to himself at Garden Square, leaving him plenty of time to ruminate. Even without alcohol, he could conjure up conspiracies. We were starting to think, that in the end, he was just a screw-you kind of guy. He was polite and respectful and seemed to enjoy talking to us; but his periodic bursts of vindictiveness seemed to be the ulcerous eruptions of another persona.

A few days after July 4th, Becky came home in tears. A huge thunderstorm, so typical of summer afternoons in Colorado, darkened the sky. We sat on the patio in front of the house. "He's out of his mind, today," she said. "He opened the paranoia folder and pulled down the file marked, 'They kidnapped me.'"

"What happened?" I asked, as the sky darkened even further. I thought idly how the lawn really needed the rain.

"He said, 'I'm out here because Freddie wants to steal my apartment.'"

A "SCREW YOU" KIND OF GUY, AROUND 1948.

"What did you say to that?"

"I told him that if we had wanted his apartment, we would have left him in the nursing home in the Bronx. He said he wants to go back to his apartment where he has more room. 'Maybe I can make new friends. I often went dancing.'"

"Dancing? He thinks he went dancing?"

"Right, and he was so angry. His face was white and intense with rage. He said, 'I'm ready to walk out now. I wanna go back to New York.'"

"What did you say to that?"

"But, Sonny, when you're alone at home you drink. You get drunk."

He shook his head and ran his hand over the few strands of his wispy gray combover. "No, that's not true, Becky. I haven't had a drink for a long time."

"But you do. It happened often."

He looked at her with intensity and hatred. "You can't stop me. I can walk out of here any time I want." When he got in these moods, he was hateful, bitter, distrusting, and paranoid. Although he was pleasant enough with his low mutters of "Thanks Fred," when I opened the car door, or "Thanks Fred," when I produced a grande mocha frappuccino. When the distrustful and angry persona surfaced, it always took us off balance. Which Uncle Sonny will we see today?

Something Is Wrong Here!

However, just when we had accepted his basic nastiness, he became all sweetness and light. On a whim, he bought a bouquet of flowers for Becky "just because I want to do something nice for her."

One Friday night late in August, Becky, Melanie, and I took him to dinner at the Olive Garden. He immediately inhaled a double scotch on the rocks, which went right from his empty stomach to his head. He grinned broadly. "I'm high," he said. "That was one strong drink." Then he drank another.

As usual he enjoyed the meal and was in great spirits. "It's a wonderful night when I can spend it with the people I love," he said, sipping the minestrone soup. "Melanie you are a beautiful young woman," he said kissing her and then biting down on the garlic laden shrimp scampi. When he talked to Becky it was always, "Thank you, sweetheart."

Uncle Sonny was a sweet old Morrie-type guy.

But three days after the "high" at the Olive Garden, he told everyone at Garden Square that "the people I love" and that "sweetheart" Becky forced him to come to Colorado so they could sell his apartment and pocket the money.

That's What You Expect in the Bible Belt

By the end of August, we weren't quite sure who Uncle Sonny was. He was at times, deceptive, cagey, erratic, two-faced, a liar, hostile, demented, passive, sweet, resigned, logical, illogical, loving, hating, inquisitive, happy, sad, aesthetically inclined, in awe of the universe, passive, or raging.

Was he nasty and angry, a sad old man at the end of a miserable life? Paranoid and hateful? Sweet and philosophical? Angry and hopeless? Poignant and tragic? Schizophrenic? How about all of the above?

I visited him one Sunday in June in his room at Garden Square. He sat on his walker riveted by the World Series of Poker on the TV screen.

"How are you doing?" I asked brightly.

"So, so."

Uh, oh. "What's the matter?"

"Freddie," he said, in that strong baritone voice. "That's what you expect in the Bible Belt."

"What do you mean?"

"This woman at lunch asked me if I was staying for dessert."

"Okay, so what's the problem?"

"It's what you expect here in the Bible Belt. Look, I walk down the hall and don't see any New York names: no Italian, no Jewish, no Polish names."

"You're losing me, Uncle Sonny. What does that have to do with the woman at lunch?"

"It's something you expect here. Look, I've experienced anti-Semitism throughout my life."

"What did this woman do?" I asked.

"She asked me if I was Jewish."

"That doesn't mean she was anti-Semitic," I offered.

"Of course it does. Freddie, I'm telling you, it's not my imagination. People stare at me here, like the girl who came to my room. It's Jew baiting.

"What girl?"

"One who works here. She came into my room and said, 'I know you've been smoking, Sonny.'"

"How is that Jew baiting?"

"She smiled at me."

"Maybe she was just trying to be nice."

He shook his head and blinked wildly. "Freddie, I know it when I see it. She was smiling in a way that said Jew Bastard. Believe me, I know anti-Semitism, I experienced it in the army."

Indeed he had, as he had written about his war time experiences in a long therapeutic letter to us the previous decade:

I was sleeping, and I heard some cheering & shouting & walked to the front of the barracks & asked the men out there what the celebration was all about. Their answers were Jew Bastards, kill the f------ Jews; they agreed with the Nazis. I was shocked and reported to Captain Crueger what had happened. He said he couldn't stop anti-Semitism as it was rife in the army. The cheering was for the D-Day invasion which had taken place a few hours earlier.

I had three fist fights with some anti-Semites & so did Stan

Hayes, a powerfully built young Jewish soldier. One day on the chow line someone made an anti-Semitic remark to Hayes. He grabbed the guy, threw him down and was digging the fingers of both hands in the guy's eyes. The other guys were moving in on Hayes so I jumped in, grabbed a ladle of boiling water and held them off. And I told Hayes to gouge his f------ eyes out. Soon after the captain had us transferred out. He said either you'll kill someone or they'll kill you. For defending ourselves we were sent to the notorious Litchfield replacement camp which sent recovered & wounded & raw recruits to the Battle of the Bulge. Everyday I'd fall out for roll call & the sadistic sergeant called us Motherf---ers & gold bricks & told us if we heard our name called we were to fall out to the right for immediate orders to go to the front. I fell out for roll call for 1 month & developed a serious anxiety as I didn't get called & became a non-person, an invisible man.

Spiritually Dysfunctional Jews

Uncle Sonny had been complaining for two months about the lack of Jewish people, so early in October I located the small Jewish commu-

UNCLE SONNY IN THE ARMY WHERE ANTISEMITISM WAS RIFE.

nity in town, and we went to the temple for Yom Kippur services. He wore an old double-breasted suit a couple sizes too big for his shrunken frame.

"Maybe we should bring a pen," he said as we made our way down the corridor at Garden Square, his walker, as always keeping him stable.

"Why?"

"To write things down," he said with a hard edge to his voice, as if any idiot would know what to do with a pen.

"Well, what do you want to write down?" I asked, maintaining the role of idiot.

"I dunno. Whatever."

The moment we walked into the lobby of the temple and heard the congregation singing in Hebrew, I was immediately sad, nostalgic, and guilty. We donned skullcaps and found two empty chairs. Well over a hundred people attended the services. It was a real Jewish service with a rabbi and cantor. There were Jewish kids, young Jewish parents, Jewish old folks, and Jewish teenagers. I felt a sense of comfort knowing there were still real Jews in the world—unlike my family who had long ago abandoned the faith. My uncle and I stared at the prayer book as if we had any idea of what was going on. We were simultaneously strangers in a strange land and the prodigal sons returning. At once outsiders and insiders, belonging but not belonging, paradoxically uncomfortable with the familiar. We were simultaneously Jews but not Jews, two spiritually dysfunctional men, spanning two generations of a vague and ongoing religious ambiguity.

After the service we indulged in a great spread of food. The room was full of chatter, and we talked with the people at our table. Or more to the point, I talked while Uncle Sonny occasionally joined in with an apropos anecdote from his mental files. But for the most part, his face was a chiseled mask. His anxiety was palpable.

Out in the parking lot, he sat on his walker smoking. Car after car ignited, headlights cutting into the darkness, motors roaring. In short order all was quiet. The sky was full of stars. I expected him to make his usual comment about the possibility of life in the universe, but something else was on his mind. He flicked an ash and said, "I don't know how to make small talk. People are suddenly talking to each other, and I don't know what to say. How do you make small talk?"

"Just ask people questions. What do you do? Where are you from? People love to talk about themselves."

He nodded and looked out into the almost-empty parking lot. Now I understood why he wanted to bring a pen. He had hoped to write down names and phone numbers of Jewish people whom he might see later, but he was no more capable of making new friends than he was of taking a rocket to Alpha Centauri, which, he'd be quick to tell you, is four light years from earth.

31

chaos as the road
to salvation

Those who see their lives as spoiled and wasted crave equality and fraternity more than they do freedom. If they clamor for freedom, it is but freedom to establish equality and uniformity.[1]

—Eric Hoffer, *The True Believer*

On August 14, 2003, the lights went out in the Northeast: another blackout. Everyone's first thought was terrorism. But we quickly realized it was just a massive power outage. Thousands were trapped in subways. Blank traffic lights caused huge traffic jams. Elevators stalled in skyscrapers. New Yorkers responded admirably, with no reports of looting, and with a positive spirit. Television images showed tens of thousands of New Yorkers, walking for hours to get out of Manhattan. People waved and smiled at the cameras. They chatted, laughed, shrugged, and made the best of it.

Equality in Disaster

Surprisingly, most of this is normal and expected. While there is often sporadic looting, survivors of natural disasters generally respond with helpfulness, cooperation, and even cheerfulness because natural disasters bring people together in a camaraderie of purpose. The communal response to natural disasters feels good. Why? Because in the struggle to pick up the pieces, everyone becomes equal. As a result, we feel closer to our fellow man. We all have the same goal–survival. Social and economic differences fade in the face of the common challenge.

In addition, no one is to blame. We are all equal in our non-culpability. We become a community with a common purpose. As we stand there shaking our fists at the hurricane, the snowy sky, the broken dam, or the electric company, we are all equal–equal in suffering, equally blameless, and equally in need of each other. Old animosities and statuses become irrelevant. There is nothing to fight about. Working together to solve the common problem is our first and only priority. In *The Territorial Imperative*, Robert Ardrey wrote that natural disasters "produce instant mutual aid, unthinking sacrifices, smiles on the faces of strangers, intimacies exchanged which have never changed hands before, a gladness and trust that leave us sorry when the emergency has passed."[2]

Why is this worth mentioning? Because those who perceive their lives as failed and insignificant, gain in stature when chaos creates an artificial and temporary equality. Those who cannot rewrite their life scripts, gain significance and rise in importance when the rest of the world is brought down to their level.

Lovers of War

War creates feelings similar to those in blackouts. In 1940, when the Germans bombed London, the normally reserved British became friendly and talkative. One observer wrote, "Many Londoners later had an odd sensation of being more fully alive during the war than at any time in their lives before or since . . ." British sociologist Richard Titmuss noted "an unsettling vista of smiles" during the blitz.[3]

Why smiles? Because war, in spite of its horrors, gives people a common immortality project. Working together creates a shared sense of purpose in a communal transcendent cause. War brings people down to a common denominator of survival. It is a moment of genuinely felt brotherhood. Stefan Zweig's description of the nationalistic fervor in Vienna at the outbreak of World War I in 1914 sounds like the reaction of New Yorkers to the blackouts:

> As never before, thousands and hundreds of thousands felt what they should have felt in peace time, that they belonged together

... All differences of class, rank and language were flooded over at that moment by the rushing feeling of fraternity. Strangers spoke to one another in the streets, people who had avoided each other for years, shook hands, everywhere one saw excited faces. Each individual experienced an exaltation of his ego ... he had been incorporated into the mass ... and his person, his hitherto unnoticed person, had been given meaning.[4]

It's no wonder war has such appeal. To be "incorporated into the mass" is to grow in stature, importance, significance, and purpose. To become part of a greater whole is to be empowered and elevated. And then on top of that to gain "meaning" through a conglomerate holy mission harbors on the spiritual.

French writer, Roland Doregelès, concluded that for the poor people of France, the real appeal of war was equality:

What did they have to defend, these blacknailed patriots? Not even a shack, an acre to till, indeed hardly a patch of ground reserved at the Pantin Cemetery; yet they would depart, like their rivals of yesterday, a heroic song on their lips and a flower in their guns. No poor or rich, proletarians or bourgeoisie, right wingers or militant leftists; there were only Frenchmen.[5]

In war, as in natural disasters, we are all the same, sharing the same heroic immortality project.

A Blessed Moment

The camaraderie of the equal is also common at athletic events. Although a person might be individually weak, in the stadium, surrounded by tens of thousands of like-minded people, with the same goal–beating the other team–he becomes equal to everyone else. In the stadium statuses are put on a temporary hold. "It is for the sake of this blessed moment," wrote Elias Canetti, in *Crowds and Power*, "when no-one is greater or better than another, that people become a crowd."[6]

At this moment, writes Canetti, the spectator experiences "an immense feeling of relief," because he has a sense of purpose and his weakness is hidden. Outside of the arena he might be uncertain, intimidated, unhappy, frustrated, and aware of his lower status. But while he is in the arena, he enjoys what we might call *anonymity of status*. He melds with the crowd and becomes strong in its conglomerate purpose. The moment is "blessed" because for a few hours an otherwise subordinated individual is lost in the equalizing chaos of the arena. In a sense, the fan in the arena fuses with the crowd and absorbs its power. Beating the opposing team becomes a temporary and satisfying holy mission.

The death of public figures also has an equalizing effect. When John F. Kennedy was assassinated, an entire nation mourned in common. We all knew who he was and were all shocked and saddened. When a loved one dies, we grieve with a small circle of friends and family. When a public figure dies, we grieve together. This too is a "blessed moment" because in that moment of common grief we are all equal, and our feelings are confirmed by millions. So in this sense we gain certainty. We do not obsess over proper behavior. We know how to act. We know what to do to gain acceptance—we grieve.

When Princess Diana was killed in a car crash, the outpouring of grief bordered on the hysterical. Like Kennedy, the victim was young, attractive, and adored. But it seemed to go beyond grief into an entirely different emotion. I would suggest that people *enjoyed* grieving. Their public displays of mourning created a mutual and common suffering. Waiting in line all night to sign guest books, folks commiserated, cried, and were pulled together. Much of the grieving was for public consumption. The sad expressions, the tears of grief, the shaking of heads as if they were silently denying the horror of it all, gave legitimacy and acceptance to anyone who could shed a tear. There seemed to be a tacit message among the mourners: we grieve together; we are one. Doctor, merchant, and street cleaner relinquished their statuses and became equal—at least equal in grief.

All of these examples—from cheering in the arena and grieving on the streets, to wars and revolutions—provide certainty, camaraderie, power, purpose, acceptance, and equality. They provide a shared holy mission. This coming together for a common purpose makes people feel good. But for the most part, it is a temporary high because after the war, after the hurricane, after the lights go on, after we leave the stadium, and when the conglomerate grieving ends, we quickly shuffle back to our former statuses.

This Is What We Live For—Catastrophe and Chaos

Now, there are people who cannot wait for the next blackout or war. The camaraderie of the arena is much too transitory. The roles they play as "hipster," or "sports fan," or "grieving citizen," or "protesting student" are artificial and temporary. They want ongoing crises and continuing heroic roles. They want perpetual struggle and permanent disruption in order to retain a permanent sense of equality and purpose. They want the lights to go out and stay out. They crave chaos as a starving man craves food because it sustains them. "I mean," said someone in a *New York Times* interview, "this is what we live for . . . catastrophe, chaos . . . you can't always count on the occasional earthquake to jump-start your heart."[7]

In November, 2003, Sarah Chayes said something similar. The former National Public Radio reporter quit her job to become a field director to help rebuild Afghanistan. Why did she put herself in harm's way? "I was covering a three star restaurant in Paris," she explained, "that was all vegetarian. Everyone was saying, 'Oh my, it's a French restaurant that doesn't serve meat.' I had a great lunch, but I thought, what real value does this have? I don't feel comfortable in comfort. I need a little chaos."[8]

For Chayes, "chaos" meant doing something challenging that required effort and danger—something she could sink her teeth into to provide a sense of accomplishment. But for other people, a little chaos is not enough. They want destruction. Spiritually Dysfunctional True Believers—dissatisfied people fanatically devoted to causes—joyfully participate in the destruction of the existing order. When the world is destroyed, their individual failures will blend into the chaos that follows. The ordered world, with its laws and rules, showed up their inadequacies. In the chaos of the newly destroyed world, everyone is back to square one; everyone is equal. Successful people love order because they stand out in it. Unsuccessful people crave disorder because they can hide in it.

Eric Hoffer said it best. "Chaos, like the grave is a haven of equality."[9] Chaos is a warm and inviting magic blanket that wraps around the angry and the alienated, making their failures and uncertainties invisible. Chaos is a great leveler. When the lights go out, we are all the same. When civilization crumbles, we are all the same. Thus, the hidden agenda of many holy missions is to tear down civilization. They

249

fabricate devils. They foment wars and revolutions and pursue them with religious intensity. This is why militants throughout the world intensify their killing when peace movements make progress. They don't want peace. They don't want order. They want permanent chaos, permanent struggle, permanent enemies—all of which provides them with cosmic significance.

When they lash out at civilization they gain four energizing doses of existential gratification:

1. They are striking back at the world that subordinated them.
2. They have heroic roles to play that require struggle and effort.
3. They are defying the great and evil powers that surround them, and
4. They are creating the anarchy which brings everyone down to the same level.

They struggle. They sacrifice. They revel in brotherhood. They kill. Sometimes they die. Their goal is to gain equality through confusion. Nirvana for them is a world gone mad. And in their pursuit of salvation, they turn this world into a vale of tears.

A Palpable Enthusiasm for Armageddon

Those who hate civilization and hunger for chaos often make religious references. Jack McLamb who has a radio show reaching thirty states, has been agitating for twenty years. "Our work is increasing as the government becomes more oppressive, anti-God, and seeks to impose a one-world system." Like apocalyptic cults, these political groups seem to expect a crisis to come in which (hopefully for them) the American government falls and they take over. A letter to the editor of *American Survival Guide: The Magazine of Self Reliance*, asked, "I would like to see addressed in an article . . . a scenario of how things are going to fall apart in the last days." "To help readers cope with the coming chaos," wrote Mike Tharp and William J. Holstein in *U.S. News & World Report*, "advertisements in the magazine offer 72-hour supplies of food and water and Israeli gas masks."[10]

There is a palpable enthusiasm for Armageddon. They are looking forward to the coming chaos. The Phineas Priesthood is perhaps the most violent and anarchistic of the right-wing movements. They rob banks, set off bombs, and murder for the holy mission of protecting God's Law and the United States Constitution. They are Christian soldiers fighting a holy war against leftists who represent Satan and one-world government.

"Killing is normally murder . . . Theft is theft," says Walter Eliyah Thody, who is serving a life sentence at a maximum security prison. "But if you're in warfare, then those same acts are acts of war. I'm at warfare against the enemies of my country."

Who are the enemies? Jews, blacks, minorities, homosexuals, abortion clinics, and the American government. The Phineas Priesthood is waging a holy war for their own eternal souls, and will not be deterred. Bryan de la Beckwith, convicted of killing civil rights activist Medgar Evers, is reportedly a Phineas who sees such murders as an "ordained duty."

"The Phineas Priesthood, " writes Jim Nesbit, "is seen as the most dangerous credo of violence, a powerful combination of religious zealotry, racist ideology and almost fool-proof tactics."[11]

Mike Reynolds, a senior researcher at KlanWatch said of the Phineas Priesthood, "You just can't overstate the power of the religious component in all of this." Indeed, religious references pepper their comments: anti-God, the last days, the Phineas *Priesthood*, ordained duty. "These folks are willing to step over that line and stay there," Reynolds added. "They're willing to die for what they believe."[12]

Vampires Gaining Psychological Sustenance

They are also willing to kill. Anarchists, in their many and varied forms, are extraordinarily dangerous and selfish because of that "religious component." They are vampires gaining psychological sustenance from the blood of others. Charles Manson, Osama bin Laden, Timothy McVeigh, Samuel Adams, and the Phineas Priesthood were chasing after salvation; and in the process, they sacrificed the rest of us on the altar of their own cosmic significance.

Here again, we are seeing the destructive nature of the spiritually dysfunctional.

32

a candle at thanksgiving

And you my father, there on the sad height,
Curse, bless me now with your fierce tears, I pray.
Do not go gentle into that good night.
Rage, rage against the dying of the light.
–Dylan Thomas, "Do Not Go Gentle into that Good Night"

Thanksgiving came right on schedule with the usual assortment of family members over for turkey. Uncle Sonny seemed to be in high spirits sitting on his walker in the kitchen, watching us cooking, carving, and mixing. He wore an oversized suit without a tie. He seemed genuinely pleased. It was probably the first traditional Thanksgiving he had attended in decades. For my aunt and uncle, Thanksgiving was just another day. Since they didn't work, it didn't have the feel and enjoyment of a holiday. They had no relatives to join them. They had nowhere to go. Thanksgiving was like every other day: a day of nothing.

"When He Was Dying, You Stayed with Him"

My father died on Thanksgiving day in 1986, and I lit a *Jahrzeit* candle as I did every year. Sometimes when we were on the road, I'd bring the candle with us to Kansas, lighting it when I could. I lit it in our big house in Germany and in the little cement house on the Marine base on Okinawa. *Jahrzeit* candles burn over twenty-four hours, and I often blew it out in the evening so it would last longer. Sometimes late at night, as we turned out the lights, I would pause for a moment to look at the yellow glow in the kitchen and wrap my hands around the glass-enclosed candle to feel its warmth. I was always sad when it burned out, wishing it would go on forever.

Becky stood beside me in the darkened kitchen, looking at the flickering candle.

"I don't think that your dad and I ever really connected. I'm not sure he liked me very much. He didn't think I was very smart."

"How could he not have seen that. You're obviously very bright."

Becky shrugged. "Not in his mind. He had these little mental puzzles to which I never got the answers."

"But he did that with everyone. He was an engineer. He had that logical mind. Most of us can't do that stuff."

"Maybe, but the truth is that he had no idea who I was. To him I was a simple, meek religious girl. I certainly wasn't the kind of woman he would have chosen."

She was right, of course. He didn't have a clue about her—no sense of or admiration for her substance, kindness, competence, strength, strong opinions, and moral clarity.

"He once told me," she said, "that the man brings status and income to a marriage, and the woman brings glamour. What was I supposed to say to that?"

I looked at her. "I'm sure he didn't mean anything by it."

"Well, I'm not so sure," Becky said.

"And yet, when he was dying, you stayed with him."

Becky spent many hours at his bedside. He was unconscious and in a diaper. His face periodically convulsed. My family was in agony. We sat with him for hours. When the rest of us were worn out from grief and pain, Becky took her turn.

"I was less emotionally involved than the rest of you," she said, "which is why I was able to spend so much time with him."

Maybe, but I always suspected she had another reason. "You were praying for him, weren't you?"

She nodded. "I wanted to be there when it happened. It's a holy moment . . . the transition from this world to the next." But he died alone early Thanksgiving morning.

"Did you talk to him when you were alone?"

She nodded. "I told him that if he sees God not to be afraid. I got the impression he was annoyed."

"Or was he just afraid?"

Becky paused for a moment. "Oh, he was certainly afraid."

"Really? What makes you think so?"

"Don't you remember what your sister said?"

I looked over at her, annoyed. The candle still flickered, painting the kitchen in hues of yellow and gray. Shadows danced around us. "What are you talking about?"

"She said that in the days before we arrived at the hospital, she would be down the hall and he would be screaming, 'Help me, help me, somebody help me, I'm dying.'"

I was incredulous. "You're kidding? I never heard that."

"Oh, yes, he did it any number of times. 'Don't you understand,' he shouted, 'I'm dying, please help me.'"

I was shaking my head and muttering, "My god. He said that? He really said that? I didn't know." My father who never complained, who endured pain silently, who faced death silently, who was always strong, who always had an answer to every question, was afraid at the end.

"That's why I stayed with him," Becky explained almost eighteen years after his death. I was nearly in tears. He was afraid, and I hadn't done anything for him.

"You must have blocked it out," Becky said.

I'll never know what my father thought at the end, but I hope Becky allayed his fears, and if in those closing moments he turned to God, then so much the better.

Christian Empathy and Charity

Becky was right; my father didn't have a clue who she was. He didn't know that Becky was at her best when giving people comfort at times of gut-wrenching adversity.

When divorce or alcoholism or a gambling addiction or disease or loneliness or rebellious children or economic problems hit, she was the sympathetic ear giving people solace and advice. People spilled their guts to her over the phone, and she would say, "uh-huh, uh-huh, uh-huh," with a pained and sympathetic intonation. She was the warm port in the storm. When a German friend was dying of cancer, she flew to Germany. When an alcoholic son threw his mother out on the street, Becky took her in. When a friend's son turned to crime and drugs, tearing the family apart, she was always available to talk. When a member of the church was economically strapped, she coerced me into giving her money.

Christianity, empathy, and charity fit her like a pair of spandex shorts.

Although I never said anything, I secretly admired her for it. Becky never had to ponder that basic existential question, Who am I? She knew who she was.

And I hope in the end, my father did too.

Dad's Aborted Quest

But what about my dad? Who was he, and what did he want out of life? After the talk around the candle, Becky went upstairs to sleep, but I stayed in the family room to watch the news and wind down from the long day of eating and the emotionally draining conversation of my dad's last days. I recalled the spring I had returned from Spain, just a few months before I had met Becky . . .

A cool April wind and a late afternoon sun greeted me at JFK when I arrived in New York. I knew in my heart of hearts that the novel I had been working on for the past year would never get published, but I hacked away at it through the spring and summer. To fill up the days and make some money, I got on the sub list for a few Bronx high schools. In one of those schools, my father was still teaching.

At fifty-nine, Dad was coming to the end of a 34-year career in teaching. And for a few days in the spring of 1974, we taught at the same school, Samuel Gompers, an all-boys vocational high school in the South Bronx. The fact that it was a vocational school as opposed to academic, and its location in the Bronx slums, meant it was one tough minority school. I didn't mind subbing there because I was just passing through, and in a few short months, would be back in Europe. But Dad had taught in vocational schools his entire working life.

At the end of one school day I found him sitting at the end of an aisle at a faculty meeting in the auditorium. Someone was speaking to the assembled teachers, but Dad wasn't paying attention. He wasn't interested in the latest blathering on the education front, and he stared downward, his eyes deeply glazed. He might have just been resting his eyes after a long day at school. Or he might have been thinking about his retirement in Florida a few years hence. Perhaps he was wondering where life had gone.

After I startled him out of his reverie, he motioned to the guy speaking to the teachers. "He's my chairman. He's got lots of good ideas." He said this matter-of-factly, genuinely, and without the bitterness that could have been there. My father was never department chairman, never the principal, although he had the intelligence, maturity—well, gravitas—to have been the superintendent of the New York City School system. There is a reason that in spite of his organizational skills, ambition, confidence, and presence, he was still teaching geometry to sophomores in the South Bronx. And that reason is another example of the paradigm I am trying to build in this book.

In the late thirties, as the Great Depression wound down, he was slim and handsome with a full head of thick, dark hair and was pursuing my mother relentlessly. He had a chemical engineering degree and took a job as an executive with Maidenform Bra Corporation. But with his mother's guidance, and the insecurity that so many developed during the Depression years, he opted for something "safe"—teaching. He entered the profession brimming with confidence and planning to quickly rise up into administration. And then something stopped him in his tracks. A land mine exploded, forever shattering his ambitions.

It always seemed to just about everyone that there was something strange about my father not being a principal. He seemed to exude that kind of authority. Several times he told me that when I was old enough to understand, he would explain.

And eventually he did.

When he had been teaching a few years, sometime in the early 1940s, he made a mistake on a form, indicating a year of experience instead of six months. Some bureaucrat discovered the inconsistency and told him that there was nothing he could do about it now; but if my father ever went for a higher license, that he would not only be fired, but also would lose all the money he had contributed to his pension. As a result, he never pursued administration.

That's it? I thought. You mean to say you gave up your lifetime goals, your ambition, your passion for which you were eminently qualified because of an idle threat made by a petty bureaucrat so many years ago? My mother encouraged him to go for the administration license, but he just couldn't take the chance. To lose one's pension, after a lifetime of work, to be fired, to lose it all . . . he just couldn't risk it.

He gained real satisfaction from the math texts he wrote, but his working life was based on a flawed decision. Unlike those well-educated, dissatisfied, unhappy souls in the Bronson book, here was someone who knew his calling, but prevented himself from pursuing it. As a result, I suspect he went through life with the uncomfortable feeling that he would never fully achieve the significance he knew he was capable of. His life was full enough. He and my mother had several circles of friends. He had two children and was well-respected and articulate, an expert bridge player, and a successful author. But every day of his life he trudged off to the South Bronx.

He put on weight, lost his hair, and when I arrived in New York in 1974, there was nothing left of that handsome young man who was going to set the world on fire. When I went off to college in 1961, he crafted two signs in wooden letters, which he lacquered over for eternity:

FRED SINGER: PRINCIPAL
and
TRY AGAIN

He wanted me to do what he had not. His last words to me were not "Take chances," or "Be brave," or "Find your passion and don't let anything deter you," or even "Try Again," but "Time is precious." I'd like to think he was saying, "We only have one life to live. Death overtakes us quickly. Enjoy the time you have. Don't chase after false gods. Don't rewrite bogus life scripts. Make good decisions. And for god's sake, don't do what I did, do what you were meant to do and hang the consequences."

33

thorn birds at the alamo

When men take up arms to set other men free, there is something
sacred and holy in the warfare.

—President Woodrow Wilson during World War I

"Fred," Becky said. "You don't want to be a thorn bird."

We were standing about two hundred yards in front of the Alamo,
at a forward gun emplacement.

"Is that what you think? That I'm a thorn bird?"

"Well, you need more interests. You're too narrowly focused. You
need more friends. You need to make time for people."

I shook my head and looked back at the Alamo, which was surrounded by San Antonio, a city of over a million people. Across the
street was an ice cream parlor. Behind us stood a giant Marriott.

"But there is a huge difference between a thorn bird and someone
who just likes what he's doing," I protested. "Thorn birds destroy themselves. I really love what I'm doing." But even as I argued, I knew
there was some truth in what she said.

Eggs Benedict

Becky had been asked to interview for a job as principal of a Catholic
elementary school. So late in May, we flew to San Antonio to check it

out. It was something of a dream job for her, but it would mean we would be separated, as I could not leave Uncle Sonny. The fact is I was feeling bleak. Some of the rentals we'd invested in weren't rented. Uncle Sonny was carrying on about returning to New York. I certainly didn't relish the idea of living alone in Colorado.

The visit to San Antonio added to my bleakness. A young man at the church picnic said to me, "So, are you retired?"

Oh? Do I really look that old? You mean to say you can take one look at me and assume I'm retired?

The headmaster of the school, Dr. Stiegelmeister, did nothing to lift my spirits. Tall, husky, quick, and intelligent, he was thirty-five and looked seventeen. His 1950's-style crew cut made him look more like a college student than a school principal. Intense, religious, and self-assured, he was used to getting his way.

When we toured the church, Catholic chatter spilled out of his mouth with a certain studied familiarity. Once again, I was in an alien world.

Breakfast at the headmaster's house moved along smoothly as he prepared Eggs Benedict for us and an assortment of parishioners. He moved things along with efficiency, dispatch, and swagger, ordering various people to separate the yokes from the white, others to mix the sauce and so on. Personally, I would have preferred bacon, eggs, and pancakes.

The world, it seems, is getting younger and younger. Seventeen-year-old-looking kids are headmasters. I'm just the old retired guy. Becky can go to San Antonio, and I can take care of Uncle Sonny. And what would I do if I did go to San Antonio? Visit the Alamo every day?

"You could teach at the university," Becky suggested.

Maybe, but at this point in my life, I'm not looking for a major job commitment. I just want to write.

On the other hand, I don't want to be a thorn bird.

One Superlative Song, Existence the Price

The moment Becky mentioned thorn birds, I knew the idea would have to be integrated into this book because thorn birds, who are obsessed by their immortality projects, are a classic example of the spiritually dysfunctional. They put all their existential eggs into one flimsy basket. They make decisions–which they think will bring them happiness, but destroy them instead. And I had to wonder, as the sun dipped around the Alamo, if I was one of them.

The Thorn Birds, Colleen McCullough's magnificent novel of Australia, begins with the following fable.

> There is a legend about a bird which sings just once in its life, more sweetly than any other creature on the face of the earth. From the moment it leaves the nest it searches for a thorn tree, and does not rest until it has impaled itself upon the longest, sharpest spine. And, dying, it rises above its own agony to outcarol the lark and nightingale. One superlative song, existence the price. But the whole world stills to listen, and God in his Heaven smiles. For the best is only bought at the cost of great pain . . . Or so the legend goes.[1]

The characters in McCullough's book are thorn birds because they each have a single purpose that they believe will bring them happiness. They pursue that purpose relentlessly, but in every case they find themselves impaled on the thorns of life–destroying their chances for happiness.

Ralph de Bricassart, a handsome young priest, pursues his ambition to rise up the ecclesiastical ladder. He knows it's the wrong decision, but can't resist. Meggie, his occasional lover, gives up the possibility of a satisfying life because of her hopeless obsession with Father Ralph. When she finally marries Luke O'Neil, a restless and penurious cane cutter, it is also for the wrong reason: he looks like Ralph. Luke's uncontrollable ambition to be the best cane cutter in the country and to save every penny he earns, ruins their marriage from the start. Instead of finding happiness, the characters find emotional and spiritual ruin. Like the bird in the legend, they aspired to sing only one song, but existence was the price. They destroyed themselves becasue they couldn't lay their ambitions down.

Nobody Wants Athens More Than I

There is, of course, a danger in pursuing only one objective to the exclusion of everything else. Since the thorn bird pins all his hopes for happiness and satisfaction on one goal (his immortality project), he may find that achievement of the goal does not make him happier or fulfilled, does not solve his problems or heal old wounds, does not, in effect, provide salvation. As a result, the disappointment can be emotionally devastating. If, on the other hand, the thorn bird never reaches that one great goal, his life might become an endless road of frustration, failure, and regret.

Consider, for example, the tragic case of Al Heppner, who was training for the Athens Olympics as a long distance walker. "I'm focused on one thing," he said on February 8, 2004, "and that's giving it my best shot . . . No night life. No girls. I'm on a mission."[2] But it was apparently more than a mission—it was a holy mission. Taped to his bathroom mirror was a note that read, "Nobody wants Athens more than I."

Unfortunately, he didn't make it. A few days after he faltered in the Olympic trials, he jumped from a bridge in San Diego County, ending his Olympic hopes and his life.[3]

John Canzano, writing in *The Oregonian* during the Olympics, asked the obvious questions. "How can the pursuit of a personal dream turn on you? How can the Olympics become a personal demon? How does someone with so much going for him end up jumping off a bridge?"[4]

Tim Seaman, a friend and teammate had an answer. "His dream of being an Olympic athlete was so intense. I'm not sure if he thought there was anything else."[5]

We'll never know for sure, but it seems evident that for thorn birds like Heppner, once the single focus of their lives disappears so does their opportunity for gaining salvation. But what if Heppner had succeeded in gaining an Olympic berth and winning a gold medal? Would he still be considered a thorn bird? Would he then be happy? Would he be satisfied having achieved his holy mission? Would that single moment of success and notoriety be enough to carry him through a lifetime? The answers are yes, no, no, and no. Such narrow existential focus is a sign of a troubled soul, one that will never be satisfied, one who, in his own mind, will never gain salvation.

On the other hand, single-minded intensity can be positive, healthy, and fulfilling. When the ancient astronomer Ptolemy looked up at "the serried multitude of stars," when Howard Tibbals spent over three decades building his model circus, when Albert Einstein said that the mysteries of the universe "beckoned like a liberation,"

262

are we to think they are too narrowly focused? When Norman Cousins wrote that "the essence" of missionary doctor Albert Schweitzer "was purpose and creativity," should we consider Schweitzer obsessed? Should we consider aviatrix Amelia Earhart one dimensional when she justified her dangerous flights by saying she did it because, "To want in one's heart to do a thing for its own sake; to enjoy doing it; to concentrate one's energies upon it—that is not only the surest guarantee of its success, it is also being true to one's self."

These people are not thorn birds. They pursue their chosen fields partly to justify their lives but mainly because they love what they do. They experience flow. They are self-actualized. They know, as Charles Murray said earlier, that life has some kind of cosmic purpose and their work is part of that purpose. While thorn birds ruin their lives in the process of trying to gain salvation, psychologically healthy individuals gain salvation as a result of their interests.

Forget the Alamo

As we meandered back to San Antonio's Riverwalk, a canyon of restaurants and hotels towering over the river, the irony of the juxtaposition of our conversation with this location was clear: The battle of the Alamo was a destructive holy mission.

Although we love our heroic myths, the Alamo deaths were neither noble nor necessary. The Mexicans had invited American settlers to Texas on the understanding that they would learn Spanish, become Catholic, get rid of their slaves, and abide by Mexican laws. The Americans reneged on all promises, and when Mexico put a restriction on further American immigration, the Texans revolted. It was not the noblest of causes, yet if we listen to commander William B. Travis, their fight was vitally important. "I call you," Travis wrote to the United States, "for the sake of liberty, patriotism and everything dear to Americans to help us, as fast as you can. If you do not come, I have made up my mind to hold out as long as I can and die like a soldier who never forgets what he ought to do for his own honor and that of his country. We have made up our minds. Victory or Death!"

"Victory or Death" has a hollow ring. They wanted to be martyrs for a fabricated cause. They did not die for patriotism or honor or to oppose tyranny. They died to sing "one superlative song, existence the price." The Alamo was another holy mission gone bad.

A New Version of the Alamo

During the two days Becky observed in the school, I had plenty of time to wander around, and inevitably made my way back to the Alamo. I got myself a chocolate almond ice cream cone and returned to that same forward gun emplacement where I imagined what it was like in 1836 with nothing but empty space around the mission. And I wondered idly what I would have done if faced with the decision to stay or run . . .

COLONEL TRAVIS DRAWS A LINE IN THE SAND

I tied up my horse at the trough and wiped the dust from my face. Everyone was buzzing about the arrival of Davy Crockett and his men. God knows we needed reinforcements, but it wasn't enough. Santa Anna had four thousand well-trained men determined to snuff us out. Still Crockett's arrival was a boost to us all.

"Whattaya gonna do, Freddie?"

I turned to see my friend Peter, who in another life would have been a retired dentist. He was cleaning his Winchester. We were both nineteen years old.

"Whattaya mean what am I gonna do?"

Peter lowered his sweaty hat to keep the blistering sun from his eyes. "They is sayin' that Colonel Travis is gonna give us a chance to stay or run. And I'm thinkin' that I don't know what to do. I don't want nobody sayin' that I'm no coward."

I took a sip of warm, dirty water from my canteen and wondered how anyone with such bad grammar could hope to become a dentist.

"I don't want nobody thinkin' that either," I said. And then I was struck by a thought. "Peter, do you remember back when we wuz in high school settin' on the benches by the building, and you wuz tellin' me about somethin' called a values clar-ee-fi-cashun test you took?"

"Cain't say as how I do, partner."

"Well, I remember. It was a warm spring day, late in the morning, and I wasn't even sure what them values was, but seein' as how there was nothin' else goin' on, I listened to you rattle off some of them clar-ee-fi-cashun questions. I didn't pay no mind to what you was sayin' until you got to one particular question. One that I never forgot. One that stopped me in my tracks."

"Is there a point to all this, Freddie?"

"I'm getting to it, Peter. Anyways, here's the question. 'What would you rather do, kiss a pretty girl or stand up for what you believe in?'"

Peter scratched his hair, which was matted with dust and sweat. "A future generation might call that a no-brainer."

"Right, that's the point. Back in high school, kissin' a pretty girl was right up there with air and food as one of life's priorities, and yet I wasn't sure how I would answer."

"What does that have to do with us bein' here at the Alamo?"

"Just this. When I was sixteen I didn't have strong opinions, didn't know nothin' about no values or about what I believed. So choosin' between girls and beliefs was kinda like comparin' whiskey to sage-brush, and yet if I had to choose I knew I was leanin' toward standin' up for what I believed. And that didn't make no dang sense to me."

"But I bet you done figgered it out by now," Peter offered.

"Sorta. You see, I grew up in an opinionated home, so I kinda saw havin' opinions as one of them values. But on another level, in my teenage mind, I might have sensed that standin' up for what I believe in had elements of defiance and heroism and was therefore more exis-tentially gratifying."

Peter grimaced. "Where'd you learn all them big words?" Then a light seemed to go on over his head. "I see what you is gettin' at. You is sayin' that this whole Texas Revolution thing is just a bunch of pokes hopin' to be defiant heroes."

I left Peter scratchin' his head and headed over to the mess hall where I found the chef, Tom Coraggio, puttin' the finishing touches on his veal picatta in a light lemon sauce.

"Hey, Tom," I greeted.

"Hey, how ya doin'," he said in his classic New Jersey twang.

I watched him gently spicing the sauce. "What are you gonna do, Tom?" I asked.

"About what?" He seemed preoccupied as he put a large anchovy pizza on the fire.

"About fightin' to the death."

"Jeez," he said out of the side of his mouth. "Are you kiddin' me?"

"You mean you're gonna leave?"

"Darn right. I'm gonna head west and open an Italian restaurant."

I scratched my head. "But I thought history is gonna record that we all fought to the death?"

Tom wiped his hands on his apron and pulled some freshly baked bread out of the oven. "Well, not me. When Santa Anna attacks I'm gonna slip out the side. I got a wagon full of pasta and a barrel of oregano that I'm not leavin' for no Mexicans."

Almost as soon as the words were out of his mouth, Colonel Travis called all us men into the center of the mission. He was tall and husky and looked like Dr. Stieglemeister. He told us that there will be no more Eggs Benedict for breakfast.

"Them days is gone boys," he said. Then he drew a line in the sand with his sword and talked to us in a trembling voice. "Those prepared to give their lives in freedom's cause come over to me."

Every single man crossed over. Even Jim Bowie who was laid up with pneumonia, asked to be carried over the line. Well, almost everyone crossed over. When the dust settled, one hundred and eighty-five men had joined Travis to fight to the death. Only one dirty cowboy remained on the other side.

All hundred and eighty-five turned to look at me. It was a bit embarrassing. I kicked some horse dung off my spurs and tried to look cool.

Davy Crockett was the first to speak. He seemed to be about ten feet tall and looked exactly like Fess Parker, who played him in the 1950s Disney series. "You're a yellow-bellied coward, son."

I kicked at the sand with my dirty boots and squinted at Davy, not because of the sun, but because it made me look tougher. It always seemed to work for Clint Eastwood.

"That may be true, Davy," I said. "But I'm only nineteen years old. I've got my whole life ahead of me. I wanna see this country expand across the continent, survive the Civil War and become a great industrial nation. And when I'm an old man, I'll live to see cars and pictures that move and aero-planes. I wanna get married and have children. I only have one chance to live. I don't wanna give it all up for this," I added, sweeping my hand over the desolate landscape.

Now it was Jim Bowie's turn to speak. He reared up from the cot that would soon be his deathbed, coughed up a little phlegm, and laid it on me. "Son," he said, "I don't know nothin' about no aero-planes and shit like that, but I do know this—in about a hundred and thirty-two years some guy by the name of Jim Jones is gonna say it all. You know who that is, son?" he asked rhetorically. "He's the cult leader who's gonna lead almost a thousand of his followers to commit suicide. And do you know what he's gonna say, son?"

I caught a quick glance of Bowie's curved knife, but maintained my macho posture. "I'm sure you're gonna tell me, Jimbo."

Bowie squinted at me, not sure if he had just been dissed. "He said, 'To die in revolutionary suicide is to live forever.' You know what that means, son?"

"I surely do, Jim. It means he's convinced his followers that to die for the cause will bring them immortality."

"You got that right, son. And that's what we is all doin'. We may die tomorrow, and you may live to see them cars and stuff," he said spitting the last words with contempt. "But who do you think they's gonna remember in the twenty-first century? You, you sniveling worm, or us? Who they gonna sing songs about? Who they gonna make all them Alamo movies about?"

By this time I was up on my dusty painted horse, pulling on the reins so he would rear up for a dramatic effect. "Let me tell you something," I said pointing to the 185 dirty, smelly men who were hours away from oblivion. "It's people like you, with your destructive wars and holy missions that make this world such a bloody place. You're always talking about freedom and liberation and fighting for God, but you do it all for yourselves. You're right, you will gain immortality by your senseless deaths, but as for me," I said, turning my snorting horse with spurs a-jangling, "I choose a less destructive path to immortality–I'm gonna write great books. It's paper tombstones for me. See you in eternity, suckers."

As I rode off, I could hear the Mexican bugles playing the "Deguello," which meant "no mercy to the defenders." Or were they the car horns of San Antonio?

PART 4

LIFE, LOVE, AND DEATH

Judaism teaches us to understand death as part of the Divine pattern of the universe. Actually, we could not have our sensitivity without fragility. Mortality is the tax that we pay for the privilege of love, thought, creative work—the toll on the bridge of being from which clods of earth and snow-peaked mountains are exempt. Just because we are human, we are prisoners of the years. Yet that very prison is the room of discipline in which we, driven by the urgency of time, create.

——a meditation from a Jewish prayer book

34

mother melanie contemplates her life in 2081

She's already a fanatic, and so am I.

—Becky, 2004

Early in September, we got a call from Melanie who was back at the University of Wyoming starting her junior year. She hadn't had a good day. Sex, she told us, was rampant on campus. A friend was back at the dorm briefly before spending the night with her boyfriend. She had a conversation with a male friend who insisted that "everyone does it." Melanie believed in chastity. It's not that she wasn't interested, in fact, like any normal twenty-one-year-old, she had a healthy interest in the opposite sex (which, hopefully would convince her that nuns have no fun at all); but morality for her was not only sanctioned by God, but also simply the right thing to do. In a college essay she wrote:

> All of us deserve to be treated as someone of value; someone "worth waiting for." If we valued ourselves and respected the right of others to do the same, can you not see the astounding domino effect that would take place? Fewer teen pregnancies, fewer broken families, fewer STDs and cancer, more satisfying marriages and happier children are only the beginning.

Abstinence will not solve the problems of the world, but it's a start. We were made for better things than this. I challenge all of you to take back what has been stolen from you.

Burned at the Stake for Not Doing Homework

During the summer before Melanie's senior year in high school, we had visited some universities in Kansas. K-U in Lawrence was gigantic. Walking across the campus was like exploring a big city. Melanie was feeling overwhelmed and intimidated, and wondered if she could do it. She sensed she would be lost, alone, and struggling.

Benedictine University was expensive and run by monks. The counselor we spoke with wore a black robe. I was horrified at the thought of Melanie attending a medieval institution mired in superstition and fanaticism. She was already steeped in Catholicism and needed some secularism in her life.

"She's religious enough, " I said to Becky, "and doesn't need to be exposed to this stuff twenty-four hours a day. It'll turn her into a fanatic."

"She's already a 'fanatic,'" Becky replied. "And so am I."

We were sitting on campus benches overlooking a river. The sun was pleasantly warm. Melanie was in the bookstore.

"I know, I know," I said, getting increasingly frustrated. "But my point is that she needs balance."

"But Fred," Becky replied. "She doesn't want balance. She wants God in her life."

"Look, I have no problem with her being religious. It's who she is. But I don't want her propagandized night and day for four years."

"It's not propaganda. It's what she wants to hear. It's who she wants to be around." Becky put her hand to her forehead to shield her eyes from the sun. "Imagine if you could go to a school where everyone was a conservative Republican, and in every class you heard points of view that you agreed with and made you feel good. Wouldn't you want that?"

She had a point, but there was no way I was going to let Melanie go to a school where guys in black robes preached Jesus. I got the feeling they burned people at the stake for not doing their homework.

"I'm not paying $18,000 a year for the Spanish Inquisition." But what really worried me was that such an environment could put her over the edge and into a convent. The thought gave me an empty feeling in the pit of my stomach. It was Melanie who wrote, "I love you, my God! You are my savior, my lover, my heart. Help my love to grow even greater." Melanie needed balance, not more of the same from thin-lipped women in habits and eunuchs in black robes.

Long-Lived Nuns

On the way home, we stopped in Paola, Kansas, to visit the grave of Sister Mercedes, who had died at age ninety-three, and who had been one of Becky's mentors. We had visited years before, when Sister Mercedes was a feisty old nun. The convent was a complex of buildings, one of which had been a school many years before. The nuns seemed to be happy, and who could argue with that.

A friend of a friend had spent a year as a monk. It wasn't for him, but he said he could see it as a way of life. "No decisions to make, no on-the-job hassles, none of the usual life worries. It was peaceful. Life had certainty and order."

While Becky and Melanie walked around inside, I drifted out to the cemetery where generations of sisters were buried. Cemeteries are irresistible. How long did they live? Was he killed in the war in 1944? How long did the wife live after her husband's death? Of course the sisters didn't have husbands. They lived on these grounds and died on them. The other nuns were their family. And so there they rested, many going way back into the nineteenth century.

Sister Rosemary Mason 1899–1990
Sister Rafael Dillon 1906–1990
Sister Mary Charles McGrath 1895–1990
Sister Mary Augustine Lickteig 1891–1989
Sister Josephine Gorman 1895–1987

They tended to live very long lives. The pattern was clear—nuns live longer. But why? Study after study confirms that religious people and those who participate in church and related activities live longer and healthier (and probably happier) lives, and it's not hard to figure out why. If Sister Mercedes genuinely believes in God and Heaven and all that that implies, then she lives in an orderly world in which life has meaning and certainty, in which we humans exist for a purpose, in which God personally loves and cares for her. Sister Mercedes has cosmic significance. Every day of her life is comforting because she knows that God is there and salvation waits. This abiding faith in eternity, this certainty that all is right with the universe, and the lack of stress that the rest of us go through, is life enhancing. At least it was for the nuns in Paola, Kansas.

2081

During the long, boring drive through Kansas, I drifted off into the future, where a very old nun in Paola, Kansas was walking through a cemetery . . .

Mother Melanie Singer wrapped a shawl around her head and wheeled slowly out to the cemetery to pray again for him. Her round little body insulated her against the chill of this late November twilight. She was tired. God knows she was tired, and she suspected that she would soon be with the Lord. Finally. She so looked forward to seeing the Beloved Father. To actually be with Him, to touch Him, to talk to Him would be the culmination—the reward—of such a long life. Mother Melanie was ninety-nine years old.

The cemetery was a special place for her, not only because so many of the sisters she had known now lay there for eternity; but because he had been there, and she had vowed to pray for him every day for the rest of her life. Of course, she had missed many days, especially during the forty-one years she taught at the school. Those were busy years; and she knew her father would be happy to know she was out in the world—at least the parochial school world—and not cloistered.

"She needs balance in her life, Becky," he would say. "Not monks in robes."

Mother Melanie smiled. A slight wind cut through her habit. Wet leaves clung to the ground. She was certain God had heard her, but would take no chances. After all, his eternal salvation was at stake. She looked at some of the graves, stood up from the wheelchair, and shuffled over to the resting place of Sister Mercedes, her mother's old friend. She felt a strange physical emptiness sweep through her. Lord, thank you for Sister Mercedes, thank you for my mother, my wonderful Lord, I want to pray for him again.

If it wasn't for the holographs, she would have forgotten what he looked like. For that matter she would have forgotten what everyone looked like. Perhaps it was old age, but she simply could not conjure up the faces from the past. Everyone was gone now: her sisters, her cousins, many of her nieces and nephews, generations of students. All gone. Long life was a blessing, but a poignant one.

Twilight darkened. "Mother!?" a young novitiate, barely twenty years old, approached. "You'll surely freeze to death out here."

Melanie turned to the girl. Shards of dry, gray hair peeked out of her shawl. Her face was surprisingly unlined, more like white dough that had been kneaded and unshaped. She smiled at the girl. "Oh, I'll be fine, dear."

The other sisters knew why she regularly went to the graveyard; apparently this one did not.

"Did you know her," the novitiate asked, looking down at the grave. Then noticing the date of Sister Mercedes' death, added, "Oh, no, you couldn't have. My goodness, she died so long ago."

"My mother knew her," said Melanie, feeling that strange emptiness growing. She felt short of breath. Perhaps it was the cold.

The girl wasn't sure what to make of that: Melanie's mind had been fading. "You really should come in now, Mother."

Twilight edged into night. A brisk breeze brought a feathery shower of wet, brown leaves and twigs. "In a moment," she said absently. "In a moment. Just one more moment, Lord." The novitiate walked back to the stone stairs and looked back at the ancient woman whose mouth moved in prayer, and wondered what she was praying about.

Mother Melanie made her way back to the stone stairs and allowed the robotic chair to lift her up into the convent that had been her home, on and off, for over seventy years. Her breath was labored. The main hall was quiet. She heard the murmur of the sisters in the dining room, a sound as familiar as the wind. But she wasn't hungry. "To my room," she said to the robotic chair.

Once inside she activated a hologram and was instantly surrounded by her family in 1989 when she was seven years old. Decades ago, she'd had the old DVDs converted. It was Christmas in Germany. Little Melanie was blonde and missing her front teeth. Her father and sisters were decorating the tree. Jingle bells played in the background. The images were three dimensional and as clear as if it were happening at that moment. She was back in the distant past, at a time so long ago that it hardly seemed possible that it really had happened. The voices seemed to come right out of the mouths of her family. The music played from the side. Mother Melanie felt fatigued and struggled for breath. The chill seemed to reach directly to her bones. It felt as if ice water flowed through her veins. She shuddered, wheeled over to her sister Mandy, and stared at her twelve-year-old face.

"Dad, can we put something else on besides those stupid Statler Brothers?"

Dad turns from the tree. He had been singing along. "Just wait 'till the album is over."

She wheeled up to him and froze the frame for a few seconds. She circled around, viewing him from all sides. She had spent many hours in the past decade in these holographs. Sometimes she just sat there absorbing the sounds, marveling that the past could be reproduced in such stunning life-like, three-dimensional detail. Sometimes her heart ached almost to the point of anguish. Other times it brought her almost as much comfort as the Lord Himself.

She froze the holo frame and turned to examine her younger self. An ancient woman in a robotic wheelchair staring at her own seven-year-old face with its toothless grin. She examined herself from every angle. How could it be, she wondered. Life and aging were among God's most breathtaking creations. She looked over at her father, frozen in motion as he hung an ornament. He had always been in awe of just about everything; maybe that's where she got her sense of wonder. Even that crazy old uncle of his had been in awe of creation. What was his name? The one who had come to Colorado. Uncle . . . Uncle . . . She shook her head, certain that her mind was going.

Mother Melanie re-activated the holo. The Christmas music played again. She was lightheaded and ever so tired. The room began to spin. She knew exactly what was happening and was extraordinarily happy. She so looked forward to being with God.

"My sweet Lord, at last . . . Lord please take my . . ."

". . . Dad!"

"Dad!"

***

"Fred, are you deaf?!"

I looked out over the Kansas plains. "What?"

"We've been talking to you. Did you not hear?"

"Sorry, I was dreaming."

"We need to eat," Becky said from the back seat of the van. "Take the nearest exit."

"Okay." I looked at Melanie sitting next to me, not yet eighteen, not yet a nun. Not dying in a holographic image in 2081.

The Specter That Is Always with Us

As we pulled into the parking lot, I thought that if I were God, I wouldn't give people life and then allow time to chew them up, warp their brains, ruin their beauty, and then take it all away for eternity.

Death is the specter that is always with us. We try to negate it by making our lives busy and meaningful, but there is no escape. This is here and this is now. Time is precious. As the Jewish meditation at the start of Part 4 said, "Mortality is the tax that we pay for the privilege of love, thought, creative work—the tool on the bridge of being . . ." We pulled into the parking lot. I put my arm around Melanie as we headed into Wendy's, wishing she would stay this way forever.

35

life begins at sixty (but death begins on day one)

The knowledge of death is reflective and conceptual, and animals are spared it. They live and disappear with the same thoughtlessness: a few minutes of fear, a few seconds of anguish, and it is over. But to live a whole lifetime with the fate of death haunting one's dreams and even the most sun-filled days—that's something else.[1]

–Ernest Becker, *The Denial of Death*

On September 1st, 2003, at 10:50 p.m., when we turned out the lights, I glanced at the red digits of the clock and thought on some vague level of sadness that in one hour and ten minutes I will be sixty years old. In a decade I'll be seventy. After that, who knows? Those who genuinely believe in god, fear death far less than people like me who face eternal oblivion. It's such a demoralizing concept, it's best left alone. Unfortunately, we can't leave it alone because death, awareness of death, fear of death, and denial of our animal mortality underlies everything we have been talking about.

The Fuel that Stokes the Existential Fires

We human beings are in the unenviable position of being sentient. We are aware that we are alive. But awareness of life must be accompanied by awareness of death. It's an ironic package deal. And it is that awareness–and the accompanying fear–that is the fuel that stokes the existential fires. Turning sixty, or fifty, or forty, or even thirty are signposts on the road to oblivion; and whether we admit it or not, it haunts us. If earning a place in the cosmos is our unstated goal, and we know our time is limited, then the fear of running out of time before we accomplish our objective makes us terribly afraid.

Morrie Talks about Spirituality and Death

On one of those warm, noisy nights in the Bronx, when we still weren't sure if we would get Uncle Sonny on the plane, we read the chapter on death in *Tuesdays with Morrie*. My uncle's apartment on the nineteenth floor overlooked the interstate where the noise from the endless stream of cars filters up into the apartment as a permanent background rumble. New York was unseasonably warm late in April, and the windows were wide open. From our vantage point, the lights of the Bronx illuminated the bedroom with a dirty, muted, yellow glow.

"Everyone knows he is going to die," the dying Morrie told Mitch Albom, "but nobody believes it. If we did, we would do things differently."[2]

And how would we do things differently? How should we live? Morrie used Mitch as an example.

"Mitch. Can I tell you something?"
Of course, I said.
"You might not like it."
Why not?
"Well, the truth is . . . if you can accept that you can die at any time—then you might not be as ambitious as you are."
I forced a small grin.
"The things you spend so much time on—all this work you do—might not seem as important. You might have to make room for some more spiritual things."
Spiritual things?
"You hate that word, don't you? 'Spiritual.' You think it's touchy-feely stuff."
Well, I said.
He tried to wink, a bad try, and I broke down and laughed.
"Mitch," he said, laughing along, "even I don't know what 'spiritual development' really means. But I do know we're deficient in some way. We are too involved in materialistic things, and they don't satisfy us. The loving relationships we have, the universe around us, we take these things for granted."[3]

Morrie talked about spirituality and death in the same breath because they are linked, but in some respect he got it backwards. Morrie implied that if we could acknowledge death, we would be more mellow. If we knew that today was the last day of our lives, we would put away our ambitions and hatreds and jealousies, we would abandon our false materialistic values, and would love our fellow man. We would enjoy the flowers and the sun and the birds. We would appreciate life more if we could simply acknowledge that death awaits us and that we must enjoy our transient lives.

But I suggest the opposite—acknowledging death does not make us mellow. It reminds us that we must hurry to make our marks. It puts us in a subconscious frenzy. If we knew with absolute certainty that we had a thousand years to leave our footprints in the sands of time, we could kick back and relax. If our current marriage is a disaster, there's plenty of time to find happiness elsewhere. If we are stuck in a dead-end job, not to worry, the next one will be fulfilling. But what we do know with absolute certainty is that the need to make our lives worthy is a frantic race against time. We only have one brief shot at living a satisfying and meaningful life before we are lost forever in the cosmos. The transience of life, the uncertainty of an afterlife, and our limited time on earth are among the terrifying and poignant forces driving us.

Only the Gods Live Forever . . . But as for Us Men, Our Days Are Numbered

Start with the Garden of Eden. Adam eats from the tree of knowledge and God tells him, "Thou shalt surely die."

Ernest Becker tells us what that means. "In other words, the final terror of self-consciousness is the knowledge of one's own death, which is the peculiar sentence on man alone in the animal kingdom . . . death is man's peculiar and greatest anxiety."[4]

In *The Epic of Gilgamesh*, written almost four thousand years ago in cuneiform writing on clay tablets, in what today is Iraq, the death of his friend causes Gilgamesh to lament, "Despair is in my heart. What my brother is now that I shall be when I am dead . . . I am afraid of death." Gilgamesh would like to live forever, but the gods created man to ultimately die. "Where is the man who can clamber to heaven? Only the gods live forever . . . but as for us men, our days are numbered, our occupations are a breath of wind."[5]

A more recent and sophisticated version comes from Blaise Pascal:

> When I consider the short duration of my life, swallowed up in
> the eternity before and after, the little space which I fill and even
> can see, engulfed in the infinite immensity of spaces of which I
> am ignorant and which know me not, I am frightened and am
> astonished at being here rather than there . . . The eternal silence
> of these infinite spaces frightens me.

It frightens most of us. The universe is vast; time and space are
beyond understanding, and the immensity of it all is intimidating. Yet
here we are–scurrying around on the third planet which is part of
around one hundred billion star systems, which itself is among at least
one hundred billion galaxies–wanting to transcend our minuteness to
become special. We have an achingly poignant need to know that we
exist for some cosmic purpose; yet we also have a deep, often unstated
fear that there really is no purpose. While the existence of god gives us
the comfort to know that the universe has order and that we have a
specific and special place in that order, we are still terribly afraid that
our brief moment on earth will not be satisfying.

"This is the terror," wrote Becker, "to have emerged from nothing, to have a name, consciousness of self, deep inner feelings, an
excruciating inner yearning for life and self-expression–and with all
this yet to die."[6] But even worse is never to have lived, never to have
added a thing to the cosmos. Death scares us, but having not lived a
fulfilling life, scares us more. This fear is the source of so much misery
and death. As we have seen, those who fear eternity make the rest of
us suffer with their endless wars, revolutions, and destructive holy
missions.

Two Sides of the Same Coin

Spirituality and death are two sides of the same existential coin. We
seek spirituality because we fear death. Heads I live for eternity, tails I
face oblivion. Spirituality transcends death. If we are in touch with
god–or the false gods of our holy missions––then the terror of death is
mitigated. The point then is that fear of death, denial of death, and
denial of our "creatureliness," as Becker terms it, transmutes into a

fear of adding nothing to eternity. Consequently, if we engage in heroic pursuits for whatever god we choose, then we are earning our way into eternity, which eases, if not erases, our fear of death. Once again, we turn to Ernest Becker who concisely summarized the intertwining of heroism, meaning, God, and death.

> . . . I don't think one can be a hero in any really elevating sense without some transcendental referent, like being a hero for God, or for the creative powers of the universe. The most exalted type of heroism involves feeling that one has lived to some purpose that transcends one. This is why religion gives the individual the validation that nothing else gives him.[7]

Death is indeed the fuel that stokes the fires of our existential dread.

Becky Destroys My Entire Argument

"The trouble with all this," said Becky, "is that death doesn't frighten me."

We touched on this in the prologue, and now need to elaborate. Statements like this are incomprehensible to me because like Becker, I'm terrified of death and think about it all the time. "How could you not be afraid? I just don't get it."

"Because," Becky said, weighing her words, "I've already encountered an Eternal Presence. I trust Him with my now and I trust Him with my forever."

"So you're not afraid because you'll live forever in eternity?"

"No, not really. I'm not worried about living forever. I don't think about it at all."

"You're telling me you never think about Heaven."

"Well, I occasionally try to imagine what that means. But because eternity is timeless, it's a whole different experience than time, and probably impossible to imagine."

"Okay, so you have 'forever' covered. But you must be afraid of dying. You can't just not care about it," I said, more of an accusation than a question.

"Well, of course I don't want to die; but on the other hand, I don't think, 'Oh, I'm so glad I won't cease being after I die.' I never think about it. Finding God and loving Him and building my life with him

—that's what I think about. Mostly I want to stay close to God and hear what He is saying to me."

36

significance, disease, and death

One of these days the cancer research people . . . who have worked so frantically and intensively on the problem for the past 30 years will wake up to the fact that psychology has an influence on tissue cells.

—Dr. Karl Menninger

During the second week in September a kind of bleakness set in. Uncle Sonny's vitriolic rantings were increasing. He was now using the F-word on the phone with me, and all over the place at Garden Square. "I don't deserve this," he said. "I don't deserve to be locked up. I never said I wanted to go to Colorado." He was defiantly smoking in his room despite continued warnings. Garden Square was forced to confiscate his cigarettes, which he sometimes reacted to with bitter, profane anger, and at other times with a gentle acquiescence.

He also wasn't happy about his haircut at the assisted living facility. For as long as I could remember, he'd had a wispy combover. "They cut all my f'n' hair off," he told me; but later admitted it actually looked better. He had his ups and downs. One day he rinsed his infected eye—not with eyewash—but with aftershave lotion. "I didn't know what was happening. It burned like hell. I was screaming and screaming."

Communication at his dining room table at Garden Square was another problem. "Ben is amazing," my uncle said. "He talks through the whole meal, yet manages to finish everything." Ben also took naps during meals. His head would start edging downward ever so slowly until it hit his plate. Jack, watching the descending head, would bang his hand on the table to wake him up. Jack was a thin, wispy man with a permanently strained wispy voice. He could barely put two words together in a sentence. When Ben said something in his mumbling monotone, Jack who couldn't talk, explained it to my Uncle who couldn't hear. Somehow they managed.

The ninety-degree temperatures of summer dipped into the sixties and seventies, and the first snows hit the mountains, bringing joy to the hearts of skiers and the ski industry. I was always reluctant to let summer go. It was kind of like dying—the leaves die and fall, the grass lies brown and dormant, the increased hours of darkness and cold have a feeling of ending and mortality.

Indeed, disease and death were around us.

We learned that week that Malcolm had died of cancer earlier in the summer. Malcolm was the Woody Allen-looking guy in the Bronx VA nursing home who had been instrumental in convincing Uncle Sonny to go to Colorado. Intelligent, very thin, articulate, and sad—I think he knew it was coming. I had chatted with him a few times that week. He never smiled. His expressionless face connoted resignation. The day we left, he joined us for pizza in the nursing home cafeteria, and later sat in his wheelchair in front of the nursing home as we loaded up my uncle for the long trip west. As I pulled away from the curb, I caught a glimpse of him in the mirror watching us as we drove off.

Malcolm was fifty-nine, the same age as I am. While I'm in perfect health, he had terminal cancer and looked ten years older. We long for cosmic justice. We want the universe to be orderly and make sense. We want life to be fair and to know why it isn't. There is no joy in such a conclusion, just a wistful longing for some pattern.

Cancer—A Disease of Insignificance

Later that fall, a longtime friend of ours, Michelle (not her real name), was diagnosed with ovarian cancer. A considerable amount of evidence suggests that cancer is caused by a multiplicity of psychological factors, all of which have to do with the quest for significance. Strange as it may seem, both anecdotal and clinical evidence indicates a link between cancer and personality traits.

The tragedy of so much of human life is that many of us make decisions and take life paths that we think will make us happier, more respected, important, and purposeful; but these actions often have the opposite effect. Bad decisions can turn our lives into hell and ruin our chances for satisfaction and meaning. When we rewrite our life scripts and things get worse, when we fabricate new chapters that only backfire, when our fictitious selves don't fool anyone—then we begin to get a sense of hopelessness about ever achieving a life worthy of eternity.

When our attempts hurt us instead of elevate us, the crushing psychological defeat is enough to make us sick and even kill us. For when we lose hope of ever gaining symbolic immortality, disease often follows. Thus, *instead of gaining immortality by creating a meaningful life, our quests for significance may destroy us.*

Consider, Michelle. Her marriage to a short, insecure, and unstable young man ended quickly in divorce, leaving her with a three-year-old son, Randy. Sixteen years later, when Randy was nineteen, he got a girl pregnant. The girl, Brittany, was emotionally erratic, but Michelle insisted they marry to avoid embarrassment. Unfortunately, the marriage only compounded the problem. Randy, unable to cope with the situation, escaped by dropping out of college, joining the army, and deploying to Afghanistan.

If this wasn't enough, Michelle's volunteer work at the local homeless shelter added more stress because she was often called to help at inconvenient times. The volunteering and her regular job greatly reduced her family time. In addition, the people she worked with were hateful and psychologically abusive, spreading rumors, for example, that she was having an affair with another staff member.

Why did she stay with the homeless shelter? Perhaps it gave her a sense of accomplishment, of doing something important, something needed, even a little heroic.

The combined stresses, I'm sure, contributed to the cancer. In a tragic sort of way, her illness was self-induced. So many of her decisions were supposed to make her life better, but made instead they made it worse. When stress heaps on stress, when our own actions hurt instead of help, our immune systems get the message, and we open ourselves to disease and death.

This is not a new observation. In 1926 Elida Evans wrote, "Cancer is a symbol, as most illness is, of something going wrong in the patient's life, a warning to him to take another road."[1]

Dr. Gotthard Booth described his cancer patients as having been dominated since childhood by the feeling that their opportunities for satisfaction are very limited and that they would succeed only with great effort in creating a meaningful existence for themselves."[2]

Dr. Lawrence LeShan described the cancer-prone personality thusly: "The central orientation appeared to be a bleak hopelessness about ever achieving meaning, zest or validly in life."[3] When LeShan asks his patients what it is they've done to make themselves so angry, or guilty, they generally answer, "No, I've done nothing. You don't understand, Doctor. It's not that I've been or done anything. It's that I've done nothing and been nothing."

Cancer, I would suggest, is a cellular manifestation of quiet desperation. It is like a vulture circling above, waiting to strike at those who have lost their way, who are straggling on life's road, who lack spiritual purpose, who feel helpless and hopeless, who feel, in a word, insignificant.

Why Is Uncle Sonny Still Alive?

If all of this is true, why is Uncle Sonny still alive? Why didn't he die of cancer forty years ago? His life had been characterized by disease and psychological pain. When he was ten years old, he was hit by a car, he contracted spinal meningitis twice, he was a lifelong smoker, a diabetic, and an alcoholic. He lacked direction and purpose. He didn't have a career; he didn't feast on ambrosia but nibbled on snippets and leftovers. The crushing psychological pain of watching his children slowly die, and the periodic bouts with depression should have been enough to weaken his immune system and allow disease to have its way.

During the last decade, he had expended huge amounts of psychic and physical energy in his rage against a multiplicity of people and organizations. His anger at the insurance company, his neighbors, his landlord, the Mafia, Jewish lawyers, local congressmen, my mother, sister, Becky, and me had been volcanic. With no past to remember fondly, no future to work towards, and a bitter present to ruminate upon, Uncle Sonny should have been dancing with the angels a long time ago. Yet, there he was, turning eighty-four years old, often bitter, often angry, uninterested in other people, socially inept and aware of it, surviving on pills that kept him somewhat mentally stable, and unable even to read books, which had provided some solace and escape during those lost decades. He was pretty close to absolute zero. It seemed as if only his bitterness kept him going.

Uncle Sonny, as it turns out, had an answer for his longevity. "It must be in the genes." After all, his sister was doing even better–energetic, socially connected, a regular bridge player, loving to dance, and having endless friends. And when her friends died, she found new ones, and new ones after that. My mother fit the psychological profile of the long-lived; her brother did not. "It has to be the genes," he repeated.

But it might be something else: awe. Recall Einstein's comment:

> The most beautiful experience we can have is the mysterious. It is the fundamental emotion which stands at the cradle of true art and true science. Whoever does not know it and can no longer wonder, no longer marvel, is as good as dead, and his eyes are dimmed.[4]

If I learned one thing about my uncle, it was that he was in awe of just about everything. He marveled at the clouds and the sunsets and the mountains. He marveled at the Canadian geese that flocked by the hundreds to the lake across the street; he wondered about parallel worlds, and the DNA of chimps, and cell phones, and animal behavior, and life on Mars, and medical science, and the derivation of words and the possibility of God.

But most of all he was in awe of the universe, and in that area, at least, we were kindred spirits. On at least twenty-five different occasions, he raised the subject of the vastness of the universe, the impossibility of traveling to other stars, and the possibility of life on other planets. When a new planet was discovered in our solar system out beyond Pluto, he wrote it down and then became upset when he forgot where he put it. Whenever something amazed him he would smile slightly and mutter, "It's unbelievable." His brain may have been damaged from alcohol and age, and his life had been unfocused, but his sense of wonder remained intact.

289

The mystery of creation held his interest and may be part of the reason he was still alive.

37

a bridge is broken

There is a majesty and an eloquence in the death of the aged that nothing can touch. A link with the far past is gone. A bridge is broken. A heart which has throbbed for years has ceased to beat, like the engines of a mighty liner when, after a long and tempestuous voyage, it drops anchor in its home port.

—Robert Morris Washburn

July 18, 2004, at 5:30 in the morning, Melanie, Ashlie, and I drove to a reservoir in Denver to watch Melanie compete in a women's triathlon. It was the beginning of a very long day.

A Dry, Dusty Scorching Field

The triathlon traffic, with its twenty-five hundred competitors and thousands of spectators, turned the early Sunday morning traffic into a rush hour stall. After parking in a huge field that had been converted into a parking lot, we walked over a mile to the race site, where Melanie, a little nervous, toddled off to wait two hours for the swim, bike ride, and jog.

The typical July day was dry and scorching. Ashlie and I caught glimpses of Melanie as she transitioned from one event to the other. The race started late because of the traffic, forcing Ashlie to jog back to the road to catch a cab to her Air Force job.

The problem began at the end of the race. I couldn't find Melanie. I should have gone to the finish line, but thought we would meet elsewhere. After forty minutes, I ambled up to the long, long line of bikers and friends snaking their way back to the parking field. Still no Melanie. Because it was a mob scene of thousands of people, I walked back to the car as the logical meeting place. Still no Melanie. A slight tinge of worry crept through me. I sat in the car, baking in the Colorado sun, and watching hundreds of cars edge slowly out. After an hour, the field was almost empty. Only a smattering of cars remained. I walked around the field. Then walked around again. What if she had collapsed in the race? Maybe she'd had a heart attack? Maybe she didn't finish the race and was off somewhere crying by herself. She should have been here by now.

I walked around the field yet again and peered down the road toward the racing site. The last of the bikers were making their way back to the parking field. *She should have been here by now.*

I didn't want to move. If I just stay here eventually she'll come to the car. But I couldn't wait any longer. I jumped in the van, drove across the field and . . . there she was, wheeling her bike: brown, fried, wet, steaming, exhausted, and on the verge of tears. She stood there fuming at me for not meeting her at the finish line, which had added another two hours to her exposure to the blistering sun.

At that exact moment, a few minutes after two, as Melanie and I faced off in the dry, dusty, scorching field, Uncle Sonny died.

I Miss My Family

I said at the outset of this book that there would be no poignant death scenes, which was my original intent. But time and again, we were forced to come back to it. And here we are one more time.

I've been lucky in exposure to death. My grandfathers died before I knew what was going on. My grandmothers passed as a matter of course, as something that happens to the very old. Dad's death was an agony that clouded most of 1986, although I was overseas most of the time. But Uncle Sonny's death was something else again. We saw him almost every day for fourteen months and were intimately involved in his reminiscences at Starbucks, his interests, his appetites (he loved marshmallow cookies), his aches and pains, his moods, and his periodic rages.

"How was he today?"

"What did you talk to him about?"

"I took him shopping."

"He was out of his mind, this afternoon."

"We had a pleasant lunch at Garden Square."

"He was great, just great."

We were also aware of every detail of his health. We talked with a parade of doctors, psychiatrists, and social workers who drifted in and out during the year. We made medical decisions, and then witnessed his last eruptions as he did indeed rage and rage against the dying of the light.

We had been to the emergency room with him a half dozen times during the previous fourteen months, and he always bounced back. Becky called him "the energizer bunny." But this time there was no energy left. He struggled furiously and finally fell into a sedative-induced sleep from which he never awoke.

When we arrived at the hospital at seven in the morning, he was struggling mightily for every breath he took. The oxygen mask and respiratory treatments helped, but every breath was a labored gasp. He was clearly frightened.

Uncle Sonny looked up at me and put out his hand, a way perhaps of saying "Thank you. Thanks for being here. I'm afraid, and you're the only one I can rely on." I shook his hand. His grip was firm, and I said as much. He grinned through the oxygen mask and shook his head, amused but still flattered.

On the TV screen one of the New York weathermen was doing his usual morning schtick with the crowds who were screaming and waving placards as the camera panned them. Some were jumping up and down. Others grinned excitedly. I wish I could have been the weatherman.

Me: Sticking a microphone in a woman's face: "So what's your name?"
Woman: Forty-ish, heavy-set, excitement rippling across her face: "Loretta."
Me: "Why are you so excited, Loretta?"
Loretta: "Because millions of people will see me on television."
Me: "But Loretta, none of the millions of people will remember you. It's meaningless. Will you stop waving and screaming?"
Loretta: "But it's not meaningless. It makes me special, important. Maybe even a little famous."

Me: "Loretta, do realize that at this very moment there is a man dying in a hospital room, and that someday you will be in that very place? And do you realize when you are breathing your last, the fact that you were on television will have had no meaning? Go out and do something worthwhile.
Loretta: "Hi Mom!"

Hospitals are cold, sterile places where machines and tubes keep us alive. Uncle Sonny would have died long ago were it not for the technology, and they tried once again. Becky explained the options—tube down the throat and into the lungs, find the source of the bleeding that is keeping the oxygen from getting around his body.

"It's the only option, do you want to do it?" Like Johnnie fifteen years earlier, he didn't hesitate.

Before he went under, he said to Becky, "I miss my family."

I Really Am a Jew!

He spent the last four days in a hospice. The purpose of hospice is to allow people to die in comfort and peace. The tubes were minimal. Oxygen in the nose helped him breathe. The social workers and nurses provided morphine for pain and kind words for the family.

They also provided a rabbi.

"It was a challenge," said the social worker, proud of the fact that she was able to find one at such short notice.

Uncle Sonny was having a bad day when the rabbi arrived. Unable to speak, my uncle responded to questions with a quick shaking of the head. How much he heard, how much he understood, what he was feeling—fear, anger, bewilderment—we'll never know. But one thing was clear: he was agitated. Perspiring, struggling to breathe, eyes half open but unfocused, he periodically moaned and roared. A cold compress on his head had little effect.

"We're here, Uncle Sonny. Freddie and Becky are here." In the prior week we had told him that the tube would be out soon, and he'd be going home. Now there was not much to say except that "we're here," and touch his hands.

Do you talk about death with someone who's dying? Can he even hear and comprehend? Would it frighten or comfort him?

294

"We're glad you came to Colorado this year, Uncle Sonny," Becky said rubbing his arm. "And your life with Johnnie and Richard and Millie will never be lost; it will always be a part of our family history."

With Uncle Sonny groaning and moaning and flailing, the rabbi arrived.

Short and slight, with a dark beard, longish hair, and a large beret sitting rakishly to the side, he looked a Jewish Che Guevera. The rabbi, who was perhaps twenty-seven, was a gentle, soft-spoken creature with an amazing aura of spirituality about him.

He removed his corduroy jacket, introduced himself in a very quiet voice, and turned his attention to my uncle who was struggling, moaning, trying to sit up. He seemed to be near death, and the rabbi, who was a dreamy, heavenly presence, noted that this "is a very spiritual moment."

Once again, I felt embarrassed and uncomfortable around a "real" Jew. So many of us had abandoned the faith, had married outside the faith, and had become so integrated into American culture that after multiple generations, we are no longer Jews, no longer in touch with our four thousand years of culture, faith, and suffering. And the rabbi knew it.

The prayers he sang over Uncle Sonny were barely audible, but somehow powerful. He talked to Becky. "Are you Jewish?" he asked in a soft voice. "You seem very spiritual." How he knew that, I'll never know.

Then he turned to me.

"Are you Jewish?"

"Yes, of course."

"Do you know the *sh'mai*? It's the last prayer one should hear before they die."

As soon as he said "sh'mai," I knew that I knew it. Uncle Sonny was struggling, moaning, rearing up, raging, and roaring against the dying of the light. "Yes," I told the rabbi. "I know it. I do." And I knew the tune. I could sing it. *You see,* I wanted to say to the rabbi who was young enough to be my son, *You see, I really am a Jew.*

Too Personal to Share

Uncle Sonny didn't die that day; he passed the weekend peacefully, and we spent most of the time with him in the quiet of the hospice room. His signs were stable, his color was good, his breathing settled down. Maybe, we thought, the energizer bunny had a few more miles in him. I spoke to Becky from the triathlon. Maybe we need to have another conference with the doctors. Maybe he'll wake up. But then he began crashing. Becky raced to the hospice. I didn't have a cell phone. Melanie was somewhere out there running and biking. By the time we got to a phone, he was gone.

A month after his death, when our lives were back to their usual rhythms, while the 2004 Olympics formed an ongoing background noise, I asked Becky about his death. She had told me that she had sensed it was the end, and at the moment he was taking his last breath, the nurse walked in. Uncharacteristically, Becky told her to leave.

"You need to leave now, you have to get out. You have to get out *now*."

"I didn't want any strangers there," she said.

With a 400-meter swimming relay splashing on the TV screen, I asked, as I had about my father, "So did you want to send him off to god?"

"It's not something I want to talk about."

"Well, it's not like I'm a complete stranger. I'm really interested."

"I know you are," she said, "but I'm really not going to talk about it. It's something between me and God and Uncle Sonny."

A Gaping Black Hole

By the time I arrived at the hospice room, he had been dead for three hours. I touched his head. It was still warm. His door was closed. The name plate SONNY was down. Sonny didn't live there any more. Sonny no longer existed. And there he was at peace: a small, bald, gray, ancient, skeletal man. Eyes closed. No longer struggling for breath. Arms folded. Hands swollen from intravenous feedings. *Gone.*

His mouth hung open—a gaping black hole—and one had the feeling of utter emptiness inside, the kind of void that only death can bring. Within that blackness is nothing; it's not hollow, but empty. There is no life in there. The body is a shell. The soul has departed.

We human beings are fidgety creatures. We are always moving, blinking and gesturing, looking this way and that. From the moment we come screaming into the world, we are wiggling, talking, writing, walking, running, reading, eating, looking, cooking, grooming, picking, thinking, working, scratching, sniffing, and gesticulating. We are perpetual motion machines. And in that regard, Uncle Sonny had been different. He generally sat very still, staring forward, almost amphibian-like. He didn't twitch and fidget. He didn't look around. He moved slowly and deliberately.

Death is striking for any number of reasons—the finality, the unknown, the fear, the grief of survivors—but the stillness and emptiness were most striking to me. In death the restlessness is over. There is nowhere to go, nothing to do.

> *No itch to scratch. No train to catch.*
> *No meal to take, no cake to bake.*
> *No lawn to rake, no love to make.*
> *No thought to think, no eyes to blink.*
> *No books to read, no field to seed.*
> *No lunch to eat, no man to beat.*
> *No hair to brush, no place to rush.*
> *No games to play at end of day*
> *No war to fight, just black of night.*
> *No talk to talk, no walk to walk.*
> *No race to run.*
> *When day is done.*

The hospice room was silent. All the machines had been turned off, and the tubes had been removed. I looked at this ancient man and remembered a picture I had found of him when he was around fourteen. His expression and body language evoked swagger and spunk. The self-assured arrogance of youth was in full display. Squinting at the camera he seemed to be saying, "I'm a tough New York City kid, so don't mess with me."

The transformation from that moment in the Bronx to this moment in Colorado is striking. How can it be that the boy in the picture and the aged man in the bed are the same? I'm sure that boy—like all of us—couldn't have imagined that time would pass, and he would be old. Uncle Sonny would have shrugged and said, "It's amazing."

Closing Prayer

It was late Sunday afternoon. Becky wanted to stay with the body until

UNCLE SONNY (L) AROUND 1933 WITH FRIEND.
A TOUGH NEW YORK CITY KID.

the mortuary picked him up for the plane ride back to New York. I had errands to run. The funeral home needed proof of his military service to ensure the honor guard would be there for his burial. They also told me, to my surprise, that he had opted for an orthodox Jewish burial. But before I headed out, there was one thing left to do.

"I want to say that prayer for him. The one the rabbi said should be the last words he hears."

Of course Becky was fine with that but wondered why.

"I guess because I actually know the prayer. I don't know. It's just something I want to do." I turned to her, exhausted from the long day, the long drive, losing Melanie in the searing heat. "But I want to do it alone. I just feel so uncomfortable saying any kind of prayer." She squeezed my arm and exited, closing the door behind her.

Jewish men are supposed to pray with their heads covered. I put on the baseball cap I had been wearing all day at the triathlon and looked down at him for the last time.

"I'm sorry you had a miserable life. I'm sorry you made bad decisions. I'm sorry you could never be happy. I wish it were all true. I wish you and the boys were together and young and healthy and whole." And then, in the silence, for a very brief moment, I was a Jew again. My voice was weak and shaky.

Sh'mai Yisrael, adonoy, elohanu, adonoi echod.
Hear O Israel, the Lord our God, the Lord is One

38

a short visit to a parallel universe

There but for the grace of God go I.

—Anonymous

Forty-eight hours after his death, on a scorching and humid Tuesday afternoon, we sat in the shade of an awning in a Westchester, New York, cemetery to bury Uncle Sonny.

The Beauty of the World

Only a handful of people showed up. My sister's family attended, along with a half-dozen of my uncle's acquaintances. Steve, the one-eyed neighbor, couldn't make it because his wife was ailing. Many of his old friends had preceded him in death.

Uncle Sonny was wrapped in a shroud. His eyes were covered by tiny stones. He would be buried as an orthodox Jew.

He was also buried as a veteran. Two army corporals draped the coffin in an American flag, played a recording of taps, and slowly saluted. I had always been interested in his war stories. He had actually landed on the beaches of Normandy! He saved a heavily laden GI in front of him from drowning as they slogged from the landing craft to the shore. He caroused and brawled and fought the anti-Semites even more than he fought the Germans. He was part of the Greatest Generation, which was rapidly fading away. The little group sitting in the shade under the awning was uncomfortably silent. Perspiration dripped and soaked every dress and every shirt.

As the rabbi went through his spiel, my eyes wandered over to the other graves. He was now joining Richard, Johnnie, and Millie in eternity, and I said as much in the eulogy. "There are many versions of Heaven, many perceptions of what it might be. And I think I know what my uncle's would be. In Sonny's Heaven, his boys are healthy and happy. He and Millie are helping them with their homework, watching them grow up, watching them play ball, go out with girls. He would be sitting at dinner, asking the boys what they did in school that day. The boys would be marrying and having children of their own. I can't imagine that his Heaven would be any different than this. There is nowhere else he would rather be than with his family."

Then Becky spoke, revealing what she had said to him in the last moments of his life, a few minutes after two, on July 18, 2004.

"'Uncle Sonny,' I said, taking his hand, 'do you remember all the talks we used to have about the beauty of the world, like a cloud that drifted across the wide open sky? We looked at the different shades of green on the trees across the street on the lake. We talked about the variety of all the world's animals and all their strange noises and shapes. We talked about the incredible flavors of all the world's fruits. We used to agree that the world is a beautiful place.'

"And then I said to him that 'life too, is beautiful, isn't it, Uncle Sonny? In spite of the heartache of your life (she was crying now), you found life beautiful. You found beauty in the love of your children, your wife, and in the love of your friends gathered here around you.

"'Life is beautiful, you lived in the beauty of life; you *gave* to life. It was a good life, Sonny, a *good* life.'

"A few minutes later, as I held his hand, God took him home."

Becky turned in the direction of the coffin, poised over the freshly dug grave, and still crying, said one last thing. "Sonny, you were a part of all of our lives, you will leave a hole in our lives. You will be missed. *You will be missed.*"

I hope he heard Becky's last words in the hospice and was comforted by them. But I couldn't help thinking as we drove back to my sister's house in the rented car, that in spite of what Becky had said, he could have been stronger, he could have transcended the tragedy and done so much more.

"True enough," Becky said, "but none of us knows how we would deal with such a thing. It would take a very strong person to not be overwhelmed by it. I wouldn't have had the strength for it."

"You would have done fine," I said, enjoying the relief of the car's air conditioning. Becky has an inner strength that surfaces in times of tragedy. Me on the other hand? I would have crumbled. I would have raged at a non-existent god. Driving home, it wasn't hard to imagine what life could have been like . . .

A Short Visit to a Parallel Universe

"How was she today?" I asked Becky when she arrived home at six. It was Wednesday–her day to visit our youngest daughter Melanie.

Becky dropped her purse on the floor and sat at the kitchen table. She didn't say anything, but stared through the window into the setting winter sun.

How was she today? was the question we had asked each other almost every day for twenty-six years, first with Mandy, then with Ashlie, and now finally with Melanie.

"So?" I said with a slightly hardening edge to my voice.

Becky sighed and went to the refrigerator. "We prayed."

"Well, you always do that."

Becky stiffened. "Don't even start."

"Whattaya mean, don't even start. All I said was . . ."

"I know what you said, Fred. I know what you think about our praying."

I shook my head, my stomach began to get that empty feeling that reflected the emptiness in my soul. "How many times do I have to tell you, I don't care about the praying–I'm happy you pray–I'm happy if it brings her comfort."

Becky let out a huge sigh. "I'm sorry, I . . ."

"What is it?"

Becky hesitated. "I think she's ready to die."

I sat down at the table. Of course it was always just a matter of time, but we had both had a sense that time was drawing near. "What happened?" I asked.

"She said she was looking forward to being with God."

"But she always says things like that."

Becky shook her head. "This time it was different. She told me how much she loves Jesus and that she can't wait to be with him."

"Did you talk to Stevenson?"

She nodded. "The doctor said there was no way of knowing. She could go on for a few more years or . . ." she let the sentence drift away.

I leafed through the mail. It was early December and the Christmas letters were rolling in. I hated Christmas letters. They were always the same–parents bragging about how their kids made the honor roll or were playing soccer. The pictures of beaming families were reminders of what we didn't have. What we would never have. What I was cheated out of.

"Look at this," I said to Becky. It was a Christmas letter from my cousin Johnnie. I hadn't heard from him in years. His oldest son had just graduated from Cornell and was heading to law school. His two daughters beamed out from the photo with friendly, open faces. Johnnie, at forty-six, was in his prime as an aeronautical engineer.

"Remember my Uncle Sonny?" I asked Becky.

She nodded absently. We hadn't seen him since his grandson's Bar Mitzvah eight years earlier. "Well, he just turned eighty-four."

It was hard to believe. My memories of him were of a vigorous man roughhousing with his boys in their yard. My uncle made some good money writing a book about industrial grinding. He had been a popular shop steward for many years, and then retired early on the profits from his book. He and the boys always seemed to be tossing footballs around in the yard or playing handball. Now he was an old man.

I clicked on the news. Americans continued to die in Iraq. Bush was talking about Social Security reform. I didn't care about Iraq or health plans for seniors or Social Security. I only cared about Melanie. I wondered what life would be like after she was gone. Tending to her needs, her education, her doctors, the shrinks, the Muscular Dystrophy specialists had consumed more than two decades.

Before that, we had taken care of Mandy and Ashlie. For a while, we had three dying girls at home. Mandy died at nine, autistic and crippled. Ashlie's mind was fine, but her anger at her condition knew no bounds. Her fiery spirit had manifested itself as rage. She knew with absolute certainty that she could have done so much in this life; the unfairness of it all burned at her every moment of every day. At the age of seventeen, she just gave up. Becky's comforting words, ongoing love, and talk of God could not penetrate the bitterness that had encrusted over Ashlie's hopelessness. She stopped talking, stopped relating, and soon died.

Melanie lived the longest. Perhaps her faith in God had kept her going. I really don't know. But now—inevitably—the end was near for her. I feared that after she died, what little was left of our marriage would quickly disintegrate.

Our bitterest fights had been over God's role in all this. "How can you believe in a god that would do this to us—especially to you. This is how you get paid back for being such a good Christian!"

We had been through the why-did-god-do-this-to-the kids conversation so many, many times. I eventually came to realize it was not god I was angry at. How could I be angry at a non-existent god? No, I was angry at Becky for clinging to a god that had ruined our lives.

After dinner she got back to her computer where she continued to hack away at her PhD in theology. She had long ago completed the masters. The work was therapeutic. It's better to be busy than miserable.

I also tried to keep busy. I had always wanted to be a writer, but teaching and then looking after the crippled children consumed all my time. How could I write when every other day I drove to Denver to be with little Mel? We are her lifeline, her friends, her companions. She was our lifetime project; in a way, she was my lifeline too.

I passed Becky at her desk in the basement and headed upstairs. Grabbing an apple, I drifted around the empty bedrooms—the rooms we were going to fill with children. Mandy's old room was reserved for the occasional guest, Ashlie's we used for storage. Melanie's room was more or less as she had left it after she'd had the emergency tracheotomy and ended up permanently in Goldwater Memorial Hospital. I sat on the bed looking around at the dolls and games. After the other girls died, we showered her with stuff. She was now the only child left, and we spared no expense in making her life happy. We knew it was just a matter of time before that horrible disease would again take its inevitable toll.

I meandered into Ashlie's room, now piled with boxes. Ashlie the

Angry, I used to call her in jest. There was a time when I could make her laugh, but in that last year she was emotionally void. She never laughed, never cried, never believed in a god who could do this to her. With each child we knew we were taking a chance. The doctors told us we probably would never have a healthy child. Becky wanted to adopt, but I wanted my own progeny. Melanie was our last hope, but she too was doomed from the moment of birth.

I crawled into bed and watched the news before turning out the light. A half hour later, Becky quietly slipped into the other side of the bed, as far from me as possible. When she came to bed, I was thinking about how I hated Christmas and about Melanie and the drive I would make to Denver the next day. I needed to talk to one of the nurses about the device she uses to signal for help with her tongue. And I was thinking about how things could have been.

"Don't forget to talk to Stevenson tomorrow," Becky said, sensing I was still awake.

"Okay," I said almost inaudibly.

"What's on your mind?" she asked.

I was surprised by her question. We rarely talked about anything meaningful. We coexisted. We cohabited. And we were both in constant pain. Becky accepted it as part of God's plan, but I hated god's plan. Hated it. Nevertheless, although we had long since abandoned each other, Becky occasionally tried to reach out to me.

"What's on my mind," I repeated, turning and looking out through the curtains to the faint light of a moonlit winter. "I was just lying here thinking that . . ." I hesitated for a moment, wondering at the pointlessness of what I was going to say. "I was thinking that somewhere there is a parallel universe where Melanie is healthy and . . ."

"Fred, don't do this," she said softly.

"Don't tell me what to do," I exploded. "You asked, didn't you? You asked what I'm thinking, so I'm damned well going to tell you."

I tossed the covers off the bed and stood in my pajamas in the chilly room. Becky turned away from me, softly crying. "You know," I said, "you always talk about god and the supernatural, so why not indulge me for a minute. Why not imagine a parallel world in which we had a house full of kids. Mandy would be married and maybe we'd be grandparents. Ashlie would be busy and productive. Melanie would still be in college, going out with friends, wondering who she would marry. And you and I wouldn't be hating each other and . . ."

Another Version of Count Your Blessings

In a strange sort of way, this terrible parallel universe provides a reasonably satisfying explanation for why a benevolent god would allow human suffering. Without the suffering and heartaches of life, we would be unable to distinguish between good and bad, and therefore could never fully appreciate the good things we do have. If there was a god, and he wanted us to appreciate the eternity into which we are heading, then giving us a life of suffering, insecurity, confusion, fear, and disease—and then bringing us out of it and into heaven—would certainly make us grateful for our eternal existence. So, perhaps all of life is a time to teach us humility, a time to teach us how bad things can be before we learn how good things can be. Perhaps we are created to deny and fear death, so when we emerge into the afterlife and are given some kind of immortality, we can better appreciate it. For we could not be sufficiently thankful for existence, for heaven, and perhaps for immortality, without having first feared that we would never get them, without having anxiety over our own demise, and without having first struggled through the pain and uncertainty of this best of all possible worlds.

39

morrie returns from the dead for one last chapter

If Professor Morris Schwartz taught me anything at all, it was this: there is no such thing as "too late" in life. He was changing until the day he said good-bye.[1]

—Mitch Albom, *Tuesdays With Morrie*

This book was close to completion about a year after Uncle Sonny's arrival in Colorado, but I was waiting for a dramatic ending, a climax, a satisfying conclusion. I could have novelized the ending, could have made something up, but instead allowed circumstances to provide closure.

A Change for the Better

In every good story the character changes. It seems to be a literary requirement. The story isn't satisfying unless the character comes to some realization about prioritizing his values. In film after film and book after book, the main character's values and outlook change for the better. Consider Tom Hanks in the film *Castaway*. As a Fed Ex executive he is obsessed with speed. He talks fast and he makes a lot of money. He expects packages to race around the world at a breathtaking pace. After his plane crashes and he spends four years alone on an island, he finally makes it back to civilization–but he's *changed*. Nothing that mattered before matters now. His pace is slow and deliberate.

He takes time to appreciate the little things. Working for the company no longer matters. He returned from the dead and now only wants to enjoy life . . . slowly. His ordeal mellowed him.

Perhaps the best-known character shift in literature is Charles Dickens' Scrooge, a bitter, miserly old man who humbugged his way through Christmas. But the nocturnal, ghostly visitors led him to the realization that he was missing out on love and relationships. One of the reasons we love *A Christmas Carol* is because Scrooge recognized his faults, became aware of his mortality, recognized his time was limited to make amends, and became a better man for it.

Why are we moved by character change? Because the protagonists were taken down a peg. They learned the meaning of suffering and were better for it. We want to see deep and fundamental changes —a realization, an epiphany, a move toward humility and human kindness, a paring down of ego or a value shift to, well, "what's really important."

Morrie and Mitch Change

Morrie admitted he was a different person than he had been. Mitch asked him: If someone were to wave a magic wand and make him all better, would he become, in time, the man he had been before his illness?

Morrie shook his head. "No way I could go back. I am a different self now. I'm different in my attitudes. I'm different appreciating my body, which I didn't do fully before. I'm different in terms of trying to grapple with the big questions, the ultimate questions, the ones that won't go away."[2]

Mitch made it clear that his experience with Morrie had changed him for the better. When he first visited Morrie he was—like the Tom Hanks character—a man on the move, knee deep in work, and racing with the clock.

> I had a cup of coffee in one hand and a cellular phone between my ear and shoulder. I was talking to a TV producer about a piece we were doing. My eyes jumped from the digital clock—my return flight was in a few hours—to the mailbox numbers on the tree-lined street. The car radio was on, the all-news station. This was how I operated, five things at once.

But the sight of Morrie got his attention.

As the car stopped, I caught a glimpse of a large Japanese Maple Tree and three figures sitting near it in the driveway, a young man and a middle-aged woman flanking a small old man in a wheelchair.

Morrie.

At the sight of my old professor, I froze.

"Hello?" the producer said in my ear. "Did I lose you?. . ."

. . . "Yeah, yeah, I'm here," I whispered, and continued my conversation with the TV producer until we were finished.

I did what I had become best at doing: I tended to my work, even while my dying professor waited on his front lawn. I am not proud of this, but that is what I did.

At the conclusion, Mitch wrote:

I look back sometimes at the person I was before I rediscovered my old professor. I want to talk to that person. I want to tell him what to look out for, what mistakes to avoid. I want to tell him to be more open, to ignore the lure of advertised values, to pay attention when your loved ones are speaking, as if it were the last time you might hear them.

. . . if Professor Morris Schwartz taught me anything at all, it was this: there is no such thing as "too late" in life. He was changing until the day he said good-bye."[3]

Morrie Returns for One More Tuesday

Since character change is so important, I'd like to see one more chapter in *Tuesdays With Morrie.*

THE SIXTEENTH TUESDAY:
WE TALK ABOUT WHAT'S REALLY, REALLY, REALLY IMPORTANT

"Mitch?"

Morrie! I thought you were . . .

"Dead. I am . . . But God let me come back for one last Tuesday. And just call me coach."

Okay, *coach.*

Sure enough, it was my old professor, looking like his old self again. What should we talk about? I asked.

"Life, death, immortality, salvation."

Okay.

"But, Mitch?"

Yes?

"You're not gonna like what I have to say. Is that okay?"

Sure, that's okay, coach.

I remembered how Morrie was at the end; helpless, unable to wipe himself, but still positive, cheerful, and accepting of his fate. Now he seemed the same, yet somehow different. It's not just that he had his health back, but something had changed in Morrie, something vital.

"You remember my basic message, Mitch, about how loving people is more important than careers?"

Yes, I remember.

"Well, I was wrong."

I looked at Morrie, stunned. What made you change?

Morrie smiled. "God. God made me change. He set me straight."

You mean you actually talked to God?

Morrie shook his head and grinned. "Well, of course, Mitch. That's what we do up there, make things right with God. And I had a lot of explaining to do."

About what, I asked, not really wanting to know the answer.

"Well, Mitch, we both pretty much ignored the Man Upstairs in our talks and in your book. I mentioned spirituality, but didn't define it. I talked about What's Really Important but left out the whole concept of God. I didn't talk about how people need a sense of purpose and accomplishment to give their lives meaning. I didn't discuss that although loving other people is nice enough, we also need the existential sense that our lives were worthy. I was off base with . . ."

Well, Morrie, I really have to be going.

"Did I upset you, Mitch?"

Why should I be upset, Morrie? I sold zillions of books based on your ideas, and now you tell me I left some things out. I really have to be going.

"But I need to tell you something else before you go."

I sighed.

"I can tell you where to find the truth about human existence. In a new book called *Spiritually Dysfunctional* and . . ."

So Who Changed?

Leaving that fantasy aside, did any of the characters change in *this* book? Contriving satisfying character changes would be easy. Melanie and Becky converting Uncle Sonny would make a good story line. Their basic sweetness and sincerity and total commitment to God wins him over. Knowing that death is not too far off and hungering for some spiritual relief, he starts going to church and dies content with the certainty he will be spending eternity with God.

How's this for an ending? Uncle Sonny turns out to be a sweet, old Morrie-type guy after all. Coming to the end of a long and painful life, he overcomes his paranoia and learns to love his family. He enjoys the clear, blue skies. He loves the mountains. He loves Starbucks and Carrabas and Olive Garden and Red Lobster and the Texas Road House. He poignantly realizes how much he had missed and how much he appreciates what we have done for him. The lack of alcohol and the normal daily interaction that had been absent from his life for so long strengthened his mind, and he actually improved mentally. Uncle Sonny was happy. It's a Hollywood ending as he goes on to enjoy many years of contentment.

But that didn't happen. There were times when he was genuinely tranquil and happy, as if he were on a triple dose of Prozac; but every ten days or so, the "paranoid file" would open and his anger would emerge.

Uncle Sonny never changed.

So There Would Be Something Left of Us

I have only one regret about Uncle Sonny. It has to do with the following conversation. Early in June, about six weeks before his death, Uncle Sonny and I headed over to the Walrus ice cream store for two big chocolate ice cream cones. We sat outside at the tables watching cars come and go in the strip mall parking lot. Our favorite haunt, Starbucks, was just across the lot.

"Are you still writing?" he asked between mouthfuls.

His question was a surprise. He rarely inquired about anyone. In the year since leaving New York, for example, he had only mentioned Norma twice; she was the woman who had helped them for five years. In his mellower moments, Uncle Sonny might make a comment about a news story on television, or ask about "your daughter, the one in the Air Force," or if I had finally found a renter for the empty house. On those rare occasions, his features softened, his face relaxed, his blue eyes became steady and calm. Perhaps it was the effect of the drugs he took to keep him mentally balanced. Or a normal mood swing. Maybe he was just having a good day.

"Well, I'm working on a few things," I answered, purposely leaving it vague. But then as an afterthought, "maybe I'll write a book about you."

This brought a rare smile to his face. "It wouldn't be very interesting."

I wiped some ice cream off my lips. We were both enjoying the sun. "Well, they say that every story is worth telling, that everyone's life is interesting."

"Not mine," he said, still maintaining that mellow mood. "Nothing ever happened." Uncle Sonny paused for a moment as he took another bite of the cone. He ate in the same manner that he wrote and talked, slowly and deliberately. The ice cream was melting faster than he could eat it, and he was making a mess. I offered some napkins. Then he seemed to lose himself in his inner world. His face began to tighten.

"It could have been different," he continued. "Millie wanted to adopt, but I wanted to be macho, have my own kids."

Before he plunged any further into his negative mode, I took a plunge of my own. "How would you feel if I told you that I'm writing a book about you and Millie and the boys, and your lives together?"

Uncle Sonny smiled, or more to the point, it was a Mona Lisa-type hint of a smile. His face loosened again, bringing him back from the brink of what might have been a cascade of negative thoughts. "I used to think about doing that," he said. "So there would be something left of us."

I had already finished my ice cream, but he was still struggling with his.

So there would be something left of us.

Paper tombstones, perhaps.

Immortality.

"Well, believe it or not, I'm really writing the book. If it gets published, maybe thousands of people will know about your lives, will know how hard it was, will know what Johnnie went through. I think Johnnie would have liked that."

A noisy group of kids made their way into the Walrus ice cream store. His face was relaxed again, but still hard to read. He seemed preoccupied by finishing off the ice cream cone. He wiped his mouth with yet another napkin. Then he said nothing. Had he even heard what I said?

"What do you think of that?" I asked cautiously.

He seemed to be staring across the parking lot at Starbucks. "Johnnie wanted people to know he existed, to know there was a real person named Johnnie."

Okay, Uncle Sonny, but did you hear what I said?

He turned to me, speaking in that deliberate, deep baritone. "Tell the people who read the book that shortly before Johnnie died, he told me something important."

"Okay."

"He told me that he was sure that after he died he would be whole again in Heaven."

"I hope it's true," I said, and then as an afterthought, asked, "Do you believe he'll be whole in heaven?"

Uncle Sonny's face edged ever so slightly into his trademark Mona Lisa smile. "I have to believe it," he said. "It's the only hope I have."

Regret

The regret I have, of course, is that this conversation never happened. Although Johnnie really did make that statement about his hopes for the afterlife, the rest is a fabrication. Uncle Sonny never knew about the book. In those last moments when he gasped for breath through the oxygen mask, when he shook my hand, when he said "I miss my family," in those moments, he could have been comforted by the knowledge that they would all leave footprints behind on life's beach. He *could* have been comforted, but he wasn't.

What About the Rest of Us?

Becky? No change there. She is solid as a rock. The only significant change would be for her to lose her faith. If this were fiction, that would be a miserable and pointless ending. Even in non-fiction, it would be a miserable and pointless ending. "Ah, now I know what life is all about, death and oblivion."

What about Melanie? Losing her faith is a total impossibility. So she becomes a nun. There's a story line there. It's still a possibility. We don't talk about it, but I can feel it in my bones. I love Melanie to death, but to become a nun removes one from the world. Ashlie thought that Melanie becoming a nun would be "neat."

"*Neat?!*" I said to Ashlie the atheist. "What in the world is neat about wearing a habit and turning your back on marriage and family."

"But if that's what makes her happy, then why not."

She certainly has a point, after all the nuns in Paola, Kansas, lived long, happy, and centered lives. What more could I want for Melanie?

How about Ashlie? Little by little she returns to the church. Becky always thought that was a possibility. But knowing Ashlie as I do—intense, independent, confident, opinionated, strong, and a confirmed atheist—that scenario is not likely. Ashlie as a Christian might make a good ending and would certainly constitute a character change, but is far from likely.

Perhaps the most satisfying ending would be for me to become a Christian, to suddenly see the light so typical of religious conversions. It's the kind of book Christians love. Sinners and unbelievers converting are powerful tools for proselytizing and might indeed make this book, as Becky predicted, popular with Christians. This is an impossibility. Genetically and cognitively, I'm just not programmed for the supernatural. Besides, god will never meet me on my own terms.

40

the childhood
of eternity

Thou art my own, my darling and my wife;
And when we pass into another life,
Still thou art mine. All this which Now we see
Is but the childhood of Eternity.
−Arthur Joseph Mundy (1828-1910)

One snowy night in December, I came up with an ending to this book, which on the one hand was horrifying, and on the other would provide closure, a satisfying character change, and the existential certainty we crave.

As Soon as I Heard Her Sister's Voice, I Knew

Early in December, Becky made another one of those solo drives to Kansas to visit her sister. We are all worriers in our family. We always assume the worst, yet Melanie always makes it safely back to school, Ashlie isn't abducted in Turkey, Mandy doesn't die in childbirth, and I return from class in Denver on a snowy night.

But not this night.

The phone rang at 11:40 p.m. As soon as I heard her sister's voice, I knew. A car crash. Instant death. Emptiness rolled through me like some kind of poison. In that moment, everything changed. I wasn't angry at god because there was no god to get angry at. My first thoughts were of the girls: How would I tell them? Mandy and Brandon were in

Seattle, Melanie at school, Ashlie in Denver. How do I tell them? What about the funeral? And how do I get the body back to Colorado?

The body.

I wasn't strong. My throat constricted. Eyes wet. My hand on the phone was shaking. *I have to be strong for the girls.* In the back of my mind I knew this was the ending for the book, and I knew Becky would understand. But in that moment, I would have traded it all to have her back. *I would have given up my immortality project for her.*

Once again, emotion trumped reason.

"Fred."

I sat on the bed next to the phone. The lamp was on. The window cracked for fresh air. Becky was at the bedroom door.

"It's okay, honey," she said. "Don't be afraid."

She came over, sat on the bed, and took my arm. I wasn't sure if I should be angry, or happy or . . . or what?

"What's going on? What's going on?"

"This is what you always wanted," she said, still squeezing my arm. "Proof of eternity. Proof of God's existence."

I hovered between anger, nausea, horror, and abject sadness.

"It's true," she said. "I died and I'm back."

My first reaction was to state the obvious, "This is ridiculous." I also knew this was no dream. I was alert and awake.

"You're right," she said, "it's not a dream."

Incredulity edged out fear and sadness. "How did you know what I was thinking?"

"Because I read the book."

All I could do is mutter, "What?"

"You wrote this scene in the book. It's one of the reasons it was published."

I edged toward anger. "What are you talking about? How could you have read a scene that hasn't happened yet?" But even as I asked the question, I knew what she was saying.

"Time," she said, putting her head on my shoulder, "is different in eternity."

I felt somehow as if I were in a stupor yet also fully alert. Becky really did die that night, and everything written here is exactly as it happened. I felt so tired. My body ached. "What's going on?" I asked, almost resigned to it.

"Fred, God wants you to write this book, and He always has."

"That's ridiculous," I started to say.

"Think about it," Becky said. "A Christian writing a book about God wouldn't impress non-believers. But you, Fred, you are so clear about what you believe that when you say it people will believe it."

"I still don't believe it. I just don't."

"You will when you realize that I'm really gone and we were together tonight."

Chills shot through me. "I don't want you to go. I don't want to be alone here without you."

Her arms were around me. "You'll be okay, trust me. You're going to be very busy."

"Busy?"

"With the book."

"You mean . . ."

"You're in for a lot of surprises."

"Like what?"

"Remember when I told you that Christians would be a big audience for your book? Well, they will be."

My reaction to everything she said was the urge to reply, "That's ridiculous."

"It's not ridiculous," she said, reading my mind again. "This is what God has wanted you to do all along."

"That's ridiculous," I said, finally saying it.

I stood up and walked to the window. In the distance, a few cars silently moved along 30th Street. The trees were bare. Remnants of the last snow lay sad and dirty on the moonlit lawn.

She stood with me at the window. Took my arm. Looked out into the night. "You've missed all the signs," she said.

"Like what?"

"Remember the Englishman you met on the beach? The one who knew what you were going through. The one who told you to keep at it. Don't you know who that was?"

I fought the urge to say *that's ridiculous*. "But why would God talk to *me*?"

"Because He knew someday you would write this book. And He wants you to tell the world He exists." She turned and sat down on the bed. "And that night in Barney Googles when you met those sailors who changed the direction of your life. You always said it was an incredible coincidence. And yet it wasn't a coincidence. God set that up. You had to go overseas and meet me . . ."

I listened silently, still looking out the window.

"And then your father's last words: *Time is precious*. He came out of a coma to tell you that. And as it turned out, that is the basic premise of your book–that the time limitations death imposes drive us to make our lives worthy. Don't you realize the significance of that?"

"Have you seen my father? Can you talk to people in Heaven?" I suddenly realized that here was Becky. My wife. And she was gone. And she had glimpsed eternity. And how I wanted to understand.

"My God, you know! You know all the answers! You know the truth about everything I've wanted to know for so long." I was extraordinarily excited. "What is it? What's the truth. What's out there?"

She signed. "It's impossible to explain."

"Try me."

"Fred, try explaining your book to a three-year-old. There is no frame of reference."

"That's a cop-out and you know it. You can make it intelligible. Like is there sex in Heaven?"

She laughed. She always laughed at my jokes.

"I'm so sad for you," she said, "but I know you and the girls will be fine."

That shook me back to the reality of what was happening. The girls. And Becky.

"I'm going to go now," she said.

"I want you to stay."

"I know."

I wanted to talk to her. I wanted to go over our lives together. I wanted to talk about the girls, and how I would tell them and . . .

"We'll talk again," she said.

"Can I hug you one more time?"

"I'd like that."

I held her for a full minute. She was real and solid. The heater kicked on. I knew that I had glimpsed eternity; that it was all true and that I should be happy that there is some kind of consciousness after death, that God exists. What better news could any transient and sentient creature hope to hear? And yet I was not happy. I was achingly, horribly sad as I quietly sobbed. I wondered if God had done this, had killed her to get at me.

"It's more complicated than that," she said. "Don't be angry at God. God's Kingdom is so complex, so multi-layered, so different from anything anyone has imagined."

We separated. "You'll be okay," she said. "That much I can tell you."

She walked to the bedroom door. "I'm so happy you were my husband."

"We'll always be together," I said.

She walked down the stairs, opened the front door, and was gone.

I picked up the phone to call Mandy.

What in the World Should We Make of That?

I conjured up that scene one night when Becky was driving to Kansas, but put off actually transcribing it to the written word because it was so offbeat and strange.

"I can't do it," I told Becky. "I'd be jerking the reader around. You can't write a scene like that and then put a figurative elbow into the figurative ribs of the reader, wink, and say, 'just kidding.'"

But there it is. The question is why? And how does it fit with the spiritual themes?

First, the fantasy provides wish fulfillment—I wasn't wishing for Becky's death, but the ending and answers I was searching for.

In a literary sense, it would provide a satisfying character change and a genuine conclusion. After searching for the answers for hundreds of pages, the protagonist indeed finds the truth. And what a satisfying truth it is: That God exists, that we as individuals and as a species exist for a reason, and that we survive in some form after death. In effect, salvation and immortality await us all! That's what we all want.

What about all those signs I missed? The Englishman, the sailors at Barney Googles, and my father's last words. It isn't hard to impute to them supernatural design. But these things happen. The Englishman was meaningless, the sailors a coincidence, and my father's words were clearly those of a dying man wishing he had more time.

So in the end, this character remains the same—wishing it were true and knowing it isn't.

The Last Atheist in the Foxhole

On the other hand, did I write the Becky-death fantasy as *another type* of wish fulfillment—the hope that it's all true? Is the fear of death and insignificance so great that in the end we all succumb to the hope that we exist for a purpose and eternity awaits us? What did my dad think in those declining moments when Becky spoke to him? Was he annoyed? Hopeful? Peaceful? Afraid? Or in the end, did he too succumb? We'll never know; I probably don't want to know. And when my time comes, will I remain consistent like Voltaire or crumble like Becker? When I'm the last atheist in the foxhole will I sand up and be counted? Will I accept Jesus in those closing moments to make Becky happy? Or will I do it because, well, what the hell, just in case . . .

But I do know this. My dad's last words are the essence of everything I've been trying to come to grips with. I know that time is precious. I know that we are racing against it to make our one shot at existence worthy of the cosmos. I know that we fool ourselves with complicated mental gymnastics to polish our images for eternity. I know we are lost in the vastness of time and space. I know I can never understand creation. I know we created all gods to allay our fears and to give us hope. I know we hunger—poignantly ache—for cosmic meaning, and I know it isn't there. I know this world is a vale of tears because killing becomes easy when the spiritually dysfunctional connect with their destructive holy missions. I know that if Melanie becomes a nun, it will break my heart; but I know I'll have to accept it. I know that I would never have been so kind to Johnnie if it had not been for Becky. I know that we can live full, loving, and productive lives with or without god. And I know that writing this book is an immortality project.

And I know one other thing. I know that in my heart of hearts, I want it all to be true. I want this piece of cosmic dust to mean something in creation. And I'm still waiting for answers that make sense.

notes

Introduction: A Stormy Night in Venice
1. Morris Bishop, "Petrarch," in Plumb, J.H., *Renaissance Profiles,* ed. J.H. Plumb (New York: Harper Torchbooks, 1961), pp. 16-17.

PART 1: AN ASSORTMENT OF CHARACTERS ON THE SPIRITUALITY SPECTRUM

Chapter 1: First Date: Love and Evolution 1974
1. Information on the Scopes Monkey Trial from L. Sprague de Camp, *The Great Monkey Trial,* Garden City, NY: Doubleday & Company, 1968.

Chapter 2: His Miserable Life Was an Inspiration
1. Harold S. Kushner, *When Bad Things Happen to Good People,* New York: Schoken Books, 1981, p. 6.

Chapter 3: If This Is the Best of All Possible Worlds, Then How the Heck Can I Get Off?
1. David Montero, "The Faithful Plumb Whys, Wherefores of Disasters," *Rocky Mountain News,* September 24, 2005, p. 6A.
2. Kushner, *When Bad Things Happen to Good People,* p. 2.
3. Eric Gorski, "40 Days' Formula Inspires Churches," *Denver Post,* Nov. 2, 2003.
4. All quotes from Rick Warren, *The Purpose Driven Life: What Am I Here For?,* Grand Rapids, MI: Zondervan, 2000, pp. 22-23.
5. Kushner, p. 129.
6. Ibid., p. 134
7. Armand M. Nicholi, Jr., *The Question of God: C.S. Lewis and Sigmund Freud Debate God, Love, Sex, and the Meaning of Life,* New York: Free Press, 2002, p. 202.
8. Viktor Frankl, *Man's Search For Meaning,* New York: Pocket Books, 1963, p. 187.

Chapter 4: Mere Christianity
1. C. S. Lewis, *Mere Christianity,* (original pub. date 1943), Reprint ed.: New York: Simon & Schuster, Touchstone Books, 1996, p. 57.

2. Ibid., p. 191.
3. Ibid., p. 56.

Chapter 5: Odd Characters in the Bronx
1. Ogden Tanner, *Stress*, New York: Time Life Books, 1976, pp. 48-49. The study was done in the 1960s.

Chapter 7: Johnnie, Death, and God
1. Ernest Becker, *The Denial of Death*, New York: Free Press, 1974, p. 160.
2. Mitch Albom, *Tuesdays with Morrie*, New York: Doubleday, 1997, pp. 173-174.

Chapter 8: Popcorn and Free Will
1. Nicholi, *The Question of God*, p. 206.
2. Dean Hamer, *The God Gene: How Faith Is Hardwired into Our Genes*, New York: Doubleday, 2004, p. 6.

Chapter 9: Some New Characters on the Spirituality Spectrum Arrive on the Scene
1. All Einstein quotes from: Einstein, Albert, *Ideas and Opinions*, New York: Bonanza Books, New York, 1954, p. 11.

Chapter 11: Do Things Happen for a Reason?
1. Po Bronson, *What Should I Do With My Life? The True Story of People Who Answered the Ultimate Question*, Random House, New York, 2002, p. xv.

Chapter 12: Uncle Sonny Contemplates the Universe or How Can We Go On If We Don't Believe in God?
1. Carl J. Jung, *Man and His Symbols*, New York: Dell Publishing, 1964, p. 76.
2. *Rocky Mountain News*, July 23, 2003.
3. Stephen M. Barr, *Modern Physics and Ancient Faith*, South Bend, Indiana: University of Notre Dame Press, 2003, pp. 158-164.
4. Marvin Perry, et al, *Western Civilization: Ideas, Politics & Society*, Boston: Houghton Mifflin Company, 2004, p. 90.
5. Ibid., p. 90.
6. DennisPrager.com, "Is God Enough?" September 18, 2002.

Chapter 13: Uncle Sonny and the Little Old Ladies
1. Albom, *Tuesdays with Morrie*, p. 159.

Chapter 14: Uncle Sonny Deals with the Big Question: Who Am I?
1. William Glasser, *The Identity Society*, Revised Edition, New York: Harper & Row, 1972, p. 21.
2. All quotes from Bronson, *What Should I Do with My Life*; Noah, pp. 38-43; Tim, pp. 49-55; Bart, pp. 73-79; Ashley, pp. 84-89.

notes

PART 2: THE QUEST FOR IMMORTALITY

Chapter 15: A Brief History of Modern Spirituality

1. Eric Hoffer, *Truth Imagined,* New York: Harper & Row, 1983, p. 93
2. Edward O. Wilson, *On Human Nature,* New York: Bantam Books, 1978, p. 176.
3. A. de Tocqueville, *The State of Society in France Before the Revolution of 1789,* 3rd ed., London, 1888, pp. 9-11.
4. Quoted in Joachim C. Fest, *Hitler,* New York: Harcourt Brace Jovanovich, 1973, p. 66.
5. Roland Doregelés, "After Fifty Years," in *Promise of Greatness,* George A. Panichas, editor, New York: John Day, 1968, pp. 14-15.
6. Quoted in Barbara Tuchman, *The Guns of August,* Macmillam, New York: 1962, p. 145.
7. Jose' Ortega y Gasset, *The Revolt of the Masses,* South Bend, Ind.: University of Notre Dame Press, 1985, p. 123.
8. Ibid., p. 128.
9. Ibid., p. 123
10. Ibid., p. 123
11. Ron Fournier, "Country Craves Purpose, Dems Say," the Associated Press, Dec. 12, 2005.
12. David Myers, *The American Paradox: Spiritual Hunger in an Age of Plenty,* Yale University Press, New Haven, 2000, pp. 5-6. And, Gertrude Himmelfarb, *One Nation, Two Cultures,* Alfred A. Knopf, New York, 1999, p. 25.
13. Christopher Whipple, "Chrissie," *Life,* June 1986, pp. 64-72. Cited in Myers p.259.
14. Aleksandr Solzhenitsyn, *A World Split Apart,* New York: Harper & Row, 1978. Cited in Myers p. 258.
15. George H. Gallup, Jr., "A Nation in Recovery," *PRRC Emerging Trends,* December, 1994, pp. 1-2; cited in Myers, p. 260.
16. Remarkable Surge of Interest in Spiritual Growth Noted, as Next Century Approaches," *Emerging Trends,* December, 1998, p. 1; cited in Myers, p. 260.
17. Arianna Huffington, *How To Overthrow The Government,* New York: Harper Collins Publishers, 2000, p. 177.

Chapter 16: What Do People Want?

1. Albom, *Tuesdays with Morrie,* p. 175.
2. Nicholi, *The Question of God,* p. 100.
3. Quoted in Marvin Perry, et al, *Sources of Twentieth Century Europe,* Boston: Houghton Mifflin, 2000, pp. 39-41.
4. Christopher Monte, *Beneath the Mask: An Introduction to Theories of Personality,* New York: Praeger Publishers, 1977, p. 181.
5. Karen Horney, *Our Inner Conflicts: A Constructive Theory of Neurosis,* New York: W.W. Norton & Company, 1945.

6. Ibid.
7. Ibid., 109.
8. Nathaniel Branden, *The Psychology of Self-Esteem*, Los Angeles: Nash Publishing Corporation, Bantam Edition, 1969, p. 109.
9. Ibid., p. 10.
10. "Maslow on Self-Actualizing Persons," Adapted from C.H. Patterson's *The Therapeutic Relationship*, Monterey, CA: Brooks/Cole, 1985, on http://personcentered.com/selfact.html.
11. Glasser, *The Identity Society*, p. 61.
12. Ibid., p. 22.
13. Frankl, *Man's Search for Meaning*, pp. 117-118.
14. Ibid., p. 121.
15. Ibid., p. 154.

Chapter 17: Image Boosting

1. Will & Ariel Durant, *A Dual Autobiography,* New York: Simon & Schuster, 1977, p. 150.
2. Christopher, F. Monte, *Beneath The Mask: An Introduction to Theories of Personality,* New York: Praeger Publishers, 1977.
3. Durant, *A Dual Autobiography*, p. 150.
4. Sheldon Kopp, *If You Meet Buddha On the Road, Kill Him*, New York: Bantam Books, 1973, pp. 199-201.
5. Ibid., p. 201.
6. Deborah Tannen, *You Don't Understand: Men and Women in Conversation,* New York: Ballantine Books, 1990.
7. Vincent Bugliosi, *Helter Skelter: The True Story of the Manson Murders,* New York: W.W. Norton & Company, 1974, p. 234.
8. Susan Stern, *With the Weathermen*, Garden City, New York: Doubleday, 1975; pp. 2-11 and p. 65.

Chapter 18: I Will Not Be Anything Other Than What I Am

1. Erich Fromm, *Escape From Freedom,* New York: Avon Books, 1941.

Chapter 19: Immortality Projects

1. Ken Wilber, *Up From Eden: A Transpersonal View of Human Evolution,* New York: Doubleday, 1981, p. 17.
2. Ken Wilber, *Up From Eden*, pp. 12-16, discusses something similar, what he calls the "Atman Project." Using eastern terminology, he refers to "Atman" as Ultimate Wholeness and the Atman Project as "the *impossible* desire that the individual be immortal, cosmocentric, and all important, but based on the *correct* intuition that one's real Nature is indeed infinite and eternal." What he is saying is that since Atman–immortality and genuine significance–is beyond reach, then the Atman Project, which is the attempt to gain the cosmocentricity, serves as a substitute for it. He

also argues, as I would, that the immortality project, or the Atman Project, moves history.

3. Erich Fromm, *Escape From Freedom*, New York: Avon Books, 1965, p. 177.
4. Alan Harrington, *The Immortalist: An Approach to the Engineering of Man's Divinity*, 1970, p.101; in Becker, p. 148.
5. This concept is covered in detail in Eric Hoffer's study of followers of mass movements, *The True Believer*, New York: Harper & Row, 1951. Specifically on pp. 25-28.
6. Fromm, *Escape from Freedom*, p. 177.
7. The phrases "holy heroes" and "holy missions" in this context originated with Eric Hoffer, *The True Believer*, New York: Harper & Row, 1951, and was discussed at length by Becker in *The Denial of Death*.
8. Hoffer, *The True Believer*, p. 22.
9. John Kifner, "Mystery of McVeigh Laid Bare by Bombing," *The New York Times,* January 3, 1996.
10. Daniel J. Boorstin, *The Discoverers: A History of Man's Search to Know His World and Himself,* New York: Random House, 1983, p. 596.
11. Jacques Barzun, *From Dawn to Decadence: 500 Years of Western Cultural Life,* New York: HarperCollins Publishers, 2000, p. 201.
12. Will & Ariel Durant, *Rousseau and Revolution,* New York: Simon & Schuster, New York, 1967. p. 19.
13. Kurt G. W. Ludecke, "I Knew Hitler–The Story of a Nazi Who Escaped the Blood Purge," from Marvin Perry et al., *Sources of Twentieth Century Europe*, Boston: Houghton Mifflin Co., 2000, pp. 168-169.
14. Ludecke, quoted in Perry, *Twentieth Century Sources,* 2000, pp. 168-69.
15. Arthur Koestler, "I Was Ripe to Be Converted," in Perry, *Sources of Twentieth Century Europe*, 2000, pp. 206-209.
16. Hoffer, *The True Believer*, p. 21.
17. John H. Hallowell, "The Crisis of Our Times," in *Main Currents in Modern Political Thought,* University Press of America, 1984. Reprinted in Perry, 2000, *Sources of Twentieth Century Europe,* p. 296.

Chapter 20: Heroism

1. Becker, p. 217.
2. Perry, *Sources of Twentieth Century Europe,* p. 147.
3. All information in this section on military frauds is from Dick Foster, "Tale of Vietnam Heroics Unravels," *The Rocky Mountain News,* August 22, 2001, p. 5A.
4. Becker, *The Denial of Death,* p. 6.
5. Sam Keen, "The Heroics of Everyday Life: A Theorist of Death Confronts His Own End," *Psychology Today,* Apr. 1974, p. 72.
6. "A Long, Strange Trip to the Taliban," *Newsweek,* December 17, 2001, pp. 30 - 36.
7. Clarence Page, "Walker's twisted trek to treason," *Chicago Tribune,* December 13, 2001.

8. Jeannie Mills, *Six Years With God: Life Inside Reverend Jim Jones' People's Temple,* New York: A & W, 1979.
9. Willa Appel, *Cults in America: Programmed for Paradise,* New York: Holt, Rinehart and Winston, 1983, p. 135.
10. Edward O. Wilson, *On Human Nature,* Cambridge, Massachusetts: Harvard University Press, 1978; Bantam Edition, New York, p. 160.
11. Homer, *The Iliad,* trans. E.V. Rieu, Baltimore, MD: Penguin Books, 1950, p. 4, cited in Perry, *Western Civilization,* 2004, p. 56.

Chapter 21: The Holy Missions of War and Revolution

1. Will and Ariel Durant, *The Lessons of History,* New York: Simon & Schuster, 1968, p. 81.
2. Becker, *The Denial of Death,* p. 190.
3. Lynn Montross, *The Reluctant Rebels,* New York: Harper Brothers, 1950. Cited in Cass Canfield, *Sam Adams' Revolution,* New York: Harper & Row, 1976, p. 6.
4. Chaka Ferguson, "Parole of 1960s Radical Stuns Victims' Families," *Associated Press,* in *The Rocky Mountain News,* August 22, 2003.
5. "Boudin Says She Was a Joan of Arc," *The New York Post,* September 7, 2001, p. 23.
6. All information on Susan Stern on pages 2-11, *With the Weathermen* by Susan Stern, Garden City: NY, Doubleday, 1975.

Chapter 22: Feasting on Ambrosia: Good Immortality Projects

1. Quoted in Daniel Boorstin, *The Discoverers,* New York: Random House, 1983, p. 21.
2. Norman Cousins, *Anatomy of an Illness, as Perceived by the Patient,* New York: Bantam Books, 1979, p. 79.
3. Will Durant, *The Pleasures of Philosophy: An Attempt at a Consistent Philosophy of Life,* New York: A Touchstone Book, 1929, pp. 178-179.
4. Charles Murray, *Human Accomplishment: The Pursuit of Excellence in the Arts and Sciences, 800 BC to 1950,* New York: Harper Collins, 2003, p. 388. This concept derives from the work of Mihaly Csikzentmihalyi
5. Ibid., p. 408.
6. Ibid., p. 393
7. Ibid., p. 394
8. Ibid., p. 394

Chapter 23: Waiting for the Secular Messiah

1. Eric Hoffer, *Truth Imagined,* Harper & Row, New York, 1983, p. 94.

Chapter 25: The Joy of Martyrdom Versus Veal Piccata Sautéed Lightly in a Lemon Sauce

1. Frankl, *Man's Search for Meaning,* p. 106.

2. Jennifer Coleman, "Activist Ends Stay atop California Tree," *Associated Press*, Dec. 12, 1999.
3. "God's Work Facing Man's Judgment," *The Denver Post*, July 20, 2000, p. 1.
4. All statements by the nuns from the *Greeley Daily Tribune*, April 5, 2003.
5. Jim Spencer, columnist, *The Denver Post*.
6. *The Greeley Daily Tribune*, July 26, 2003, p. 12A.
7. All information on the Quakers from Daniel J. Boorstin, *The Americans: The Colonial Experience*, New York: Random House, 1958, pp. 35-40.
8. Laura Sukhtian, Associated Press, in the *Rocky Mountain News*, Aug. 20, 2003, p. 29A.
9. John Toland, *Adolph Hitler*, New York: Ballantine Books, 1977, p. 190.

Chapter 26: Mandy in the Middle
1. Sheldon Kopp, *If You Meet Buddha on the Road, Kill Him*, New York: Bantam Books, 1972, p. 128.
2. Becker, p. 55.

Chapter 27: Ernest Becker and Temple Grandin: A Slam Dunk Confirmation of Spiritual Hunger
1. Becker, *The Denial of Death*, p. 133.
2. Becker, *The Denial of Death*, p. 4.
3. Sam Keen, "The Heroics of Everyday Life: A Theorist of Death Confronts His Own End," *Psychology Today,* Apr. 1974, p. 71-80.
4. All information on Grandin from Oliver Sacks, *An Anthropologist on Mars*, New York: Knopf, 1995, pp. 253-296.

PART 3: FROM THE BRONX TO THE ALAMO

Chapter 31: Chaos as the Road to Salvation
1. Eric Hoffer, *The True Believer*, p. 37.
2. Robert Ardrey, *The Territorial Imperative*, New York: Atheneum Publishers, 1966, p. 319.
3. Ogden Tanner, *Stress,* Alexandria, VA: Time-Life Books, 1976, p. 97.
4. Stefan Zweig, *The World of Yesterday*, New York: Viking, 1970, p. 223.
5. Cited in Perry, *The Sources of Western Tradition*, Vol. 2, 5th ed., New York: Houghton Mifflin, 2003, p. 302.
6. Elias Canetti, *Crowds and Power*, New York: Continuum Publishing Corp., 1960, p. 18.
7. Jacques Barzun, *From Dawn to Decadence: 500 Years of Western Cultural Life*, New York: HarperCollins, 2000, p. 789.
8. Vickie Hallet, "From NPR to Kandahar," *U.S. News & World Report*, Nov. 24, 2003, p. 16.
9. Hoffer, *The True Believer*, p. 91.
10. All quotes from Mike Tharp and William J. Holstein, "Mainstreaming the Militia," *U.S. News & World Report*, April 21, 1997.

11. Jim Nesbitt, "Mixing the Bible with Bullets," Newhouse News Service, the *Denver Post*, Aug. 22, 1999.
12. Ibid.

Chapter 33: Thorn Birds at the Alamo
1. Colleen McCullough, *The Thorn Birds*, New York: Harper & Row, 1977.
2. Paul Smith, "Say It Ain't So, Al," racewalkinginternational (RWI) online, Feb. 8, 2004. wwww.worldwidewalers.net.
3. Clay Latimer, "When Failure Isn't an Option," *Rocky Mountain News*, Aug. 27, 2004, p. 6s.
4. John Canzano, *The Oregonian*, July 18, 2004.
5. Ibid.

Chapter 35: Life Begins at Sixty (But Death Begins on Day One)
1. Becker, *The Denial of Death*, p. 27.
2. Albom, *Tuesdays with Morrie*, p. 81.
3. Albom, *Tuesdays with Morrie*, pp. 83-84.
4. Becker, *The Denial of Death*, pp. 69-70.
5. *The Epic of Gilgamesh*, with introduction by N.K. Sanders, Baltimore, MD: Penguin Books, 1960, pp. 69, 104.
6. Becker, *The Denial of Death*, p. 87.
7. Sam Keen, "The Heroics of Everyday Life: A Theorist of Death Confronts His Own End," *Psychology Today*, Apr. 1974, p. 71.

Chapter 36: Significance, Disease, and Death
1. Elida Evans, *A Psychological Study of Cancer*, New York: Dodd, Mead, 1926. Cited in Bernie S. Siegel, *Love, Medicine and Miracles*, New York: Harper & Row, 1982, p. 92.
2. Gotthard Booth, *The Cancer Epidemic: Shadow of the Conquest of Nature*, New York: Edwin Mellow Press, 1974; cited in Lawrence LeShan, *You Can Fight for Your Life*, New York: M. Evans & Co., 1977, p. 71.
3. Lawrence LeShan, *You Can Fight for Life*, New York: M. Evans & Co., 1977, p. 22.
4. Einstein, *Ideas and Opinions*, p. 11.

Chapter 39: Morrie Returns from the Dead for One Last Chapter
1. Albom, p. 190
2. Ibid., p. 190.
3. Ibid., p. 190.